CASES ON BORN GLOBALS

ELGAR CASES IN ENTREPRENEURSHIP

Elgar Cases in Entrepreneurship offer an instrumental resource to fulfil the needs of instructors in entrepreneurship. Spanning numerous discrete fields, *Elgar Cases* cover state-of-the-art developments in real-world entrepreneurial endeavours, providing expert analysis with an international focus. *Casebooks* are edited by leading instructors, who bring together experienced and knowledgeable case writers to illustrate and analyse contemporary entrepreneurial scenarios. Each case offers a strong foundation for constructive discussion and includes learning objectives and summary questions to guide classroom discussion. Teaching notes for each case provide opportunities for instructors to further develop understanding and promote class engagement. An invaluable boon to course leaders and students alike, Elgar Cases in Entrepreneurship combine practicality, student engagement and international expertise to bring entrepreneurship alive!

For a full list of Edward Elgar published titles, including the titles in this series, visit our website at www.e-elgar.com.

CASES ON BORN GLOBALS

EDITED BY

ERIK S. RASMUSSEN

Professor, Department of Business and Management, University of Southern Denmark (SDU), Denmark

ELGAR CASES IN ENTREPRENEURSHIP

Edward Elgar
PUBLISHING

Cheltenham, UK • Northampton, MA, USA

Published by
Edward Elgar Publishing Limited
The Lypiatts
15 Lansdown Road
Cheltenham
Glos GL50 2JA
UK

Edward Elgar Publishing, Inc.
William Pratt House
9 Dewey Court
Northampton
Massachusetts 01060
USA

Paperback edition 2024

A catalogue record for this book
is available from the British Library

Library of Congress Control Number: 2023948404

This book is available electronically in the **Elgar**online
Business subject collection
http://dx.doi.org/10.4337/9781803924410

ISBN 978 1 80392 440 3 (cased)
ISBN 978 1 80392 441 0 (eBook)
ISBN 978 1 0353 5305 7 (paperback)

Printed and bound by CPI Group (UK) Ltd, Croydon, CR0 4YY

CONTENTS

FIGURES

TABLES

CONTRIBUTORS

Emmanuel Kusi Appiah received his PhD in 2022 from the University of Vaasa, Finland. His dissertation deals with the internationalisation of new ventures in the digital context. Emmanuel's research interest is in early internationalisation at the interface of digitalisation. He has presented his papers at top scientific conferences, such as the Hawaii International Conference on System Sciences (HICSS), the Academy of International Business, McGill International Entrepreneurship, and the European International Business Academy (EIBA). Emmanuel has previous consulting experience in digital and social media marketing. He has worked as a reviewer for the *International Marketing Review*, a reviewer for several conference proceedings, and a reviewer for several books.

Charles Aymard holds a doctorate in Management Sciences from Aix-Marseille University, France, and is an associate researcher in the Labor, Economics, and Sociology Laboratory. He graduated with a Master's degree in International Economics and a Master's in Human Resources Management. His research falls within the field of international management and focuses on the internationalisation of SMEs. Charles works with different actors: think tanks, companies, institutions, and associations to promote research and scientific spirit. He also supports companies' development by being a partner at Okay Doc as head of innovation consulting & strategy and at Battle tested Consultant in charge of international development programmes.

Véronique Boulocher-Passet is a Senior Lecturer in Marketing at the School of Business and Law, University of Brighton, UK. She received her PhD in 2000 from the University of Lille, France. She researched marketing didactics, focusing on social representations' role when teaching marketing. This research was the first to be assessed by a multidisciplinary Marketing and Education Sciences professor panel. Her current research revolves around the internationalisation of start-ups in a digital world, Born Global firms, demarketing and sustainability marketing strategies, cross-cultural consumer behaviour, teaching case study method and marketing education. She has published in business journals such as *Supply Chain Management: An International Journal, The International Journal of Entrepreneurship and Innovation* and *Journal of Management Development* and presented at many conferences. Her expertise in marketing education also led her to write many teaching case studies in marketing, published as journal articles, book chapters or within textbooks.

Félix-Antoine Chavanelle is employed by Québec International, Canada, as a foreign direct investment (FDI) advisor. He has been working with companies mainly concentrated in the Americas, and his goal is to get the best implementation of strategic subsidiaries. With a proven track record of achieving results, he is confident of significantly contributing to projects. Currently pursuing an MBA, Félix-Antoine intends to use his skills and knowledge to positively impact on a large scale.

Peter Daly is a Management Professor and Director of the MSc in Management & Leadership at EDHEC Business School, France. Peter holds a BA in Modern Languages from DCU, Dublin, Ireland, an MA in Linguistics and Communication from UCC, Cork, Ireland, and a PGCE in Online Education from the University of London. His doctoral research in higher education at the University of Sheffield analysed business apprenticeship's social, institutional and self-discourses. His current research revolves around CEO speak and legitimisation, language in international business and management learning. He has published in many business and education journals such as the *International Journal of Technology and Human Interaction, Economics of Governance, Accounting, Auditing and Accountability Journal, European Journal of International Management, Journal of Management Development, Journal of International Education in Business, Academy of Management Learning and Education, Industry and Higher Education.*

Sílvio Luís de Vasconcellos is a Full Professor at the Graduate Program in Business Administration at Escola Superior de Propaganda e Marketing (ESPM), São Paulo, Brazil. He has a PhD (2016) and Master's (2012) in Administration from UNISINOS. He graduated in Administration with a qualification in Foreign Trade from UNISINOS (1985). He completed a doctorate at Florida International University, Miami (2014–15). He developed his postdoctoral research at the University of Vale do Itajaí, SC (2016–17). He was the scientific editor of *Revista BASE* in the area of international business and *Revista BAR* in the area of entrepreneurship. Between 2018 and 2020, he was an assistant professor at FURB. He is a postgraduate guest professor at UNIVALI in Global Customer Relationship Management and Strategy and Competitive Advantage and at FEEVALE in International Market Prospecting.

Étienne Desfossés is the trading room coordinator at the UQTR Business School, University of Quebec, Canada. Currently a candidate for the MSc in Financial Economics, Étienne is mainly working on the impact of governance on firms' performance in a recession context. He also worked on public policies and the international political economy's impact on international firms. Étienne has worked at an internationalisation consulting firm and was a reviewer for the *International Journal of Entrepreneurship and Innovation.*

Véronique Favre-Bonté is a Full Professor of International and Innovation Management at the University Savoie Mont Blanc, France, where she is the director of a Master's degree in Export Area Management at the IAE Savoie Mont Blanc (a school of management). As a researcher at the IREGE institute, her field of research is mainly centred on international entrepreneurship and small businesses. She has published in entrepreneurship and management journals such as *International Small Business Journal, International Journal of Entrepreneurship and Small Business, M@n@gement, European Management Review* and *European Planning Studies.* Véronique has worked as a reviewer for many journals; she is an associate editor for the international journal of small and medium-sized firms (*Revue internationale PME*), a member of the scientific committee of the *Entrepreneurship Review*, and a member of AEI (Academy of Entrepreneurship & Innovation).

Nicolaj Hannesbo Petersen is an Assistant Professor, Department of Applied Research in Business and Technology, UCL University College, Denmark, He is working on entrepreneurship, internationalisation and business model innovation from a theoretical and practical perspective. Former head of incubation at UCL. Nicolaj is presently member of the board of advisors at Business Hub Fyn. He received his PhD in 2018 from the University of Southern Denmark on the theme of network position and identities emerging in interactions within and around a Danish public-funded cluster: does it create innovating and internationalising SMEs? He co-edited the *Handbook of Research on Business Model Innovation through Disruption and Digitalization* and was special issue editor of *Sustainable Entrepreneurship Management and Digitalization* at *Sustainability Journal*. In 2021 he was awarded the best paper presentation as co-author at the IEEE TEMS conference on Technology and Entrepreneurship – Leading Digital Transformation in Business and Society.

Rifat Kamasak is a Professor of Management and Strategy at Yeditepe University, Istanbul, Turkey. He also holds board membership positions in several companies listed on Istanbul Stock Exchange (Borsa Istanbul, BIST). For nearly 20 years, he worked in the food, confectionery, carpet, textile, aluminium, metal, retailing, trading and consulting industries. He has researched, consulted and trained at many organisations and runs his family's traditional hand-made carpet business. Having completed a Bachelor's degree in Economics and postgraduate diploma in International Management at the University of Istanbul, he received an MA in Marketing from Middlesex University London, MA in Management from Durham University, MSc in Applied Linguistics from the University of Oxford and PhD in Management Studies from the University of Exeter (2014). His primary interest areas are strategic management, knowledge and innovation and diversity management.

Berk Kucukaltan completed a PhD in Business Management at Brunel University London, UK, with the Dean's Prize for Innovation and Impact in Doctoral Research in the Brunel Business School. He holds the Associate Professor title in Turkey and has a fellow position in the UK. His research interests include performance management and measurement, digital transformation strategies, strategic decision-making, logistics, innovation and technology management and entrepreneurship subjects. In academia, he has editorial board memberships in several journals listed in the Web of Science (WoS) and has many publications in ABS-listed/WoS-indexed journals and widely known conferences. In practice, he has an active mentorship portfolio for start-ups and established businesses.

Tairi Leis is a doctoral student at the School of Economics and Business Administration, University of Tartu, Estonia. Tairi aims to receive her PhD in 2025 from the University of Tartu on the theme of failures in internationalisation during and after VUCA (volatility, uncertainty, complexity and ambiguity). Her research focuses primarily on the influence of decision-making logic and network relationships on internationalisation failure.

Giorgia Masili has been employed as Postdoctoral Researcher at the Department of Management and Law, Tor Vergata University of Rome, Italy, since 2020. She received her PhD in 2020 from the Carlo Bo University of Urbino on the theme of the role of entrepreneurial ecosystems in the internationalisation process of Born Global companies. She spent six months as a doctoral student at the Department of International Marketing at the Warsaw School of Economics (SGH) in 2018. Her current research focuses on digital transformation, agile and innovation management, and her current research projects are on low-code and Blockchain technologies. Giorgia is a reviewer for the *International Journal of Export Marketing* and a member of the Italian Society of Management (SIMA), British Academy of Management (BAM) and European Academy of Management (EURAM).

Pierre-Louis Meuric is a PhD student in Management Sciences at the Management and Economics Research Institute (IREGE), Savoie Mont-Blanc University, France. His thesis and research focus on international entrepreneurship, specifically the European Investment Fund (EIF) international high-growth firms and how they support their international dynamics. He applies the dynamic capabilities approach's micro-foundations to understand better how EIF enhances organisational agility to succeed quickly in international markets.

Fabio Musso is a Professor of Business Management and Vice-Rector for Knowledge Transfer and Public Engagement at the Carlo Bo University of Urbino, Italy. He is Vice-President of the Italian Society of Management (SIMA) and was Chairman of the MS in Marketing and Business Communication at the Department of Economics, Society and Politics of Carlo Bo University from 2008 to 2022. He has over 25 years of experience in teaching and research. His research interests are international business strategy, international marketing, marketing channels, retailing, logistics, corporate social responsibility, behavioural economics and health economics. Fabio has more than 230 research publications in various refereed international journals/conferences and has published 18 books. He teaches International Marketing and International Business Management at the Carlo Bo University of Urbino. He is editor in chief of the *International Journal of Economic Behavior* and a member of the Scientific Board of several academic journals. He is a member of the British Academy of Management (BAM), Italian Society of Management (SIMA) and Italian Society of Marketing (SIM). He previously worked as a marketing manager in the automotive and furniture industry.

Ulrik Nielsen is a Senior Project Manager at the Danish Technological Institute, and an external Lecturer at the Department of Marketing and Management, University of Southern Denmark. His research focuses primarily on international business and emerging markets. He received his PhD in 2020 from the University of Southern Denmark on Foreign Direct Investments in Emerging Markets. Ulrik has published papers in journals such as the *International Journal of Emerging Markets* and the *International Journal of Export Marketing*, and serves as a peer reviewer for many journals such as the *Scandinavian Journal of Management*, *International Journal of Business and Emerging Markets* and *Journal of International Entrepreneurship*.

Mustafa F. Özbilgin is a Professor of Organisational Behaviour at Brunel Business School, London, UK. He also holds two international positions: Co-Chair Management et Diversité at Université Paris Dauphine and Visiting Professor of Management at Koç University in Istanbul. His research focuses on equality, diversity and inclusion at work from comparative and relational perspectives. He has conducted field studies in the UK and internationally, and his work is empirically grounded. International as well as national grants support his research. His work focuses on changing policy and practice regarding workplace equality and diversity. He is an engaged scholar, driven by values of workplace democracy, equality for all and humanisation of work.

Deniz Palalar Alkan is an Associate Professor of Organizational Behavior at Yeditepe University, Turkey. She earned her baccalaureate from Florida Atlantic University, majoring in International Business and Trade. She got her Master's degree from Lynn University and her PhD from Istanbul University. While attending Florida Atlantic University, she volunteered to work with students with disabilities. After obtaining her Bachelor's degree, she worked at several international banks, including Citibank N.A. and global insurance brokerage firms. She has been an instructor since 2011 and teaches courses including Leadership, Business Management and Entrepreneurship at Yeditepe University. Her primary interest areas are organisational behaviour, leadership and diversity.

Erik S. Rasmussen is employed at the Department of Business & Management (DBM) (University of Southern Denmark) as Associate Professor. He received his PhD in 2001 from the University of Southern Denmark on the theme of Fast Internationalising, Danish Small and Medium-sized firms. His research focuses especially on international entrepreneurship and Born Global firms. In later years, he has particularly focused on the international entrepreneurs who are able to avoid domestic path dependence by establishing ventures, which already from the beginning develop routines for managing a multi-cultural workforce, for coordinating resources located in different nations, and targeting customers in several geographic places simultaneously. Erik S. Rasmussen has worked as a reviewer for a large number of journals, e.g., *International Marketing Review, International Small Business Journal, Journal of International Business Studies, Journal of Small Business and Enterprise Development*, and as editor and reviewer for several books.

Sabine Ruaud, PhD, is a Professor in the Marketing Department at Edhec Business School, France. Her current academic interest is focused on colour and the influence of humorous colour naming on consumer behaviour. The results of her research have been presented at national and international conferences and published in refereed journals. Sabine collaborates closely with international entrepreneurs and companies to lead new projects to increase their strategic success and competitive effectiveness. Based on this work, she has developed significant expertise in creating pedagogical case studies and their use for enriching students' learning experiences. They have been co-published in leading business texts such as *The International Journal of Entrepreneurship and Innovation, Principles and Practice of Marketing* – McGraw-Hill, *Cases on Digital Strategies and Management Issues in Modern Organizations* – IGI Global, *Case Research Journal*; several of them have been nominated or won awards at French and international conferences.

Gérson Tontini is a Full Professor in Business Management at the Regional University of Blumenau (FURB), Brazil. He has a PhD in Engineering from the Federal University of Santa Catarina (1995). Gérson has Posdoctorate in Business Management. He was Visiting Professor at California St. University, USA (2003) and Halmstad University, Sweden (2014). He was Chairman of Fritz Mueller Foundation (2000–2002 and 2006–2010). FURB Planning

Coordinator (1998–2002 and 2006–2010). Awards: JICA (Tokyo, 1993), BALAS (Madrid, 2006), SIMPOI (Brazil, 2013), QMOD (Denmark, 2017).

Alessio Travasi is a PhD student in Global Studies at the Department of Economy, Society, and Politics, (Carlo Bo University of Urbino, Italy. After his Bachelor's degree in Economics and Management, he specialised in Marketing and International Business, earning two Master's degrees in International Marketing and Business Communication, respectively, from Hult International Business School, in 2018 and the University of Urbino, in 2020, on the role of the 'physical point of sale in an omnichannel scenario'. Alessio's current research focuses mainly on international entrepreneurship and Born Global companies. In particular, he has focused on the role of digital technologies in shaping the business models and internationalisation processes of Born Global enterprises.

Clarice Zimmermann has a Master's degree from the Regional University of Blumenau (FURB), Brazil.

PREFACE

Erik S. Rasmussen

INTRODUCTION

This book aims to present case studies related to the type of firm called Born Global. Born Global firms (and similar concepts like International New Ventures) have been studied for more than 20 years, and many case studies exist on these firms. These case studies have not been linked, and as more attention is directed towards this type of firm, a book with case studies will be helpful. The cases in the book cover a broad span of industries and countries and can, in this way, show the different themes in the Born Global internationalisation research.

BACKGROUND FOR THE BORN GLOBAL RESEARCH

For several decades the internationalisation processes of firms have been the topic of much research in international marketing. Two parallel research streams have emerged in Europe and the US. In a review article (Andersen, 1993), these original models are labelled as The Uppsala Internationalisation Model (U-M) (see, e.g., Johanson and Wiedersheim-Paul, 1975; Johanson and Vahlne, 1977; Johanson and Mattsson, 1988) and The Innovation-Related Internationalisation Model (I-M) (see, e.g., Bilkey and Tesar, 1977; Cavusgil, 1980). Both streams of research – often labelled 'rings in the water' – contend that firms become international slowly and incrementally, which may be due to a lack of knowledge about foreign markets, high-risk aversion, high perceived uncertainty or similar factors. The U-M sees internationalisation processes as involving time-consuming organisational learning processes; the I-M tends to analyse the process as an innovative course of action, hence a question of adopting new business methods.

Both streams of research conceptualise the internationalisation process as an incremental process involving a varying number of stages. The empirical data has often supported the notion that firms internationalise like 'rings in the water' trying to gain market knowledge gradually and hence reduce uncertainty and risk over time for each country's market. The internationalisation of a company is seen as a gradual and combined expansion through geographical, product and operational development (from indirect export to joint ventures). However, many researchers have criticised models for being too deterministic and of limited value. The limitations have been shown clearly. An increasing number of firms that do not follow the pattern of the traditional stage in their internationalisation process have been identified.

In contrast, firms may aim at international markets or maybe even the global market right from birth. Such companies have been termed *Born Globals* by Rennie (1993), Knight and

Cavusgil (1996), Madsen and Servais (1997), Madsen et al. (1999); *Global Start-ups* by Oviatt and McDougall (1994); *High Technology Start-ups* by Jolly et al. (1992) and Keeble et al. (1998); *Infant Multinationals* by Lindqvist (1991); and *International New Ventures* by McDougall et al. (1994), Oviatt and McDougall (1997, 2005a, 2005b). This book will use the term Born Global about these companies.

Themes in the Born Global research

History of the Born Global concept

The concept 'Born Global' was coined in a survey for The Australian Manufacturing Council by the consultants McKinsey (see Rennie, 1993). Tamer Cavusgil clearly states the consequences of the discovery of this new type of exporter in the first scholarly article about Born Global firms in 1994 (Cavusgil, 1994, p. 18).

> There is emerging in Australia a new breed of exporting companies, which contribute substantially to the nation's export capital. The emergence of these exporters though not unique to the Australian economy, reflects 2 fundamental phenomena of the 1990s: 1. Small is beautiful. 2. Gradual internationalisation is dead.

The Australian project involved analysing new exporters amongst small and medium-sized production firms. The focus was not on new – entrepreneurial – firms, as seen in the other research on Born Globals, but on firms that recently have begun to export. Furthermore, the focus was on firms with a growing export within the last five years before the survey was conducted – the so-called emerging exporters. More than 700 emerging exporters were identified, and of these, 310 answered a questionnaire and 56 were interviewed (Rennie, 1993). The sporadic exporters and highly international firms were excluded from the survey. The characteristic of this new type of exporter (even the older firms) was that they did not see export and foreign markets as a necessary evil. Instead, they looked upon the world as one large market. The most important result of the survey was, however, that two types of exporters clearly could be distinguished.

The home market-based firms, which are well established in Australia with a market share, have built up over time and have a stable financial situation. These firms have established a solid base in the home market with many years of experience, but exporting is a significant choice if they want to expand. Thus, the wish for growth drives these firms to export, while reduction of costs or competition seldom is seen as the motive for export.

The other group – approximately 25 per cent of all the firms – were called the Born Globals. They were young firms, but they were responsible for approximately 20 per cent of the total export. This type of firm typically starts to export less than two years after the firm's foundation. Characteristics of the firms were that they viewed the world as their marketplace from the outset and saw the domestic market as a support for their international business.

Among Australia's Born Global firms were several high-tech firms, but the typical firm used well-known technology. They have experienced higher growth rates than other industries in Australia and considerable growth in their export compared to their home-market sales.

A significant factor in explaining the phenomenon of Born Global is the management's commitment to internationalisation – an explanation also found in later research (e.g., Harveston et al., 2000; Rasmussen et al., 2001; Harveston et al., 2004). Another major factor is the firm's ability to standardise production and marketing in a global niche instead of – as expected – developing customised products.

Cavusgil (1994) interprets the McKinsey report that 'gradual internationalisation is dead'. Everybody – even the smallest firm – has access to information about the export markets and can begin to export right from the birth of a new firm. With a few years' delay, the scientific world discovered the Australian results and began to draft similar research on Born Globals in different countries.

Definition of Born Global

The term Born Global has typically been defined as a newborn company (founded after 1976 for practical reasons) exporting 25 per cent or more of its total sale shortly (within the first year) after the firm has been founded (Knight and Cavusgil, 1995; Knight et al., 2004; Rialp et al., 2005; Cavusgil and Knight, 2015; Knight and Liesch, 2016; Falahat et al., 2018).

Similar concepts

Before introducing the Born Global concept, similar discussions of firms with rapid internationalisation occurred. It was typically researched, taking its point of departure in the 'stage models' of firm internationalisation. The term used in this discussion was often 'leapfrogging' (see Hedlund and Kverneland, 1985) to describe the situation when a firm jumps over stages in the classical stages model. The argument for this behaviour was that the export markets become more homogeneous and that internationalisation is a central part of the firm's strategy. The theme of the discussion was – as later on – often whether this was true for all firms or just for a high-tech firm (Young, 1987).

During the 1980s, several small studies (including case studies) documented the existence of internationally oriented firms right from birth. Ganitsky (1989) calls these firms 'innate exporters' as a contradiction to the 'adoptive exporters'. The innate exporters are more flexible and have a more significant degree of international outlook in management. On the other hand, they are often limited due to their lack of experience and resources. An early article on this topic is Jolly et al. (1992), which builds on several case studies of high-tech firms. High Technology Start-Ups, as these firms are called, are such extreme cases that it can be discussed whether it is possible to make any generalisations from the case studies. Characteristic for the case firms is that persons from several countries were the founders and followed a strategy directed towards international niche markets. These firms represent a type of firm that may have to be international from the beginning due to their high-tech product.

Up to the middle of the 1990s the research on firms with rapid internationalisation was characterised by a few case studies of primarily high-tech firms. More precise empirical and theoretical work was missing, especially regarding the nature and types of these firms. This was changed by the work of McDougall and Oviatt, who labelled these types of firms as International New Ventures (INV). They defined an INV as a firm that seeks a competitive advantage right from birth by using resources from several countries and selling its products in several countries. Their work aimed to formulate a theory of international new ventures by combining existing theories on entrepreneurship and case studies. The definition of an INV is rather broad but more precise than seen before (Oviatt and McDougall, 1994, p. 49).

> We define an international new venture as a business organisation that, from inception, seeks to derive significant competitive advantage from the use of resources and the sale of outputs in multiple countries. The distinguishing feature of these start-ups is that their origins are international, as demonstrated by observable and significant commitments of resources (e.g., material, people, financing, time) in more than one nation.

Several other authors have, during the 1990s, studied the phenomenon of rapid international-isation at newborn firms. Bell (1995) departs theoretically from the stage models and studies small computer software firms in Finland, Ireland, and Norway. The results show that between 30 and 50 per cent did not follow the stages suggested in the traditional models. The reasons were that the firms had to follow a client abroad, worked in a highly specialised niche or sector, or that the software markets primarily lie in Germany, the UK or the US. Almost all the firms in the survey worked through agents abroad and showed no intention to progress to other market entry modes.

In Knight and Cavusgil (1996), the term Born Global is discussed at length for the first time in a scholarly publication. The data for the article stems from several surveys, Gary Knight's unpublished dissertation, and anecdotal evidence from newspapers. Theoretically, the article is interesting because it discusses possible reasons for the existence of Born Global firms, mainly because of the suggestions for an empirical definition of a Born Global. In Madsen and Servais (1997), the systematic work on defining a Born Global and discussing the trends behind developing a rising number of Born Globals was continued. Especially the manager (and founder) was placed in focus in this discussion. Theoretically, the authors following the model by Johanson and Mattsson (1988) place the Born Globals amongst 'the late starters' and 'the international among others'. Madsen and Servais (1997) argue that the theory behind the stages model can still be used to understand the internationalisation of small firms. A principal part of this model is the firms' uncertainty regarding the new markets abroad. This uncertainty can be reduced due to the founder's knowledge of the export markets, and in this way, the firm can leapfrog to markets far away. The differences between traditional exporters and the Born Globals come from differences in the founder's background and the market conditions:

> However, the founder characteristics and the market conditions are different which is the reason why the manifestation of the internationalisation processes of Born Globals must be deviating from the 'rings in the water' model found to be a valid description of internation-alisation processes of firms in many empirical studies. (Madsen and Servais, 1997, p. 570)

The manager's and the founder's personal experience, relations and knowledge is thus crucial for the existence of Born Global firms. An alternative explanation mentioned in Madsen and

Servais (1997) is to take a closer look at the networks in which the firm (and the founder) is active during the founding period:

> ... when studying a Born Global firm, the time perspective should be extended beyond its birth. Probably, many of its 'genes' have roots back to firms and networks in which its founder(s) and top managers gained industry experience. Basically, in many instances it may be doubtful whether a Born Global can be considered a new company. In a legal sense the company may be new, but were it skills and capabilities not often born and matured prior to its legal birth? (Madsen and Servais, 1997, p. 573)

As Madsen and Servais (1997) state, maybe the definition of a 'home market' should be changed to be the market in which the founder of a new firm feels comfortable. Several other authors have touched on the idea of Born Global firms such as Jones (1999), who calls these types of firms 'international entrepreneurs'.

Why Born Global

Knight and Cavusgil (1996) describe different trends facilitating the Born Globals. One of these trends is the increasing importance of niche markets, forcing small firms into small niches in several countries in order to be competitive. Another significant trend was the development of process technology and the opportunities created by the rapid development of advanced communication technology. Further technology diffusion in increased speed and the importance of global networks and alliances were described as factors triggering the development of Born Global firms.

The founders

In the case of Born Globals, we may assume that the background of the decision-maker (founder) has a considerable influence on the internationalisation path followed. Factors like education, experience from living abroad, and experience from other internationally oriented jobs mould the mind of the founder and decrease the psychic distances to specific product markets significantly.

As Keeble et al. (1998, p. 327) stress:

> ...researchers argue that early-stage internationalisation reflects exceptional awareness by usually highly qualified entrepreneurs of high-return international market opportunities. In turn this reflects the entrepreneur's particular competencies derived from previous employment, technological expertise, and existing in international networking links (Coviello and Munro, 1995). They are therefore alert to new international opportunities in ways that most domestically focused entrepreneurs are not. In-depth discussions with many of the high-tech entrepreneurs and directors in the sample confirmed that the pattern typical is targeting of a specific technology-based niche for which demand in the U.K. alone was insufficient. Market internationalisation at an early stage was therefore essential for firm survival and growth.

Born Global firms can be viewed as boundary-spanning units connecting international markets or networks with the local network in which they are located. The implication is that the founder may not see national borders as an obstacle from the firm's inception but instead perceives international markets as open, waiting to be exploited. Hence, it is not necessarily so that the firm initially has to be engaged in a primarily domestic network. It may follow that the previous experience and knowledge of the founder extend the network across national borders, opening possibilities for new business ventures.

Glocal

Even though the companies are Born Global, they can be very local in their founding process when looking at the market for their products and services. In this way, the companies can be 'Glocal' as Johannisson (1994) calls it, founded in a local environment – an industrial district – and with a global market. In the same vein, Keeble et al. (1998) demonstrate that, far from substituting international for local networks, technology-intensive firms which have achieved high levels of internationalisation also exhibit high levels of local networking concerning research collaboration and internal industry networking.

Small and medium-sized enterprises' (SMEs) successful establishment and growth are often argued to benefit from location within a geographical cluster. Hayter (1997) refers to two paths of development; The seed-bed start-up, where the motivation is the desire to live in one's locality. The rationale is that new entrepreneurs are familiar with their home locales and are likewise known within these locales. As such, they have contacts with local financial institutions, knowledge of local markets, and an understanding of the characteristics of local labour, available equipment and suppliers and logistics. The home of the entrepreneur provides a ready-made company headquarters and may, for a while, host manufacturing, and local entrepreneurs, therefore:

> …inherit considerable knowledge about their local environment as part of their birthright. To locate elsewhere would involve all the costs and uncertainties in collecting and understanding information on unfamiliar places. (Hayter, 1997, p. 224)

The second path is the incubator hypothesis, where an industrialised section of an area offers new firms a supply of building access to cheap accommodation, suppliers, markets and various business services. By concentrating together, new and small firms create external economies of scale by buying and selling among one another and sharing close access to storage facilities, transportation and wholesalers, which facilitate export and imports. Such locations also provide access to labour pools and employee-related services such as public transportation and shops. On the other hand, newcomers might become entrepreneurs. The incubator start-up situation might be more concessive (e.g., ethnic groups that facilitate nurturing immigrant entrepreneurs). Especially regarding technology-oriented complexes, the incubator hypothesis has found usage in the study of science parks and is closely connected to the term industrial districts.

Growth

In recent years there has been an intense discussion of how Born Global firms behave after the foundation period and especially why and how they grow – or why not (see, e.g., Meuric and Favre-Bonté, 2023). One theme often discussed – also in the cases in this book – is whether early internationalisation is an advantage for an entrepreneurial firm (Puig et al., 2018). Another theme is how the transnational entrepreneur can facilitate the international growth of a newly founded firm (Liu, 2017). A solution for many Born Globals has been to link up to a more prominent firm and 'piggyback' on this (Gabrielsson and Manek Kirpalani, 2004).

THE CASES

In this book, 11 cases of Born Global firms are presented. They represent a broad span of industries and countries and can, in this way, show the different themes presented above. The cases are briefly presented here.

Chapter 1: The show's over at Cirque du Soleil discusses how the well-known new circus was born as a global company from its roots in Montreal, Canada, and what led it to close down and how it was re-born. The case can also be used to discuss alternative methods of financing.

Chapter 2: Born Globals or born nomads? The case of medical cannabis producers in Denmark. This case exemplifies a highly restricted, regulated and emerging business. With an outset in firms operating in the Danish medical cannabis industry, this case study provides an opportunity to examine and discuss how emerging and sometimes conflicting legislative and regulatory frameworks influence the internationalisation process of firms without a home market.

Chapter 3: GASTECH, a French born-again global firm, presents an example of the type of firm that can be labelled 'born-again global' (Bell et al., 2001). The case firm started in the home market but had to develop its internationalisation fast because of some critical incidents leading to a managerial crisis. The cases can be used to discuss the managerial capabilities needed for fast internationalisation.

Chapter 4: CLOUDTECH, how to grow a Born Global firm focuses on the growth of the Born Global firm and how – and why – periods of intense growth and stagnation shift. The case discusses why linear growth is not always the typical development in a Born Global firm and the managerial challenges related to this.

Chapter 5: A decacorn in on-demand delivery: the case of Getir from Turkey is set in the context of on-demand platforms in the e-commerce field and explores the online grocery delivery system through an illustrative case study of Getir, an international e-commerce company headquartered in Turkey. The chapter explores digitalisation and its impact on business and the unprecedented growth of the platform economy through a case study from a developing country.

Chapter 6: From dying SME to re-born global to multinational: Vendlet looks at different periods of growth at a Danish wholesaler and manufacturing company. The case of Vendlet is exciting and relevant to discuss because it questions our often implicit understanding of the linearity of growth and perceived drivers of internationalisation. The company experienced different periods of gazelle growth, generational change, threatened bankruptcy, acquisitions and rapid global internationalisation.

Chapter 7: Reinventing the footwear industry: the role of digital technologies in the market development strategy of an Italian Born Global firm is an example of a small company that developed a disruptive business model by relying on digital technologies to reinvent the dynamics of the footwear sector. The company is identifiable as a Born Global as it started its internationalisation since its establishment. It developed an omnichannel marketing strategy and has demonstrated resilience during recent crises.

Chapter 8: The digitalisation of internationalisation activities: is social media the next international entrepreneurial opportunity recognition tool for Born Globals? This chapter presents a business case integrating perspectives on entrepreneurial opportunity recognition and digitalisation in the internationalisation of a Finnish Born Global company operating in the cleantech sector. It contributes to the studies on the impact of digital technology on internationalisation in the international business field.

Chapter 9: The influence of decision-making logic on the internationalisation of Born Globals: Bolt. Bolt is the first European mobility super-app, offering ride-hailing, shared cars and scooters, food and grocery delivery. The company is operating in over 500 cities in more than 45 countries in Europe, Africa, Western Asia and Latin America and in 2022 was worth €7.4 billion. This chapter presents a case study of Bolt from the perspective of the decision-making logic's influence on the internationalisation of Born Globals.

Chapter 10: Cabaïa: can an eco-branding sustainability strategy foster the internationalisation of a Born Global? Two young French entrepreneurs, Bastien Valensi and Emilien Foiret, founded Cabaïa in 2015 to revolutionise the fashion accessories industry and internationalise quickly. The case discusses the first steps of their international development and addresses the internationalisation process of Born Global companies. It questions the role of marketing capabilities, eco-branding strategies, and the choice of a target market to succeed in rapid internationalisation.

Chapter 11: Boris & Rufus: hotspot on screen and costs on the backyard. Boris & Rufus is a Brazilian animation series produced by Bell Studio in Blumenau, aimed at children aged six to ten. This teaching case addresses the company as a born-again global firm, its rapid spread across Disney channels in Latin America and digital platforms, and the dilemma of turning the characters into licensable products worldwide. Furthermore, the case presents the dilemma of how to keep the company's business growth over the years to come.

REFERENCES

Andersen, O. 1993. On the internationalisation process of firms: A critical analysis. *Journal of International Business Studies*, 24, 209–31.

Bell, J. 1995. The internationalization of small computer software firms: A further challenge to 'stage' theories. *European Journal of Marketing*, 29, 60–75.

Bell, J., Mcnaughton, R. & Young, S. 2001. 'Born-again global' firms; An extension to the 'born global' phenomenon. *Journal of International Management*, 7, 173–89.

Bilkey, W.J. & Tesar, G. 1977. The export behaviour of smaller sized Wisconsin manufacturing firms. *Journal of International Business Studies*, 18, 93–8.

Cavusgil, S.T. 1980. On the internationalization process of firms. *European Research*, 8, 273–81.

Cavusgil, S.T. 1994. A quiet revolution in Australian exporters. *Marketing News*, 28, 18–21.

Cavusgil, S.T. & Knight, G. 2015. The born global firm: An entrepreneurial and capabilities perspective on early and rapid internationalisation. *Journal of International Business Studies*, 46, 3–16.

Coviello, N.E. & Munro, H.J. 1995. Growing the entrepreneurial firm: Networking for international market development. *European Journal of Marketing*, 29, 49–61.

Falahat, M., Knight, G. & Alon, I. 2018. Orientations and capabilities of born global firms from emerging markets. *International Marketing Review*, 35, 936–57.

Gabrielsson, M. & Manek Kirpalani, V.H. 2004. Born globals: How to reach new business space rapidly. *International Business Review*, 13, 555–71.

Ganitsky, J. 1989. Strategies for innate and adoptive exporters: Lessons from Israel's case. *International Marketing Review*, 6, 50–65.

Harveston, P.D., Kedia, B.L. & Davis, P.S. 2000. Internationalisation of born global and gradual globalising firms: The impact of the manager. *Advances in Competitiveness Research*, 8, 92–9.

Harveston, P.D., Osborne, D. & Kedia, B.L. 2004. Examining the mental models of entrepreneurs from born global and gradual globalising firms. In *New Technology-Based Firms in the New Millennium, Volume III*. Amsterdam: Elsevier, pp. 247–61.

Hayter, R. 1997. *The Dynamics of Industrial Location: The Factory, the Firm and the Production System*. Chichester, UK, Wiley.

Hedlund, G. & Kverneland, A. 1985. Are strategies for foreign markets changing? The case of Swedish investment in Japan. *International Studies of Management & Organization*, 15, 41–59.

Johannisson, B. 1994. Building a 'glocal' strategy: Internationalizing small firms through local networking. *International Council on Small Business 39th Annual World Conference, Strasbourg, June 27–29*.

Johanson, J. & Mattsson, L.-G. 1988. Internationalisation in industrial systems – a network approach. In N. Hood & J.-E. Vahlne (eds), *Strategies for Global Competition*. London: Croom Helm, pp. 287–314.

Johanson, J. & Vahlne, J.-E. 1977. The internationalisation process of the firm: A model of knowledge development and increasing foreign market commitments. *Journal of International Business Studies*, 8, 23–32.

Johanson, J. & Wiedersheim-Paul, F. 1975. The internationalisation of the firm – four Swedish cases. *Journal of Management Studies*, 12, 305–22.

Jolly, V.K., Alahuta, M. & Jeannet, J.-P. 1992. Challenging the incumbents: How high technology start-ups compete globally. *Journal of Strategic Change*, 1, 71–82.

Jones, M.V. 1999. The internationalisation of small high-technology firms. *Journal of International Marketing*, 7, 15–41.

Keeble, D., Lawson, C., Smith, H.L., Moore, B. & Wilkinson, F. 1998. Internationalisation processes, networking and local embeddedness in technology-intensive small firms. *Small Business Economics*, 11, 327–42.

Knight, G. & Cavusgil, T. 1995. The born global firm: Challenge to traditional internationalisation theory. In T.K. Madsen (ed.), *Proceedings of the Third Symposium of the Consortium for International Marketing Research*. Odense, Denmark: Odense Universitet.

Knight, G.A. & Cavusgil, S.T. 1996. The Born Global firm: A challenge to traditional internationalisation theory. *Advances in International Marketing*, 8, 11–26.

Knight, G.A. & Liesch, P.W. 2016. Internationalisation: From incremental to born global. *Journal of World Business*, 51, 93–102.

Knight, G., Madsen, T.K. & Servais, P. 2004. An inquiry into born-global firms in Europe and the USA. *International Marketing Review*, 21, 645–65.

Lindqvist, M. 1991. *Infant Multinationals: The Internationalization of Young, Technology-Based Swedish Firms*. Doctoral dissertation, Stockholm School of Economics.

Liu, Y. 2017. Born global firms' growth and collaborative entry mode: The role of transnational entrepreneurs. *International Marketing Review*, 34, 46–67.

Madsen, T.K. & Servais, P. 1997. The internationalization of Born Globals: An evolutionary process? *International Business Review*, 6, 561–83.

Madsen, T.K., Rasmussen, E.S. & Servais, P. 1999. *Differences and Similarities between Born Globals and Other Types of Exporters*. Odense, Denmark: University of Southern Denmark-Odense University.

McDougall, P.P., Shane, S. & Oviatt, B.M. 1994. Explaining the formation of international new ventures: The limits of theories from international business research. *Journal of Business Venturing*, 9, 469–87.

Meuric, P.-L. & Favre-Bonté, V. 2023. International high-growth of early internationalising firms: A feedback loop experience. *Journal of Small Business Management*, 1–47. doi:10.1080/00472778.2023.2169705.

Oviatt, B.M. & McDougall, P.P. 1994. Toward a theory of international new ventures. *Journal of International Business Studies*, 25, 45–64.

Oviatt, B.M. & McDougall, P.P. 1997. Challenges for internationalisation process theory: The case of international new ventures. *Management International Review*, 37, 85–99.

Oviatt, B.M. & McDougall, P.P. 2005a. The internationalisation of entrepreneurship. *Journal of International Business Studies*, 36, 2–8.

Oviatt, B.M. & McDougall, P.P. 2005b. Toward a theory of international new ventures. *Journal of International Business Studies*, 36, 29–41.

Puig, F., Gonzalez-Loureiro, M. & Ghauri, P.N. 2018. Running faster and jumping higher? Survival and growth in international manufacturing new ventures. *International Small Business Journal: Researching Entrepreneurship*, 36, 829–50.

Rasmussen, E.S., Madsen, T.K. & Evangelista, F. 2001. The founding of the Born Global Company in Denmark and Australia: Sensemaking and networking. *Asia Pacific Journal of Marketing and Logistics*, 13, 75–107.

Rennie, M.W. 1993. Global competitiveness: Born global. *McKinsey Quarterly*, 45–52.

Rialp, A., Rialp, J. & Knight, G.A. 2005. The phenomenon of early internationalising firms: What do we know after a decade (1993–2003) of scientific inquiry? *International Business Review*, 14, 147–66.

Young, S. 1987. Business strategy and the internationalisation process: Recent approaches. *Managerial and Decision Economics*, 8, 31–40.

TABLE OF CASES

1
The show's over at Cirque du Soleil

Étienne Desfossés and Félix-Antoine Chavanelle

CASE SUMMARY

This case is based on a real company operating in the entertainment field, specifically in the circus field. It is a decision-making case. The students are asked to play the role of advisors to Daniel Lamarre, the organisation's general manager at the time. They are asked to analyse the situation described and to make recommendations regarding the financial difficulties experienced by the Cirque. The students quickly noticed the Cirque industry's great need for capital to operate, while on the other hand, the company had often changed hands, with some shareholders being greedier than others. Thus, the students' journey will take them through the key themes of innovation financing, working capital, international finance and branding. The case is set in Canada in 2020 and the entertainment sector. The data used in this case was collected in the first half of 2022. The data is from secondary sources and was obtained through an extensive press review and various interviews given during the disclosure of Cirque's problems. The names of the individuals and companies involved in this case are actual, as the facts are public knowledge.

A Canadian company, Cirque du Soleil, was founded in 1984 and quickly expanded internationally, offering its shows on tour around the globe and recruiting artists from all around the world. In March 2020, the COVID-19 crisis had a major impact on the Circus, forcing it to pause all these shows and placing it under Companies' Creditors Arrangement Act of Canada. In the fall of 2021, the Circus will see the light of day again, reborn from its ashes, with more funding than before the crisis and a renewed management team. But what happened to the Circus? Why did the curtain fall on the Circus? Your students have been hired to see this through and propose solutions to the financial distress the Cirque is experiencing.

LEARNING OUTCOMES

The main learning outcomes of this case study are to:

- Show the impact of a global crisis on a Born Global operating in the entertainment industry.
- Highlight the importance of legislation and health policies differences between countries, in a context of global management.
- Present the importance of international finance management on Born Global.

- Mobilise essential concepts in innovation financing and working capital management.
- Understand the interaction of marketing and finance, by the nexus of the brand attractivity.

The secondary objectives are as follows:

- Develop and integrate technical vocabulary in the field of international financial management.
- Deepen one's culture and knowledge of the entertainment industry and global terminals.
- Distinguish between key and secondary mandates.
- Identify and isolate useful data in the context of abundant information.
- Collaborate, discuss, convince and communicate.
- Follow a thoughtful decision-making process.

INDUSTRY OVERVIEW

Although entertainment shows have their roots in Ancient Rome, the idea of mixing the acrobatic choreography of African civilisations, the jugglers of Ancient China and the dancers of Ancient Greece came to fruition with the cavalry Sergeant Major Philip Astley in 1768. He believed horsemen could show their prowess by performing tricks with their horses. In the same year, he decided to open his riding school. From a performance in front of King Louis XV to a show for Queen Marie-Antoinette, Mr Astley made a splash in Europe by adding clowns, rope dancers and jugglers to the performances. It was at this point that the world's first circus was born in 1782, The Royal Circus. The word 'circus' etymology comes from the word 'circle', which was the shape of the first amphitheatre that Sergeant Major Astley had his employee Charles Hughes build.

It didn't take long for the art of the circus to be exported to America. The American idea was to create family entertainment through the circus. Victor Pepin was the first to imagine this new trend. Over time, many showmen began to use trained exotic animals in addition to horses to entertain the audience. The industry became prosperous, and everyone wanted a piece of the action.

It was in 1881 that the big players began to emerge in the field. PT Barnum, a successful street performer in New York, joined forces with James Anthony Bailey to form the Barnum and Bailey Circus. Renamed 'The Greatest Show on Earth', Barnum and Bailey's circus became an attraction using acrobats, elephants, seals, clowns, and people with unique abilities. It was in the early 1900s that Barnum and Bailey Circus's main competitor, the Ringling Brothers, acquired the company, which had made its mark by using the uniqueness of some of its performers. In the UK, circuses such as Bertram Mills and Billy Smart, major players in the European industry, were influenced by innovations and shows in the US.

In China and the Soviet Union at the time, the circus industry was nationalised. In 1919, Lenin nationalised all of the circuses on the territory of the USSR and created national circus schools. Later, in 1949, the Chinese industry received a boost from the state. The Chinese government believed that the performances of its artists could bring in valuable foreign currency. With this in mind, circus schools were established throughout the cities of the Middle Kingdom.

It was not until the 1980s that the circus as we know it underwent a major transformation. Born in France from the first circus schools created in 1974, the new circus came from students graduating from these schools. Wishing to represent a new genre, these new shows did not present animals but rather a linked theatrical narrative breaking with the simple act and putting forward a dramaturgy presenting tableaux linked to a common thread. This is the creative circus. Cirque du Soleil, Cirque Plume, Archaos and The Pickle Family Circus were born during these years.

In 1995, Le Cri du Caméléon made its mark on the artistic scene by establishing itself as a work that blends dance, theatre and circus. Breaking the established codes of circus tents, circus rings and various disciplines, the show sets the table for what is known as the circus arts. Throughout this period, diabolo acts, balancing and contortion were added.

Until 2006, the circus arts were transformed, eventually leading to a new movement. The contemporary circus, as it is known today, carries the heritage of the circus arts and the new circus to form one. It has a network of institutions that can train the next generation in the production, distribution and promotion of shows. The programming of theatres, the cities that host festivals, and the schools are all stakeholders that can define the market through its diversity.

Yesterday's Ringling Brothers and Barnum and Bailey's Circus have given way to today's Cirque du Soleil, Archaos (Pôle National de Cirque), the Moscow State Grand Circus, Eloize, Cirque Knie and the Baku State Circus. Although these offer a contemporary flavour, with a thoughtful programme and a common thread, some circuses still exist as fairs. These use animals such as elephants and lions. Born Free is an organisation that campaigns and lobbies governments to end the use of animals in captivity. Some 30 countries have banned the use of animals in circus acts throughout their territory. While several countries worldwide have followed suit, circus strongholds such as France, the US, following the example of certain single state policies, and Canada have still not legislated on banning acts featuring animals.

FROM SMALL QUEBECER TO INTERNATIONAL GIANT

Cirque du Soleil is an entertainment company with a unique approach to integrating circus, art and music. A leader in the field, Cirque employs more than 4,000 people, including 1,400 performers from around the world, and generates close to a billion dollars in annual sales. Cirque du Soleil is a Quebec-based company headquartered in Montreal but has performed in over 450 cities in 60 countries worldwide. This movement has amazed nearly 200 million spectators since its creation.

The story of Cirque du Soleil began in the early 1980s when a troupe founded by Gilles Ste-Croix took to the streets of Baie-Saint-Paul, Quebec, showing off their talents. Initially known as Les Échassiers de Baie-Saint-Paul, it was under the direction of Guy Laliberté, a member of the original troupe, that the Cirque changed its name and became what it is today.

Cirque emerged in the wave of new circuses, questioning the uses of circus arts and borrowing more and more from the theatre, abandoning the stereotypes of the more classical circus.

In 1984, for the celebrations of Jacques Cartier's 450th anniversary of Canada, Laliberté launched a provincial tour. Never one to shy away from anything, the performances revolutionised the circus world of the time by presenting acts without animals while emphasising dramatic, beautiful and thought-provoking acts. From the quirky costumes to the various light shows combined with an original soundtrack, the energy and youthfulness of this new circus era can easily be represented by the Sun and, more importantly, will become a trademark element in the name.

It wasn't long before Cirque expanded, winning the hearts of Quebecers and citizens worldwide. Cirque carved out a place for itself in Quebec from city to national circus and then embarked on its first world tour in the late 1980s. In 1987, the first American tour was marked by performances at the Los Angeles Festival and sold-out shows in San Diego and Santa Monica.

Building on the success of Cirque du Soleil, the Mystère show became the first permanent show in the company's history in 1993. The complexity of the acts meant that the show was presented in a custom-built venue on the Las Vegas Strip. Mystère thrills the entertainment capital of the world with its breathtaking performances. Over the years in Las Vegas, Cirque has made its mark and become a must-see for anyone visiting the city. The circus is well known for its big top performances; however, it embarked on a diversification process in 2015, creating a dozen subsidiaries. These include Outbox, an event ticketing system, and 45 DEGREE, an event entertainment service. Today, Cirque du Soleil has expanded and can be found in Asia, Europe and South America. Always intending to delight audiences, the creative process behind each show and tour attracts contemporary circus fans to amphitheatres around the world.

THE CREATIVE PROCESS: THE DNA OF THE CIRCUS

The creative process owes its success, in part, to its renowned director, Franco Dragone. Leaving his small native village in southern Italy, Dragone studied at the Conservatory of Mons, where he developed a passion for commedia dell'arte and political theatre. The director moved to Quebec in the 1980s to join the early days of Cirque du Soleil. He played a decisive role in Cirque as creative director. With ten shows in 12 years, the Italian-born artist reinvented the circus by creating his own transdisciplinary genre. Mixing circus performance, choreography, music and technology, all linked by a simple story, Franco Dragone is changing the art of the circus in his lifetime. Dragone's vision is clear: to create spaces for the most sophisticated innovation without giving up on touching the audience at heart. This unique creative process is essential to the creation of a show in order to fulfil the vision.

In 1994, Cirque du Soleil's biggest show was born: Alegria, one of the biggest shows Dragone has put on. Inspired by the concept of power, Alegria will take us into a world in transition. The story of Alegria resonates with current world events at a time when monarchies are giving way to democracies. This show will be the only one to be given a makeover. Stopped in 2013, after no less than 19 years of service, the show will see the light of day refreshed in 2019. It is also its best-known production to date.

13 June 2018: The editors begin discussing their vision with the production team for a revamped Alegria. Barely six days later, auditions have begun, thanks to the editors who saved the scriptwriting! After that, all the steps followed quickly: creating costumes, acrobatic training, meeting artists, recording soundtracks, trying on costumes and make-up … so many steps to complete. Only three months before the presentation, in February 2019, the artists practised the mise-en-scene. Then, less than two months before the first performance, the team moves to the big top. So it is only more than ten months after the start of this great adventure that the artists will see the public for the first time. Franco Dragone, who passed away on 30 September 2022, will have left a rich legacy of creativity for those who follow in his footsteps at Cirque du Soleil and his company, Dragone.

Creating a show at Cirque du Soleil is about experimentation, the search for the new and the wonder of it all. This is the essence of Cirque and its DNA. This can range from equipment design to the development of new acrobatic concepts. As Émilie Therrien, acrobatic designer for the revival of the Alegria show, points out in an interview about the design process:

> We're more in research mode; after that, we'll really start to put the numbers together. In the same vein, an Acronet® was designed by a team of engineers for the Kurios® show, a net with bouncing properties. The Acronet® is a unique Cirque innovation that comes from a problem with the net in the Zarkana show and a high-flying troupe specialising in using this tool. Cirque invested in research and development to exploit this problem and make the net more bouncy. It may look like a simple trampoline to the spectators, but it is more complicated than it seems. Indeed, a whole team has been trained to use this invention. Six members of the Acronet® team are strategically placed on the net and are responsible for bouncing the acrobat with impulses. As one of the most complicated pieces of equipment that Cirque has in its arsenal because of its tension that must be precise to maximise performance, the Acronet® can throw trampolinists up to 40 feet in the air. The Acronet® creates a surprise effect during a show such as Kurios®, but also an infatuation of the acrobats to want to use a technology that is not seen anywhere other than Cirque du Soleil. Thus, the Acronet® represents a fine example of innovation as only Cirque du Soleil can do.

PROJECT-BASED FUND MANAGEMENT

A show project like Cirque du Soleil's is excessively capital-intensive. The remake of Alegria will have taken almost ten months before seeing its first audience, illustrating a long cash conversion cycle that requires a huge amount of cash. For ten months, designers, artists and administrative staff work hard to prepare a show worthy of the name, representing a significant investment. After this period of hard work, the troupes will finally step onto the stage, and ticket sales will replenish the coffers. In addition, these shows have significant costs: Zaia cost $150 million, while Love (a Beatles tribute show) required $100 million in renovations to the venue before any show could be designed to occupy it. On the other hand, the revenues are also there afterwards: Cirque generated $950 million in performance revenues in 2019. So, these are risky bets with large sums of money at stake, yet they can pay off big.

FROM HIRING TO CASTING

In an interview on state television, Daniel Lamarre makes no bones about the fact that the production of shows like those of Cirque du Soleil could not be possible with average employees. Thus, Cirque du Soleil has a casting approach instead of a more traditional human resources approach. Cirque du Soleil recruits the best candidate from around the world for all positions, from administrative staff to artists. The combination of such talents can only produce excellence. As a result, Cirque's staff comes from all over the world, and a multitude of languages are spoken within the troupes. In 2008, Cirque processed no less than 6,000 work permits and visas annually and had artists from some 40 countries (Turgeon, 2008). To recruit all of its talents, recruitment teams travel the globe to find the best talent for each act in each show. In addition to its recruitment teams and regional offices, a global talent attraction office evaluates needs and applications. In addition, Cirque has a separate website for recruitment, including pages detailing available positions, the artistic disciplines represented at Cirque, internal programmes and the benefits of working for Cirque. Thus, Cirque operates a skilful recruitment network in a global pool to fill equally global needs. Recruitment is more like artistic casting than hiring, as is usually the case in the corporate world.

THE CIRQUE DU SOLEIL BRAND

For more than 40 years, Cirque du Soleil has had a unique brand image based on a customer-centric approach. This approach suggests that marketing managers focus the product or service on a unique customer experience. By creating this experience, we ensure that the customer will be loyal and, what's more, will be more inclined to recommend the brand to others worldwide since they will be satisfied with their experience. Therefore, with permanent and different shows on five continents, a multi-domestic strategy is created by appealing to the local market's needs rather than adopting a more universal approach in the advertising effort and offers.

Cirque du Soleil stands out for its global perspective by creating its own markets by opting for a blue ocean strategy. This strategy allows the company to enter under-exploited markets with strong growth potential by creating a unique offering. The creativity and consistency of the shows set the company apart from its competitors by downgrading them and targeting an audience never before seen in the circus world: a recurring adult and corporate clientele. Cirque thus reinforced its position as a circus market pioneer through its innovation and a marketing approach that anticipates trends rather than reacting to them (Kim, Mauborgne, Bensaou and Williamson, 2002). The company is moving away from the traditional elements of the circus (notably the headlining artists and animal performances) towards a show closer to the theatre, including a strong narrative, quality music, a varied show and a unique show (Piotr, 2016).

This unique strategic positioning is an important part of Cirque's development. The development of Cirque du Soleil in China is a good example. When Fosun acquired 25 per cent of the company, Cirque's goal was clear: to conquer China, a country full of local circuses and, therefore, competitors. Even today, Cirque has not succeeded in conquering China completely and sustainably, although the activities there are not bad.

The pandemic proved that the Cirque du Soleil brand is strong. Indeed, Catalyst Capital, which has become the company's main shareholder, has made it its mission to relaunch Cirque. Daniel Lamarre, Cirque's boss, says that with such confidence, the Cirque du Soleil brand has nothing to envy Apple or Google. As for the Francophone name, it is a source of pride that it remains in Quebec, where the head office, with the majority of employees, is located.

INTERNATIONAL RIGHT DOWN TO THE CAPITAL

Cirque du Soleil, like many companies, has changed shareholders over the course of its history. While the shareholding was initially divided between Guy Laliberté and Daniel Gauthier, Guy Laliberté bought out Gauthier's share in 2001, becoming Cirque's sole shareholder. Thus, while it was concentrated in Guy Laliberté's hands in the early 2000s, its ownership changed over time, with Laliberté selling 20 per cent of the company's shares to Dubai World in 2008.

Thus, from its decidedly Canadian management to its globalised shareholding, Cirque also responds to Chinese and American financial interests. Since 2015, the shareholding has included the Caisse de Dépôts et de Placement (10 per cent), the Chinese company Fosun (25 per cent) and the American TPG (55 per cent), and Guy Laliberté (10 per cent). In 2015 a large dividend was paid to shareholders, and nearly $100 million in management fees have been paid to TPG since then. This is TPG's recipe: a substantial drain on the funds of these investments to ensure a quick return on investment for its clients.

In 2020, the company opened a new round of financing to replenish the coffers. Catalyst Fund Limited Partnership V, Sculptor Special Master Fund Ltd and ABRY Advanced Securities Fund III L.P. join the shareholders and now own the largest share of the pie, as revealed by the Quebec Enterprise Registry.

A VIRUS AT THE CIRQUE

In 2015, Cirque propelled nearly 20 productions around the world. In 2020, nearly 50 shows are still on the agenda, but public health will determine otherwise. 13 January: the first case of a virus that will give the authorities a hard time is discovered. Coronavirus, later renamed COVID-19, will have a big impact on the circus. Just 13 days later, the World Health Organization declared a state of international emergency. However, it was not until 13 March, two months after the crisis began, that Cirque du Soleil suspended no less than 44 productions worldwide, including all those touring in tents and arenas. Two days later, it was the resident's

Table 1.1   Productions from the last two years before COVID-19 and their years of the first performance

Alegria: Un nouveau jour	2019
Paramour	2019
Nos Divas	2020
Sous un même ciel	2021

turn to take a break. Thus, no Cirque production will set foot on the stage between 15 March 2020 and the beginning of 2021. This forced break will cause the dismissal of 95 per cent of Cirque's 4,697 employees, leaving a large proportion of them without severance pay and with weeks of unpaid wages for most of them. The pandemic also closed Cirque's box office, making its revenues almost nil. During this period, few activities were initiated at the circus. Among the few activities, there will be a redeployment of the platform.

Four of these shows have been developed in the last two years, as shown in Table 1.1. Most of these shows have been postponed to 2021, waiting for the health crisis to subside. However, some shows will take longer, such as Nos Divas, which will not be performed until the summer of 2022 in Trois-Rivières, Quebec.

In this situation, Cirque found itself in a poor financial situation, forcing it to place itself under Canada's Companies' Creditors Arrangement Act (CCAA). However, the response in the Canadian and international business ecosystem was swift: Cirque had to be saved.

- But how do you explain that a company in such good shape should be protected by the Companies' Creditors Arrangement Act (CCAA)?
- What could Cirque have done to protect itself from such risks?
- What managerial solutions would you have proposed to Daniel Lamarre, Cirque's CEO at the time?

YOU CAN'T DO TRAPEZE WITHOUT A GOOD NET

It should be noted that from the very first announcements, Quebecor, a Quebec telecommunications giant, had shown interest in acquiring Cirque. In addition, other international investors have also shown interest in the matter. Daniel Lamarre, the general manager at the time, also mentioned that this could be attributed to Cirque du Soleil's strong brand image, an image of creativity and excellence in innovation that is recognised internationally. All of this suggests that the circus has a certain potential for profitability, which is of interest to shareholders.

The company quickly resorted to a capital reinjection by shareholders. In addition, Cirque called on the National Bank to provide financial advice during this troubled period. It was not until mid-May that we learned that the Quebec government would invest no less than $200 million, associated with a right to buy back TPG and Fosun shares and an obligation to maintain the head office in Quebec. Shortly after that, Cirque's bankers reinvested $375 million, allowing Cirque's activities to resume as the intensity of the pandemic decreased. In the summer of 2022, Cirque announced record attendance at its Montreal-based Kooza show, making it Cirque's highest-attended show in the metropolis where its headquarters are located. The resumption of touring in early 2022 will also reassure investors, which Moody's rating agency reflects in an upgrade of Cirque's credit rating, noting that 'this financial rating upgrade [from Caa1 to B3 in financial terms] reflects Cirque du Soleil's solid management of the show restart, including the successful relaunch of its touring division in the first half of 2022'.

However, why did the Circus come to that point? How can Daniel Lamarre prevent it, and how can we qualify the virus at the Cirque du Soleil? You've been engaged as a consultant to sort this out, and Daniel Lamarre hopes the best for your intervention at the Circus.

TEACHING NOTES

LEARNING OUTCOMES

This case will lead the student to study the impact of a global crisis on a born global. Thus, it will highlight the importance of legislation and health policy differences between countries, but above all, the importance of international finance on born global. The case will also mobilise essential innovation financing and working capital management concepts.

TARGET AUDIENCE

This case will be mainly dedicated to advanced students in bachelor or licence (undergraduate) in the field of international management and finance. Moreover, the case could also be apropos for MBA students. Thus, this case could be useful in courses on working capital management, international financial management, and innovation financing or in courses on global business strategy.

SUGGESTED TEACHING STRATEGIES

The proposed strategy for a 60-minute discussion:

DEFINITION OF THE PROBLEM

Plenary discussion with the whole group to structure the students' suggestions after reading the case. The idea is first to clarify and isolate the mandate of the proposed case. To do this, the following questions are suggested:

- What is the real problem?
- What could go better?
- Is it critical?
- Why should the problem be addressed?
- Who should act? Who owns the problem?

The teacher will have to make a pedagogical choice about whether to go deeper into this plenary stage and investigate the nature of the problem, or to move on more quickly and leave the identification of the nature of the problem to the teamwork.

SETTING THE CONTEXT

Work in small groups to assess the nature of the problem and the roles of the different actors in relation to this problem. For this purpose, it is suggested to use Porter's force model or the '5C' analysis: Company, Context, Clients, Competitors and Collaborators. This step defines the problem precisely and eliminates secondary problems from the case. A return to the plenary is possible at this stage in order to validate the students' understanding of the problem.

POLARISATION

The options that are valid for the company should therefore be precise, which the teacher can put forward to contrast the options and invite a debate among the students. The students are then sent back to their small groups to discuss the different options and choose the solution that they feel is most appropriate to the current situation.

DECISION-MAKING

The teacher brings the students into a large plenary group and invites them to present the option chosen by their team. As a teacher, you can then take the opportunity to emphasise the theoretical elements on which the teams are based, as well as the structure of the argument. There should be many questions from the teacher at this stage to invite students to reflect on the advantages and disadvantages of their proposed solutions.

IMPLEMENTATION

Implementing managerial decisions is probably the hardest task of a manager. In this case, the student will most likely have to review the company's highest policies, which is no mean feat! In order to stimulate the students' reflections before offering them a return course in small groups to see the implementation, the teacher may consider the following questions:

- The short- and medium-term impacts of decisions on the organisation's internal and external stakeholders;
- The impact on the company's functional activities;
- The performance indicators related to the decision concerned;
- The operational implementation of the decisions (challenges to be met; resources required; implementation schedule, and financial impact);
- The relevance of a possible contingency plan (alternative solutions to be provided in case the planned solution is not sufficient);
- The means of monitoring and maintaining the selected solution.

SUGGESTED ANSWERS TO DISCUSSION QUESTIONS

As this case aims to study the financing of innovation and its relationship with working capital, as well as with the brand, we suggest the following solution path, although we recognise that there are a number of solution paths.

DEFINITION OF THE PROBLEM

As a result of the COVID-19 crisis, Cirque du Soleil experienced a sudden halt in its revenue streams, which put it in a very bad situation. A few weeks into the crisis, Cirque owed thousands of dollars in unpaid salaries, not to mention suppliers who waited a long time, some of whom never saw their money again. Faced with this situation, Cirque had to apply to the Companies' Creditors Arrangement Act of Canada. The general manager is therefore looking for ways to act and recruits you as a consultant.

SETTING THE CONTEXT

COMPANY

The Cirque du Soleil is an organisation known for its leadership in innovation. It produces high-quality shows that require large sums of money to produce. As a result, Cirque's working capital requirements are considerable, and there are many expenses before it receives its first revenues from developing a new show.

CONTEXT

COVID-19 quickly shut down all of Cirque's shows, reducing revenues to zero. Cirque had several new shows in the works for which revenues were just starting to come in, while many of the expenses had already been disbursed. In addition, Cirque tried to keep its employees employed at first, but it took a few weeks before a major layoff hit Cirque's performers, as there was no way to keep them employed.

CLIENTS

Cirque du Soleil's clientele is different from the typical clientele of other circuses: Cirque du Soleil attracts a corporate or more adult clientele in search of wonder at the artists' sets, music and prowess. In the past, before COVID-19, the clientele were very loyal to the circus, but due to health restrictions that were incompatible with the circus activities, it wasn't enough to keep the circus running.

COMPETITORS

Cirque has little to worry about from its competitors, as it is in a niche of its own. However, it is noticeable that Cirque has succeeded in carving out a place for itself with a brand much stronger than the industry average and recognised worldwide.

COLLABORATORS

Two groups of collaborators stand out in the case: Cirque's shareholders and its creditors. It is easy to see that, despite the fact that Cirque is a world-class and widely recognised company, its ownership has varied greatly over time, passing through several hands, including investment funds. This can create a rather peculiar agency conflict, in which the shareholders are interested in draining Cirque as much as possible, rather than allowing it to develop and reinvest the profits. It is, therefore, appropriate to question the goals of these shareholders, which are naturally involved in Cirque for financial reasons.

The analysis of the different facets of the case leads to a diagnosis that can be deduced as follows: the nature of Cirque du Soleil's business requires a high level of working capital, as expenses come much earlier than revenues due to the nature of Cirque's creation process. However, the shareholders do not seem to have paid particular attention to this characteristic of Cirque. In addition, COVID-19 has placed Cirque du Soleil in a particular situation where it has slowed the inflow of revenues, placing Cirque in a most perilous situation. As a result, Cirque du Soleil has run through all of its working capital and will be placed under creditor protection, approaching bankruptcy.

DECISION-MAKING

Several solutions are possible, but we recommend a new capital call through a new share issue. Indeed, Cirque is more than profitable and recognised with a strong brand. Thus, the capital issue should be done under relatively good conditions, allowing the company's working capital to be replenished. This should result in an increase in the defensive interval ratio, allowing Cirque to weather further turbulence. However, this is only a temporary solution; a longer-term change should be made by creating a fund dedicated to creating new shows. Thus, part of the income from each tour would go into the fund to pay for the design of future shows. To be effective, this fund would need to have a strong policy, including restrictive standards that prohibit taking money out of it for dividends. In the event that this fund is not sufficient, the company should explore credit facilities with its current shareholders or creditors in order to mitigate new situations similar to COVID-19, should they arise.

CASE CONCLUSION

To conclude the case facilitation in a way that maximises the learning experience for the students, it is suggested that the teacher ends on a more theoretical note. This will allow the teacher to present recently studied theories related to the Cirque du Soleil case. At this stage, we advise against taking any questions until the end to deal with the theoretical content while the case is as fresh as possible for the students and to avoid any break in the rhythm of the activities.

USEFUL LINKS

History of the circus. Accessed 26 October 2023, at https://www.theguardian.com/stage/2018/jan/19/chainsaw-juggling-human-cannonballs-and-coco-the-clown-the-astounding-250-year-story-of-circus
History of contemporary circus (in French). Accessed 13 October 2023, at https://www.artcena.fr/reperes/cirque/panorama/panorama-du-cirque-contemporain/le-cirque-contemporain-la-creation-pour-adn

BIBLIOGRAPHY

Agence QMI (2020) Les actionnaires du Cirque du Soleil investissent 50 M$ US. *le Journal de Montréal*, 5 May. Accessed 26 October 2023, at https://www.journaldemontreal.com/2020/05/05/les-actionnaires-du-cirque-du-soleil-investissent-50-m-us

Boudreault, J. (2009) Le Cirque du soleil, quelle histoire! *Cap-aux-Diamants*, 97, 10–15.

Brousseau-Pouliot, V. (2021) Qui sont les actionnaires du Cirque du Soleil? *La Presse*, 21 June. Accessed 7 October 2023, at https://igopp.org/qui-sont-les-actionnaires-du-cirque-du-soleil/

Chaoul, N., M. Diallo, R. Sardheeye, G. Gadonon and M.O. Diallo (2016) Donner seconde vie à IRIS. Project management and its context, academic report of MGP7111, 16 April, 12pp.

Cirque du soleil (2015) *KURIOS about Acronet – Episode 5*. Video published on 17 November. Accessed 26 October 2023, at https://www.youtube.com/watch?v=iPwkhg5Y9kg

Cirque du soleil (2022) À propos de nous. Accessed 26 October 2023, at https://www.cirquedusoleil.com/fr/a-propos-de-nous/historique

Cloutier, J.-F. (2020) Comment le Cirque s'est endetté d'un milliard $ US en cinq ans. *Journal de Québec*, 18 May. Accessed 13 October 2023, at https://www.journaldequebec.com/2020/05/28/comment-le-cirque-sest-endette-dun-milliard-us-en-cinq-ans?fbclid=IwAR17l9mw9OWiyI4k_AX4 jFHN6Mp2dD3SZ1QBduhq--G9ljMzjGVJDtpGDC4

Dragone (2020) Notre histoire. Accessed 13 October 2023, at https://dragone.com/fr/discover-dragone/notre-histoire/

Faucher, M., A. Chevrier and A. Béland (2020) La pandémie au Québec, en citations et en dates, 22 April. Accessed 26 October 2023, at https://www.ledevoir.com/documents/special/2020-04-22-pandemie -citations-dates/index.html

Gadner, Lyn (2018) Chainsaw juggling, human cannonballs and Coco the Clown! The astounding 250-year story of circus, 19 January. Accessed 7 October 2023, at https://www.theguardian.com/stage/2018/jan/19/chainsaw-juggling-human-cannonballs-and-coco-the-clown-the-astounding-250-year -story-of-circus

Guy, Jean-Michel (2019) Le cirque contemporain: la création pour ADN. *Centre des Arts du Cirque, de la rue et du théâtre*. Accessed 26 October 2023, at https://www.artcena.fr/reperes/cirque/panorama/panorama-du-cirque-contemporain/le-cirque-contemporain-la-creation-pour-adn

Kim, W.C., R. Mauborgne, B.M. Bensaou and M. Williamson (2002) Even a clown can do it (A and B): Cirque du Soleil recreates live entertainment. Case study published at INSEAD. Accessed 26 October 2023, at https://casecent.re/p/8195

Lamarre D. (2022). Daniel Lamarre et le Cirque du Soleil: tout feu tout flamme [entrevue télévisée]. *Tout le monde en parle*, 26 January. Accessed 2 October 2023, at https://ici.radio-canada.ca/tele/tout-le -monde-en-parle/site/segments/entrevue/386926/guy-lepage-daniel-lamarre-cirque-soleil

Lamarre, D. (2022) *L'équilibriste: Performez grâce à votre créativité*. Éditions Michel Lafon, Neuilly-sur-Seine Cedex, 349pp.

Piotr, K. (2016) *The Basic Assumptions of Blue Ocean Strategy*. 1st International Conference Contemporary Issues in Theory and Practice of Management (CITPM).

Turgeon, D. (2008) *Haute voltige au Cirque du Soleil*. Revue RH, Ordre des Conseillers en ressources humaines agréés du Québec (CRHA), 13 June. Accessed 22 October 2023, at https://ordrecrha.org/ressources/revue-rh/archives/haute-voltige-au-cirque-du-soleil

Whitney Leavens (2022) Moody's upgrades Cirque's CFR to B3; outlook stable. Rating action. *Moodys credit rating*, 23 June. Accessed 13 October 2023, at https://www.moodys.com/research/Moodys -upgrades-Cirques-CFR-to-B3-outlook-stable--PR_467257

APPENDIX 1A: TIMELINE

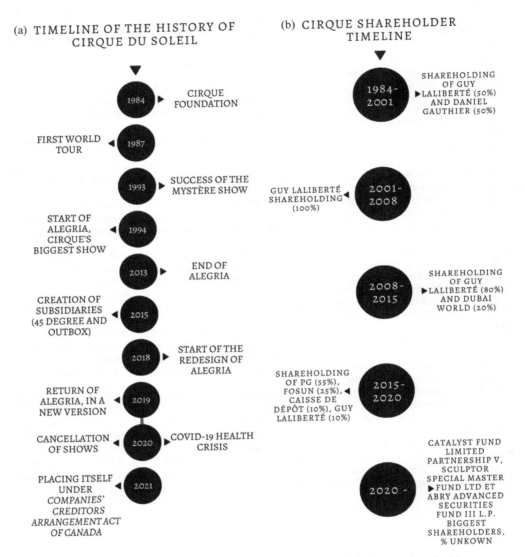

(a) TIMELINE OF THE HISTORY OF CIRQUE DU SOLEIL

1984 ▶ CIRQUE FOUNDATION

FIRST WORLD TOUR ◀ 1987

1993 ▶ SUCCESS OF THE MYSTÈRE SHOW

START OF ALEGRIA, CIRQUE'S BIGGEST SHOW ◀ 1994

2013 ▶ END OF ALEGRIA

CREATION OF SUBSIDIARIES (45 DEGREE AND OUTBOX) ◀ 2015

2018 ▶ START OF THE REDESIGN OF ALEGRIA

RETURN OF ALEGRIA, IN A NEW VERSION ◀ 2019

CANCELLATION OF SHOWS ◀ 2020 ▶ COVID-19 HEALTH CRISIS

PLACING ITSELF UNDER *COMPANIES' CREDITORS ARRANGEMENT ACT OF CANADA* ◀ 2021

(b) CIRQUE SHAREHOLDER TIMELINE

1984–2001 ▶ SHAREHOLDING OF GUY LALIBERTÉ (50%) AND DANIEL GAUTHIER (50%)

GUY LALIBERTÉ SHAREHOLDING (100%) ◀ 2001–2008

2008–2015 ▶ SHAREHOLDING OF GUY LALIBERTÉ (80%) AND DUBAI WORLD (20%)

SHAREHOLDING OF PG (55%), FOSUN (25%), CAISSE DE DÉPÔT (10%), GUY LALIBERTÉ (10%) ◀ 2015–2020

2020 – ▶ CATALYST FUND LIMITED PARTNERSHIP V, SCULPTOR SPECIAL MASTER FUND LTD ET ABRY ADVANCED SECURITIES FUND III L.P. BIGGEST SHAREHOLDERS, % UNKOWN

Figure 1A.1 (a) Timeline of the history of Cirque du Soleil; (b) Cirque shareholder timeline

2

Born Globals or born nomads? The case of medical cannabis producers in Denmark

Ulrik Nielsen

CASE SUMMARY

With the legalization of medical cannabis in various countries and states, a legitimate industry for cannabis-derived products is emerging world wide. This case study delves into the emerging medical cannabis industry, particularly focusing on LPs in Denmark. The case aims to enhance students' understanding of market opportunities and the challenges in transforming an illegal industry into a legitimate one, with businesses operating under standard market conditions and how regulatory environments can influence the internationalization process of firms. Particularly, as the firms in the industry face difficulties in generating sustainable and profitable growth. The case introduces three dominant market verticals in the legal cannabis industry and raises questions about the potential barriers to export and the unpredictability of legal reforms in the international medical cannabis market. It also disucusses the influence of macro, meso and micro-level factors on firms' internationalization strategies. By examining this real-world scenario, business students gain insights into the complexities and challenges of operating in an emerging industry subject to diverse regulatory frameworks and societal perceptions. This case encourages students to apply international business theories to a highly current and practical situation and fosters critical thinking in addressing strategic decisions in an emerging industry.

LEARNING OUTCOMES

The main learning outcomes of this case study are to enchance students' abilities to comprehend and evaluate market opportunities in an emerging industry, specifically focusing on the medical cannabis industry. Students will explore the challenges and potential opportunities of transforming an illegal industry into a legitimate one, with businesses operating under standard market conditions. The case study seeks to challenge students' understanding of the internationalization process of firms, with a particular emphasis on the importance of the home market and how varying regulatory frameworks can impact a firm's expansion into international markets.

INTRODUCTION

Cannabis sativa L. has for many years been a controversial plant. Public disputes about its recreational consumption and medical value have, since the late 1930s, resulted in the plant being classified internationally as a narcotic with no currently accepted medical value (Lebesmuehlbacher and Smith, 2021). However, since 1996, when the State of California first legalized cannabis for medical use, there has been a trend towards legalization in other regions and countries. Canada, for instance, followed suit in 2001, allowing cannabis for medical purposes, and later in 2018, expanded the legalization to include recreational use. Consequently, this global shift towards legality has given rise to a nascent industry of legitimate businesses that commercialize cannabis-derived products (Kelly et al., 2020; Shaffer, 2020). Presently, more than 24 countries and 36 US states have legalized cannabis for medical purposes, signifying a growing acceptance of its therapeutic potential. To this end, several other countries are actively working towards implementing regulatory frameworks that can accommodate the increasing demand from consumers to replace black-market cannabis products (Krause and Pullman, 2020; Lebesmuehlbacher and Smith, 2021; Parker et al., 2019). Such transformation of the cannabis industry from being illegal to a legimate and regulated market can have significant social, health and economic implications. Industry reports argue that the total legal cannabis market in North America surpassed $12 billion in 2019 (Lebesmuehlbacher and Smith, 2021) and forecasts that the European market will reach as much as €3.2 billion by 2025, growing with a compound annual growth rate of 67.4 percent (Prohibition Partners, 2021). The emergence of the legal cannabis industry has created a plethora of business opportunities. As countries continue to implement regulations to accommodate legal cannabis, entreprenuers are exploring various market verticals and value chain activities, contributing to job creation and innovation. However, despite possessing a capital advantage by being publicly traded companies, a large proportion of the most well-funded business in the emerging cannabis industry has been highly inconsistent in generating sustainable and profitable growth. A recent study has found that the performance of the ten largest Canadian cannabis companies did not improve how investors had speculated (Chen et al., 2021). This suggests that there is a gap in our understanding of how to do business in the emerging cannabis industry and the strategies that will enable such firms to adapt, compete, and survive internationally in the restricted, regulated, and still emerging industry of cannabis. Neglecting such a gap in both practice and theory runs the risk that policymakers and corporate executives miss out on realizing the industry's growth potential. Particularly, the regulatory landscape inherent in the transformation of the cannabis industry remains complex and dynamic. Policymakers face the challenge of striking a balance between ensuring public safety and addressing the needs of the industry. In order to strike such balance, there is imminent need for in-depth multidisciplinary academic research to provide insights into effective policy frameworks. With an outset in firms operating in the Danish medical cannabis industry, this case study offers a unique opportunity for international business students to bridge the gap between academic theories and practical challenges faced by firms operating in an emerging and rapidly changing industry. Thus, the case aims to provide international business students (IB) with the possibility to test and scrutinize existing IB theories in an industry that is emerging in different geographic areas at specific times, at various levels (e.g., medical, recreational, and pharmaceutical), with applicable laws being widely different.

The case will focus on licensed producers (LPs) of medical cannabis, and the abbreviation LPs will be used for these firms. To this end, the Danish medical cannabis industry serves as a catalyst for exploring the multifaceted aspects of an emerging market and its potential impact on global business practices. Through rigorous examination and analysis, students can derive valuable insights and contribute to the knowledge base surrounding this transformative industry. The internationalization process of firms is particularly intriguing due to the varying legal frameworks and cultural perceptions across different geographic areas. This case study delves into the strategic decisions made by LPs as they navigate different markets, positioning themselves for growth and expansion. The trajectory of the legal cannabis industry combined with the challenges of navigating diverse legal frameworks and consumer preferences, offers valuable lessons for international business strategy.

Market verticals of the legal cannabis industry

The emerging legal cannabis industry can broadly be classified into three dominant market verticals based on its purpose and scope of usage, as illustrated in Figure 2.1. A market vertical refers to a specific niche or segment within an industry that focuses on a particular group of customers with distinct needs and characteristics. Thus, a market vertical represents a specialized market that serves a well-defined and narrow customer base with unique requirements, products or services. Consequently, each market vertical comes with its own set of challenges, regulations, and specific requirements, making it essential for specialty businesses in the legal cannabis industry to understand and address the unique needs of the customers within that particular market vertical.

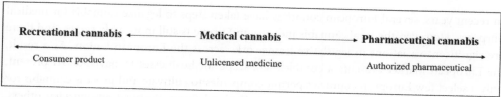

Source: Author.

Figure 2.1   Market verticals of the legal cannabis industry

The global momentum for the legalization of cannabis is driven by medical cannabis, an unlicensed cannabis-derived medicinal product sold without marketing authorization to alleviate symptoms of specific medical conditions (Parker et al., 2019). Products in this market vertical often involve using the whole unprocessed or processed plant. Products are sold as either capsules, oils, nasal or oral sprays containing either THC (delta-9-tetrahydrocannabinol), CBD (cannabidiol), or a combination of the two. The use of medical cannabis products limits legal users to patients with a doctor's prescription serving as a control mechanism for patient safety (Krause and Pullman, 2020). Another market vertical is recreational or adult-use cannabis which describes cannabis consumed for non-medical purposes. Recreational and adult use are often used interchangeably as both emphasize cannabis intended only for the consumption by adults of legal age and in legal jurisdictions that allow cannabis for reasons beyond medical ones, such as physical performance, engaging in creative activities, and spiritual purposes (Prohibition Partners, 2021). Users tend to either smoke it or consume it via edibles. The recreational or adult-use cannabis market category constitutes a significant size of the legal cannabis industry in the United States and Canada (Krause and Pullman, 2020). However, black-market products are often included in this market category as it is illegal in many countries to consume cannabis for pleasure. The third market vertical is pharmaceutical cannabis which refers to products formulated or processed using cannabinoids (either plant-extracted or synthetic). A distinct characteristic of pharmaceutical cannabis is that products have gone through full clinical trials like traditional pharmaceuticals and thus are licensed as a pharmaceutical with marketing authorization.

Since the market vertical of medical cannabis drives the global momentum for legalization, and this distinct market vertical represents the point of entry into the industry for most firms operating in countries implementing regimes to accommodate legal cannabis, these firms will arguably be forced to decide which strategy to pursue: Will it be a consumer product company that focuses on addressing consumer preferences and tastes? Or will it be a pharmaceutical company aiming for scientific breakthroughs and revolutionary medicines? The difference between the customer segments is evident and needs to be addressed by the firms to avoid a nomadic internationalization process that is hinged upon the legislative frameworks in emerging markets.

THE EUROPEAN MARKET FOR MEDICAL CANNABIS

In recent years, several European countries have taken steps to legalize cannabis for medical purposes. However, the legal cannabis industry in Europe is still in its early stages, and there are significant variations in legislative frameworks across the European Union. As a result, the European market presents a complex landscape for businesses to navigate. At present, only a select few European countries permit companies to cultivate and process cannabis for medical use. These countries include Denmark, England, Spain, Portugal, among a few others. Germany also allows for cannabis cultivation and processing for medical purposes, but it has imposed restrictions on the size of production sites for Licensed Producers (LPs), capping it at around 1,000 square meters. This limitation has led to economic challenges for businesses in the industry. France initiated a two-year pilot program for using medical cannabis in 2021. However, the cultivation of high-THC cannabis is illegal, making both France and Germany highly dependent on the import of medicinal cannabis products. The latter is the largest European market in terms of imports; 50 percent of retail sales in 2019 were sold in Germany, followed by Italy and Denmark; 19 percent of the total German imports in 2021 were from LPs in Denmark.

Medical cannabis producers in Denmark

In 2018, the Danish Parliament implemented a novel four-year pilot and development program for medical cannabis. The program's purpose was to establish a regulatory framework for the safe ordination and use of medical cannabis to patients. Initially, the pilot program only allowed firms operating in Denmark to obtain a license to import medical cannabis products from foreign markets. However, political concerns about the quality and supply of products available in foreign markets led the Danish Parliament to extend the pilot program. Thus, in 2019 firms operating in Denmark were provided with an opportunity to be granted a license to cultivate and process cannabis for medical purposes. This led Denmark to be one of the first European countries to allow large-scale production of cannabis for medical purposes. Compared to a few other European countries allowing cannabis for medical purposes, the Danish Parliament adopted a relatively liberal approach to developing the industry. Firstly, no limitations on the number of cultivation licenses were imposed, and secondly, no restrictions on the production volume were enacted. As a result, Denmark has since 2019 received a large influx of foreign direct investments from countries such as Canada, Germany, and Australia, intending to establish LPs that can serve the growing European demand for medical cannabis. A recent industry report indicates that Denmark has attracted more than 200 million euros in foreign direct investments within the medical cannabis industry. In addition to the pilot program, a development scheme was concurrently introduced in 2019. This scheme enabled firms to obtain a license to develop and practice methods for creating medical cannabis products or services based on less strict rules. For example, all cultivated cannabis by firms in the development program must be destroyed according to the guidelines of the Danish Medicine Agency. The innovative approach of letting firms experiment with medical cannabis products or services has created a vibrant entrepreneurial ecosystem of start-ups within this industry in Denmark. In November 2021, the Danish Parliament unanimously passed L 44 A, which transformed the Danish medical cannabis industry from a pilot project into a permanent industry.

Only a small number of the Danish LPs has a domestically produced product on the home markets from which it can generate revenue. A large proportion of the industry's revenue comes from export activities, particularly to the German market. The Danish market is still crucial for several smaller and newly established companies, but increased exports will primarily drive their future growth.

In a recent analysis of the Danish medical cannabis industry, several of the largest LPs highlight that the industry needs more accessible access to the Danish market. One of the reasons for the absence of Danish-produced products is, according to the LPs, the very complex regulatory conditions for medical cannabis concerning getting products approved on the Danish market. Going forward, the Danish Medicines Agency should develop one or more guidelines to help ensure a more uniform and smooth case processing of product approvals. With the new legislation, it is also possible for the companies to get their products approved as magistral medicinal products (medicines prepared in a pharmacy for an individual patient). This, however, requires a new and different permit than the ones issued under the medical cannabis pilot program, which is expensive and time-consuming. To ensure that more Danish-produced products can enter the Danish market, the Danish Medicines Agency may consider creating a FastTrack scheme for LPs, which has already been approved in the pilot program.

Consequently, will the emerging industry of medical cannabis follow the historical path of consumer products, pharmaceutical industries, or forge a unique trajectory? Sparse evidence exists of value chain activities that will evolve into high-value generating endeavors and the strategies enabling firms in this industry to adapt, compete, and thrive internationally amidst restrictions and regulations are still developing. Much IB and, in particular, the Born Global literature is based on a liberal approach to markets. In contrast to industries like robotics and software, which operate in global markets without stringent regulations, the medical cannabis industry is established upon a complex web of evolving regulatory frameworks and societal perceptions. Hence, will businesses in this industry align with the conceptualization of Born Global firms or become Born Nomad firms that will be dependent on the continuous relocation of operations to countries more conducive to their sustained expansion and profitability in the transformation of the industry to a legitimate one, with businesses operating under standard market conditions? Due to industry transformations, firms operating in the legal cannabis industry may find themselves confronted with the necessity of becoming a "nomadic enterprise". As technological advancements, changing consumer preferences, and regulatory shifts reshape the industry, the firm faces the imperative to adapt and maintain competitiveness. Consequently, the firm must strategically relocate its operations from country to country, seeking new markets, skilled labor, and favorable business environments to sustain growth and remain agile in the face of evolving market conditions. Embracing this nomadic internationalization process allows the firm to capitalize on emerging opportunities while mitigating potential risks and uncertainties associated with the transformative industry.

Licensed medical cannabis producers in Denmark

To date, the Danish medical cannabis industry consists of approximately 36 firms which broadly cover the value chain of the medical cannabis industry. To date, the industry in Denmark employs approximately 286 full-time employees, many of whom are employed in firms located on the island of Funen. From 2019 to 2021, full-time employees increased from 152 to 286. This development equates to an increase of 88 percent, illustrating a nascent but highly growing industry. On average, the industry expects an annual growth rate of more than 19 percent from 2020 to 2026.

Furthermore, the industry expects to employ more than 410 full-time employees in 2024. This growth equates to a 43 percentage point increase in full-time employees in 2021. Some of Europe's largest LPs of medical cannabis are operating in Denmark. Around half of the firms in the Danish medical cannabis industry are LPs, and more than 40 percent of the companies have activities related to product development. Additionally, 30 percent of the firms have activities within genetics or plant breeding, which illustrates that the Danish medical cannabis industry is based on a robust horticultural tradition in Denmark.

An LP is a firm that has been granted the license to cultivate and process cannabis for medical purposes. Compared to other European countries that currently allow the cultivation of cannabis for medical purposes, Denmark is offering LPs comparative advantages. For example, there is no limitation on the number of cultivation licenses that can be granted to firms, and there are no restrictions on the production volume. Hence, the regulatory system for medical cannabis production in Denmark is predominantly designed for the mass exportation of cannabis. As a result, Denmark has received a large amount of foreign direct investments from countries such as Canada, Germany, and Australia to establish productions that can serve the growing European demand for medical cannabis. The largest LPs are predominantly concentrated on the island of Funen and perceive themselves as Born Global firms due to their early focus on export sales.

Nevertheless, only a few countries with medical cannabis regimes currently allow imports. For example, Canada, the largest federally regulated market for medical cannabis in the world, still does not allow commercial imports. Furthermore, only little is known about if or when these markets will expand because the size of the addressable market is dictated by regulations governing the industry in the respective countries. Although there are changes in public perception toward increased acceptance of the perceived risk and benefits of medical cannabis, LPs face political and cultural changes to a degree not seen in many industries. Market potential does not hinge on product superiority; instead, public opinion plays a key role, as seen in the United States, where some states that have legalized cannabis have done so based on a citizen-initiated referendum (Chiu et al., 2022). Accordingly, understanding fluctuation in public opinion and government attitudes will be crucial to the necessary forecasting for doing business in the global medical cannabis industry. Consequently, the LPs in Denmark are constantly faced with decisions related to the location of value chain activities as there is a lack of insight into which industry tendency the cannabis industry will emulate and how these locational advantages will develop in the long run. Currently, many firms are fully integrated into the value chain due to regulatory uncertainties. For example, it can be observed that an established accumulation of LPs located in the region of Funen in Denmark aims to possess control of all value chain activities instead of specializing or distributing the value chain activities geographically. In contrast to horticulture, the pharmaceutical industry has experienced very different developmental paths, producing distinct industrial ecosystems stemming from the specific location advantages of the value chain activities. Thus, managers of LPs will need additional insights and guidance to situate future value chain activities to realize the full growth potential of the industry.

Currently, some of the largest LPs currently operating in Denmark are:

- Aurora Nordic (Canadian multinational enterprise)
- Schroll Medical (Danish family-owned)
- Little Green Pharma (Australian multinational enterprise)

DISCUSSION QUESTIONS

The situation in the Danish market where locally produced products are highly unavailable is quite a paradox since many Danish producers are already exporting to Germany, Poland, Italy, Australia, France, etc. In connecting to the Born Global literature, observing how this develops could lead to an interesting theoretical discussion of a firm's internationalization before being established in its home market.

1. Identify key factors and recent developments driving industry's growth, and discuss how they vary across different geographic areas and market verticals.
2. Describe the challenges and opportunities in transforming an illegal industry into a legitimate one, operating under standard market conditions. How can businesses navigate the complex and dynamic regulatory landscape while seeking sustainable and profitable growth?
3. Identify the strategies that the Danish LPs pursue to expand internationally, given the varying legislative frameworks and cultural perceptions across different countries. Do they follow the path of Born Global firms or a nomadic internationalization process?
4. Examine which countries allow exports and eventual barriers to export.
5. How fast will international import/export markets open up for unapproved medical cannabis?
6. Is it impossible to predict legal reform and regulatory development? If yes, how could such a task be solved?
7. Define the macro, meso, and micro levels of analysis.
8. How can the levels influence each other?
9. Seen from a firm perspective, how do the macro and meso levels influence the strategy?

SUPPLEMENTARY INFORMATION

Supplementary information provided in this section will enable the student to enrich the answering of the discussion questions.

Empirical observations add an extra layer to the traditional Born Global concept, which assumes homogeneous access to countries. The industry, in this case, is highly dependent on the fluctuation of various market externalities such as stigma and cultural, religious, and political trends. The entire value chain is present in the Danish context, but the route to the home market is hindered through registration, whereas foreign markets such as Poland, Germany, Italy, etc. provide less complex routes. In addition, these markets offer greater market potential, which feeds early internationalization.

Much IB and, in particular, the Born Global literature is based on a liberal approach to markets, for example, robotics and software industry that operate without global regulations. In contrast to these industries, national government and regional regulation hinder the free movement of goods for the medical cannabis industry. Of course, other industries face divergent regulative restrictions, but the medical cannabis industry is unique as it builds on a highly stigmatized (and often illegal) industry which is currently being transformed to match pharma-alike industrial standards.

REPORTS

Insight report 2019 – Medical cannabis – the City of Odense (available at the following link: https://investinodense.dk/wp-content/uploads/2020/02/Medical-Cannabis-Insight-report-2019.pdf, accessed July 2023).

Medical Cannabis in Denmark – an industry analysis 2022 (available at the following link: https://investinodense.dk/wp-content/uploads/2022/05/Medical-Cannabis-in-Denmark-2022.pdf, accessed July 2023).

REFERENCES

Chen, F., Choi, S., Fu, C. & Nycholat, J. 2021. Too high to get it right: The effect of cannabis legalization on the performance of cannabis-related stocks. *Economic Analysis and Policy*, 72, 715–34.

Chiu, V., Hall, W., Chan, G., Hides, L. & Leung, J. (2022) A systematic review of trends in US attitudes toward cannabis legalization. *Substance Use & Misuse*, 57(7), 1052–61. doi:10.1080/10826084.2022.2063893.

Kelly, K., Berry, C., Comello, M.L.G. & Ray, H.B. 2020. The regulatory and marketing environment surrounding the legalization of retail marijuana and the impact on youth. *Journal of Public Policy & Marketing*, 40, 62–82.

Krause, D. & Pullman, M. 2020. Fighting to survive: How supply chain managers navigate the emerging legal cannabis industry. *Journal of Supply Chain Management*, 57(3).

Lebesmuehlbacher, T. & Smith, R.A. 2021. The effect of medical cannabis laws on pharmaceutical marketing to physicians. *Health Economics*, 30, 2409–36.

Parker, K.A., Di Mattia, A., Shaik, F., Cerón Ortega, J.C. & Whittle, R. 2019. Risk management within the cannabis industry: Building a framework for the cannabis industry. *Financial Markets, Institutions & Instruments*, 28, 3–55.

Prohibition Partners. 2021. *The European Cannabis Report 6th Edition*. Prohibition Partners.

Shaffer, C. 2020. Medical cannabis pioneers stake their claims. *Genetic Engineering & Biotechnology News*, 40, 52–5.

3
GASTECH, a French born-again global firm

Pierre-Louis Meuric, Véronique Favre-Bonté and Charles Aymard

CASE SUMMARY

Born-again globals are firms that have joined the international entrepreneurship field, the traditional exporter, and Born Global firms. Indeed, according to Bell, MacNaughton and Young (2001), born-again global firms are companies that first focus on their domestic market before internationalising quickly. This rapid internationalisation dynamic is usually driven by a 'critical' event that triggers the SME's internationalisation. In this case, we present the story of GASTECH, which has followed the same pattern and can thus be considered a born-again global firm. First, we present its context, then the firm's main figures and finally, the three main segments of its timeline. We finish this case by asking questions about the firm's internationalisation and how it overcame some difficulties. This case discusses how managerial crises can trigger rebound effects and how specific capabilities make it possible to succeed abroad.

LEARNING OUTCOMES

The main learning outcome of this case study is to understand the path born-again global firms take. We have identified three primary outcomes to understand how firms can become born-again global after encountering difficulties. The case study results show that we can discern three phases (the inception phase and the first difficulty – the turning point – the strategy's renewal). These phases may be typical to all born-again global firms, even though contextual elements must be considered. When analysing the paths of international companies, it is necessary to identify these phases to understand which phase the firms are undergoing. For each phase, several things are helpful to analyse to formulate proper advice.

- Difficulties young firms may have in internationalising:
    - Competitive international landscape: difficulty for small, knowledge-intensive firms to compete with multinational enterprises (MNEs).

- The initial product does not necessarily fit market demand: difficulties in finding market opportunities and correctly identifying the client's needs.
- Difficulties going from a 'start-up phase' to a 'scale-up phase': from developing the product to commercialising it at a large scale.

Based on the GASTECH case, we have identified three main difficulties. These obstacles illustrate companies' troubles when they fail to adopt a global strategy. Difficulties are symptomatic of the first phase. This phase is typical of born-again globals having difficulties making a significant shift and thinking about the global market. This first phase precedes the rebound effect that managers can trigger when they have identified and solved the problems relating to global competition.

- Rebound effect – crises as a trigger for international expansion:
  - The arrival of a new, experienced CEO: a tipping point for the firm's trajectory.
  - The setting of a new strategic vision.
  - Importance of the skills and sector knowledge of the shareholders: they drive the strategy.

The rebound effect is an essential phase for born-again global firms. This phase shows that managers have succeeded in facing their difficulties in the first phase. After identifying the difficulties and finding solutions to overcome them, firms can begin the third phase related to the firm's international growth and new developments.

- The launching of a new internationalisation strategy:
  - Team composition: multicultural team with several nationalities; regular interactions between engineers and sales teams. The implementation of a new organisational setting.
  - Emphasising the CEO's role: experience, marketing capabilities, international mindset.
  - Marketing capabilities: market scouting, getting involved in international networking, visiting international trade shows.
  - The agility of the firm and the CEO to meet evolving market demand and innovate (incrementally and radically).

THE CONTEXT – INDUSTRY AND COUNTRY SETTING

GASTECH[1] is a firm based in the Auvergne Rhône-Alpes region (AURA) and was established in 2014. The AURA[2] region is France's second most economically dynamic region after the Ile de France (Paris) region. This region offers an extensive research ecosystem with two world-class universities: University Lyon Lumière and University Grenoble Alpes. Within that dynamic and competitive ecosystem is a specific institution called the CEA[3] (*Commissariat à l'Energie Atomique et aux énergies alternatives* [Commission for Atomic and Alternative Energies]). The CEA is a French scientific institution that leads programmes in the fields of energy, defence, information and communication technologies, material sciences, life sciences and health. One part of their work concerns the application of scientific work. Every year, several high-tech start-ups are created within that research ecosystem. Therefore, this organisation is an intermediary between the academic, economic and social spheres. Over ten years, the CEA has filed more than 600 patents and ranks as the leading French research organisation in the number of patent applications published. Among the firms that the CEA has created are SOITEC[4] and STMicroelectronics,[5] which have become world-leading firms in their domain.

GASTECH is another firm initiated by the CEA to respond to constraints in the energy industry. GASTECH sells chromatographs,[6] which allow gas companies to test and evaluate gas quality before it can be sold. This chromatograph is groundbreaking as it allows gas firms to test the gas quality on site. Thus, they can save gas producers a substantial amount of time and, thus, money. The chromatography market involves few but strong competitors. Indeed, some other firms are offering the same type of innovation. These companies include ABB, Siemens and Emerson, which are GASTECH's direct competitors. These competitors are multinationals that base their strategy on mass production and target a wide range of countries. All these companies target gas producers who must test their gas quality before selling it. Indeed, all gas does not have the same caloric value and thus cannot be sold at the same price. Thus, GASTECH is targeting an industry with a small number of major customers such as Total, Eni, Gasprom, Exxon Mobil, Shell, etc. In total, this industry involves around 20 actors, spread across the gas producing regions. GASTECH is therefore evolving within a highly competitive market with strong competitors, high entry costs and a low number of potential clients.

THE FIRM AND ITS COMPETITORS

GASTECH has three main competitors: ABB, Siemens and Emerson. ABB was created in 1988, has 110,000 employees and has generated a $US13.2 billion turnover. Today, ABB is mainly present in the UK, Germany, Norway, Canada and Japan. The second main competitor is Siemens. Siemens was created in 1847 and has 303,000 employees. Nowadays, Siemens has a turnover of $US62.3 billion and is present in Brazil, China, India, Germany, the US and the Middle East. Finally, the last main competitor is Emerson. Emerson was founded in 1890, has generated a turnover of US$17.4 billion and employs 87,500 employees. Emerson is present in different countries, in particular, Canada, UAE, Singapore, Australia, Brazil and Germany. We summarise this information in Table 3A.1 in the Appendix.

Concerning GASTECH, as an innovative start-up, the organisation is much smaller. Indeed, GASTECH only employs 25 people, who are mainly engineers. In 2021 the firm generated $US3.3 million of turnover ($US770,000 in 2019). Of this, $US3.3 million (75 per cent) is from international sales. This share of turnover has been constant since 2019. Thus, we can argue that GASTECH is a start-up with high-growth potential. GASTECH is using subsidiaries and distributors as entry modes. The two main market entries which have been realised since 2019 are Italy and China. Thus, GASTECH needs to find a solid and relevant competitive advantage if it wants to compete with its direct – and much more significant – competitors. We summarise this information and the GASTECH evolution in Table 3A.2 in the Appendix.

A SHORT HISTORY OF THE FIRM WITH A TIMELINE IN THE APPENDIX

The story of GASTECH can be told in three phases: inception stage, turning point and international growth.

Phase 1: the inception stage and the difficulties encountered by GASTECH

As mentioned above, GASTECH was created in 2014 by a group of scientists from the CEA and Caltech to respond to a need in the gas market. This project was supported by one of the more prominent market actors in Europe: Engie. Indeed, Engie has targeted some opportunities regarding biogas, and its managers thought it would be wise to exploit that market segment. No affordable chromatograph had been developed in that domain, so it seemed missing among the market offers. Thus, Engie and some other shareholders encouraged the firm to develop additional technological features that did not match GASTECH's initial product.

Nonetheless, they quickly realised that the biogas segment would not be enough to generate a return on investment. Indeed, the market was composed of many major players with much more capital than GASTECH. These actors included MNEs like ABB, Siemens and Emerson (described in Table 3A.1), which could benefit from an extensive network and had all the internal capabilities needed to develop the same products and technologies. Moreover, their size and worldwide reputation opened up doors to the big players in the gas and oil industry. Thus, it was clear that the balance of power was tipped in favour of the big players, and GASTECH did not immediately find its way to international growth. But where was the mistake made?

With the benefit of hindsight, the company's leader explains it:

> So GASTECH made the mistake of putting on the side their innovations ... to redevelop solutions that were sold by other chromatograph manufacturers ... and we developed a chromatograph on this basis ... it is an excellent product, it is full of exciting characteristics ... but it is positioned along with ABB, Siemens, Emerson ... multinationals who want to position themselves in this market, because it is an international mass market ...

The right strategic choice had not been made initially, especially concerning the product. Indeed, during that first phase, GASTECH teams were mainly composed of scientists and engineers who did not have any experience in the marketing field: they worked a lot on the product conception phase and thus overestimated the product's potential on the market. As GASTECH proposed a groundbreaking innovation, the CEO thought the gas industry would 'bow down' to their product. Also, the project manager did not align with the firm's need to sell the product. The engineers focused on the product development phase instead of finding solutions that allowed the firm to discover potential customers. Another grave mistake was made regarding the firm's strategic plan. Indeed, the firm was not well advised about the market segment to target or the market configuration overall. Therefore, this gap in knowledge and the misconceptions of the shareholders (founders included) led the firm close to bankruptcy. Several years after its inception, the company still had not generated consistent revenue, despite its eagerness to internationalise. The shareholders were thus worried about the company's future, leading the organisation to a management crisis: they hired a new CEO to manage the firm's sales and marketing strategy.

The following verbatim from the new GASTECH CEO illustrates the start-up's failure:

> And that's a very common mistake among start-ups too ... to underestimate all these difficulties ... So, after that ... there was ... it was a big failure ... GASTECH had invested in R&D to develop this solution and it came back without a market, with a product but without customers ... and the investors asked themselves what to do ... Did they have to reinvest? ... Did they have to stop everything? ... and that's when they recruited me ...

Phase 2: the turning point when the firm changed its strategy

The turning point occurred when the shareholders decided to change their strategy and hire a new CEO to find new market opportunities and enhance their international marketing dynamic. For doing so, they chose Mr Martin, who has a strong background in fields related to GASTECH's activities. First, as he studied engineering, he knew how to interact in this domain and had all the capabilities to lead technological projects (Figure 3.1).

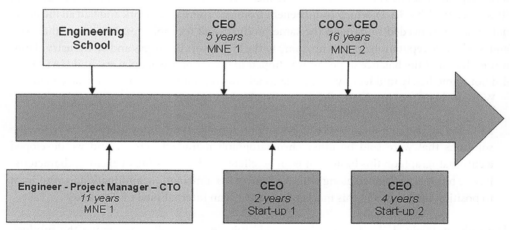

Source: Authors.

Figure 3.1   Martin's career path

He occupied different engineering and project manager roles during his early career before reaching a CEO position. Meanwhile, he had also developed sales and marketing capabilities during his career as he occupied CEO positions in several firms. His first firm was in the sector of energy services and equipment (MNE1). Martin worked as a CEO for five years before he joined a start-up in the information and communication sectors for two years. He then joined the board of another energy services and equipment MNE (MNE2), where he held a COO and

CEO position for 16 years. Finally, he joined GASTECH, an energy services and equipment start-up. Thus, Martin had extensive knowledge of the gas and oil market configuration and an extensive network in these sectors. Indeed, his career focused on the energy sectors and international business as he managed subsidiaries abroad. Thus, Martin seemed to be the perfect candidate for managing GASTECH's international growth.

Martin remembers this period:

> The fact of having the MNE2 reputation [in my CV] in the field of chromatography … led to GASTECH contacting me … because it had just undergone quite a lot of failure, in particular, the departure of their general manager … at the time as I had the experience of chromatography … and the experience of the markets in which GASTECH was trying to develop … Made them [GASTECH] offer me the job, and I thought it was pretty cool it was a good fit, and it seemed like a pretty exciting and motivating adventure …

When Martin took this new position as CEO, he immediately redefined the company's foundations and rethought the whole strategy according to his previous experience. He decided that the first priority was to differentiate GASTECH from its competitors and find a place where the big competitors like Siemens or ABB were not (a kind of 'blue ocean strategy'[7]). Indeed, according to Martin, the main mistake GASTECH made was immediately reaching out to the 'whole world' even though the firm had no chance against bigger players. Therefore, he also restructured the firm's internationalisation plan. He focused first on European markets to test their offerings before quickly moving to a more distant market (China, in this case).

Martin explains:

> We really have to target the few applications where we think we can make a difference … we have to look geographically where we are going to position ourselves … So on this geographical aspect … we make Europe a priority … it is France and Europe … France is number 1 and then some countries where there were facilities … Italy … Spain … Switzerland … some rather close bordering countries … by facility … and then … China …

Meanwhile, Martin changed the pricing strategy. Indeed, the price GASTECH was charging to make the firm profitable was very high. According to Martin, this was a bad idea: start-ups cannot charge their potential clients high prices because they have not yet built a reputation for their work. As part of this pricing strategy, he decided to change the offer. Martin decided that GASTECH should work on their services, particularly client support. For him to succeed, the organisation needed to follow 'the step-by-step' strategy, going slow to gain reputation.

Martin on the price policy:

> Then you need to have a very aggressive pricing policy … when you are a start-up, you can't claim … to charge a lot of money for something that the customer would be able to buy from a competitor for less … so you have to prime the pump … have very aggressive prices … to find the first customers … So we must … propose solutions to our customers … and

support them … that is to say lend them equipment … show them the advantages that we can provide … So we must spend a lot of energy on supporting our customers …

Finally, he also decided to restructure the engineering project programme. When Martin took his position, he quickly realised that GASTECH needed to move from an engineering approach to a commercial one. This means that the project needed to think not in terms of 'technological attractiveness' but 'technological profitability'. Martin decided that the company could not respond to all requests for adaptations from potential clients but just to those few that would make the company profitable.

Martin on how GASTECH designed products:

> We still tend to make products … I would say make products a bit to please ourselves … here we are, we're capable of that, so we do that … there's no serious confrontation with the market … for one simple reason … we don't have a good person who deals with marketing …

Phase 3: the firm's international growth and how the firm deploys its strategy

From that point, GASTECH quickly found a way to grow internationally. Among the specific points we mentioned, GASTECH succeeded as an organisation scouting specific opportunities. Indeed, the CEO quickly understood that some firms wanted to sell the product under their brand. GASTECH thus decided not to sell the entire chromatograph, selling it as 'spare parts'. Thus, its customers could sell the product under their brand. These clients then sold the same chromatograph to other firms in niche markets where they had specific knowledge and a stronger competitive advantage. Today, the two major clients of GASTECH are Italian and Chinese. Thanks to this new technique, GASTECH met its market expectations.

In the Italian market, the client was eager to develop their chromatograph to sell in the case of a security check. Thus, selling a chromatograph for its specific application in the gas production security sector was the best option. GASTECH succeeded in that mission by integrating its technology and knowledge into a brand-new product dedicated to another function.

Martin on the Italian market:

> So there is one in Italy… its business is the odorisation of natural gas … natural gas is odourless … so they add a chemical compound to it to give it odour and to detect if there is a leak. So it's an additional molecule that they add in the gas … this company was making the system that makes it possible to inject the odorant … and now he wanted to sell the system that would make it possible to measure the concentration of this molecule throughout his network … we developed a specific version for this application for them … we integrated them into a box … and we are going to sell them …

The other example concerned the Chinese market. GASTECH has been interested in the Chinese market as it presents huge opportunities for energy companies. Indeed, the Chinese government has tried to apply norms to their gas production system. For example, they are applying a lot of norms for gas quality to sell it at a specific price.

Martin on the Chinese market:

> Why China? Because first of all, this market has a huge appetite for technology … it has a certain supply of American products … and above all, the Chinese government is creating standards…. and organising its own country in terms of infrastructure … earlier I was giving the example of energy in natural gas … until now, in 2019 the Chinese when they sold natural gas it was only on volume … they realised that it was not right … so they imposed new standards … new laws … for the Chinese market … for energy measurement in the environmental field … they are the most active in the world now …

Henceforth, GASTECH seized that opportunity by offering 'capabilities' and a 'knowledge base' to Chinese firms eager to develop their chromatograph to sell, not as European or American chromatographs but as Chinese. For Martin, the secret of success for high-technology firms is to offer high-added-value products in a specific niche market.

Thanks to this strategy, GASTECH now generates 75 per cent of its turnover abroad, and the firm has experienced a 100 per cent average growth rate per year. In 2019, GASTECH went from a near 0 US dollar turnover to 735,000 Euros. It doubled its turnover in the following years to reach a 1.470 million Euro turnover in 2020 and doubled it again in 2021 to reach 3 million Euros. The company expects to double this figure again in 2022 and thus become 'profitable' at the beginning of 2023. GASTECH also tried to strengthen its international presence by setting up a subsidiary in China and hiring a new sales representative to target further markets. Indeed, today the company is seeking new opportunities in other regions producing gas. They are looking particularly at the US, which seems more open to start-ups. This could allow GASTECH to enter that market quickly and increase its turnover. Meanwhile, the firm is also interested in the food industry because, like the oil & gas industry, this industry is subject to a substantial number of product quality norms. Thus, this market segment could fit the technology developed by GASTECH.

Martin on the GASTECH market approach:

> It was the principle … we don't have any products … or we have to finalise them, so we don't have any sales … today there … We have made a little progress on this … there are products that we manage to sell … in a recurrent way, to the same people … and the same company … So that's interesting … but it's still fragile … but it's not very diversified … Because we are dependent on 1, 2, 3 big accounts … these accounts represent 80–90% of our turnover …

DISCUSSION QUESTIONS

Some questions arise in connection to the issues mentioned above. To answer these questions, you can rely on the texts above and articles on international business.

1. What were the main difficulties encountered by GASTECH in the early stages of its

internationalisation? More broadly, what difficulties do firms that internationalise early experience?

2. What are the main capabilities required for firms that want to start a new phase of internationalisation? Can you define them? How can recruiting the right capabilities at the right time generate a rebound effect?

3. What management practices would you have put in place to manage the Push and Pull strategies, develop internationally and match customers' needs with the firm's innovations?

THE PROBLEMS TO BE DISCUSSED – MARKETING, SALES, MANAGEMENT, R&D, SOURCING, ETC. – WITH A FOCUS ON THE TASKS FOR THE STUDENTS AND READERS

Throughout this case, we aim to discuss new firms' difficulties when they internationalise. We present how management crises trigger rebound effects and how marketing capabilities make it possible to succeed abroad. To discuss this case and understand how young firms internationalise, we have identified some issues related to entrepreneurs' experience and firms' evolution.

To analyse this case, we propose the following scenario: You are a member of a consulting firm mandated to support young companies in their international development. Given the contextual elements presented above, you are asked to formulate an audit around the questions asked by your clients. In order to make recommendations to enlighten business leaders on the resumption of the internationalisation process, you will insist on coherence between the practical and theoretical elements.

Based on the case of the firm GASTECH, three main issues are identified to analyse how young firms can grow internationally again after a phase of stagnation. These issues are three-fold: strategic, human and managerial.

- Strategic vision: Identify and discuss the difficulties encountered by GASTECH and, more broadly, firms that internationalise early. This issue focuses on small businesses' first steps into the international arena and their speed of internationalisation. In a general way, discuss the difficulties for firms that grow quickly into international markets.

- Capabilities and human resources management: Discuss recruiting the right capabilities to go international again. Highlight the importance of certain capabilities (team composition/marketing capabilities/CEO's networking abilities). How can recruiting the right capabilities at the right time generate a rebound effect (triggering factors)?

- Push vs Pull strategy: Discuss the managerial choices between pushing innovation and pulling the customers' needs. This issue focuses on entrepreneurs' willingness to exploit opportunities abroad (Pull) or propose a new solution/innovation to internationalise. How can firms balance between the Push and Pull strategies (challenges between engineers and sales teams: how do they interact? etc.).

LEARNING OUTCOMES – WHAT THE READER WILL LEARN FROM THE CASE STUDY

We have identified three main outcomes to understand how firms can become born-again global after facing difficulties. The primary learning outcomes focus on three points related to the path born-again global firms take. The results of the case study show that we can discern three phases. These phases may be typical to all born-again global firms, even though contextual elements must be considered. When analysing the paths of international companies, it is necessary to identify these phases to understand which phase firms are currently undergoing. For each phase, several aspects are helpful to analyse in order to formulate proper advice.

Based on the GASTECH case, we have identified three main difficulties. These obstacles illustrate the trouble companies find themselves in when they fail to adopt a global strategy. Difficulties are symptomatic of the first phase. This phase is typical of born-again globals with difficulties making a significant shift and considering the global market. This first phase precedes the rebound effect that managers can trigger when they have identified and solved the problems relating to global competition.

The rebound effect is the most important phase for born-again global firms. This phase shows that managers have succeeded in facing the difficulties in the first phase. After identifying the difficulties and finding solutions to overcome them, firms can begin the third phase related to the firm's international growth and new development.

TEACHING NOTES

TARGET AUDIENCE

This case could be taught in international business, entrepreneurship and small-business management courses. This case is appropriate for Master's degree students.

SUGGESTED TEACHING STRATEGIES

We see three possible scenarios for using this case:

a. Scenario 1: this case could be used during a course (3 to 4 hours);
b. Scenario 2: a 2-hour exam;
c. Scenario 3 (our preference): we think it is best to give the case as homework, allowing students one or two weeks to read the case and collect information about it (academic papers, internet research, etc.).

SUGGESTED ANSWERS TO DISCUSSION QUESTIONS

Q1 What were the main difficulties encountered by GASTECH in the early stages of its internationalisation? More broadly, what difficulties do firms that internationalise early experience?

The difficulties faced by GASTECH during its first phase of internationalisation are numerous. They are gathered in the six following points. These points are based on the textual elements from the interviews/'verbatims' with the top management team of GASTECH.

- Building too strong a technical knowledge base: R&D is too prominent in the inception stage;
- Misunderstanding the market configuration and expectations;
- Not finding new international opportunities or staying up to date on competitors' products;
- Not paying attention to marketing or setting up a relevant marketing strategy in terms of product, price, place,and promotion;
- Not finding the proper knowledge and capabilities;
- Not finding good shareholders (advisers) who know how to internationalise and develop the firm.

More generally, it would be interesting to compare GASTECH's difficulties with other born-again globals to assess the similarities between these different cases. We invite teachers to introduce other cases of born-again globals to identify similarities and differences with GASTECH and refer to the academic literature suggested above.

Q2   What are the main capabilities required for firms that want to start a new internationalisation phase? Can you define them? How can recruiting the right capabilities at the right time generate a rebound effect?

MARKETING CAPABILITIES

The marketing team should understand the cultural differences between the home and targeted countries. These differences in marketing expectations depend on the countries where Born Global operates.

To overcome these marketing gaps between several countries, hiring a multicultural team is helpful, as was the case for GASTECH.

To start a new phase, a firm needs teams that are mature and dynamic enough to be able to identify the specific characteristics of the targeted markets. This ability to manage different profiles within the same marketing team makes it possible to combine the experience of older managers and the agility of younger employees.

TECHNICAL CAPABILITIES

Technical skills occur at a different level than marketing capabilities. In this case, the issue is producing a good or a service that is likely to correspond to the expectations of consumers (in the case of a company operating in a B2C) or to the expectations of clients (in the case of a company operating in a B2B).

In GASTECH's case, its technical skills were not discussed during the internationalisation. On the other hand, the products offered by GASTECH didn't necessarily satisfy the customers. Therefore, it seems interesting to mention that technical skills must be aligned with marketing skills to begin a new phase of internationalisation.

End of Q2   How can recruiting the right capabilities at the right time generate a rebound effect?

THE ARRIVAL OF A NEW AND EXPERIENCED LEADER

The rebound phase is delicate. It requires the arrival of an experienced person who will have to, in a short space of time: (1) make a rapid analysis of the situation, (2) identify the problem(s), (3) provide short-term solutions because the company is in a difficult phase and time is running out, but also prepare for the medium-term future and put in place a real vision and strategy. To go further on the central role of the leader, we refer, in particular, to the numerous studies in international business highlighting individual characteristics in the management of small firms (see Hsu et al., 2013).

STRATEGIC ALIGNMENT

Moreover, these abilities must be managed: collaboration between the different profiles (technical and marketing) must be established through, for example, collective work sessions, weekly meetings, etc. Beyond 'operational' capabilities, it is essential for the company to have a strategic vision and to hire its resources according to what it plans to do. Alignment of resources and strategy is vital.

At the end of the analysis of GASTECH's case, we see several managerial practices as fundamental to an international re-launch. When recruiting a CEO who will lead the company through its 'turning point', the future CEO must have:

- A strong strategic vision, as well as the ability to implement this vision,
- Previous experience with international procedures,
- Technical abilities to guarantee the strategy's implementation and make employees feel secure.

Q3 What management practices would you have put in place to manage the Push and Pull strategies, develop internationally and match customers' needs with the firm's innovations?

The case of GASTECH reveals a double challenge for companies that want to go international: on the one hand, the innovation challenge of exploring new products or services, and on the other hand, the exploitation challenge of slightly improving and marketing already existing products and services.

The underlying question is about innovation management for companies that want to move quickly into international markets.

For GASTECH, in the beginning, the company did not know how to manage these two issues simultaneously. This lack of management competencies caused a slowdown – or a halt – in the internationalisation process. By changing elements in its management, marketing strategy and the creation of new products, GASTECH combined solutions to simultaneously respond to the challenges of creating new products (Push strategy) and customising its products (Pull strategy).

NOTES

1. For confidentiality reasons, we are using a fictitious name.
2. https://www.auvergnerhonealpes.fr/ (accessed 2021).
3. https://www.cea.fr/english (accessed 2021).
4. https://www.soitec.com/en/?__geom=%E2%9C%AA (accessed 2021).
5. https://www.st.com/content/st_com/en.html (accessed 2021).
6. In chemical analysis, chromatography is a laboratory technique for the separation of a mixture into its components. The mixture is dissolved in a fluid solvent (gas or liquid) called the mobile phase, which carries it through a system (a column, a capillary tube, a plate, or a sheet) on which a material called the stationary phase is fixed. The instrument used to perform certain chromatography is called a chromatograph.
7. Kim, W.C., & Mauborgne, R. (2005). Value innovation: A leap into the blue ocean. *Journal of Business Strategy*, 26(4), 22–8.

SUPPLEMENTARY INFORMATION NEEDED TO ANSWER THE CASE QUESTIONS

Below are key references to scientific papers and suggestions for reading that can be used in the discussion.

Bell, J., McNaughton, R., and Young, S. (2001). 'Born-again global' firms: An extension to the 'born global' phenomenon. *Journal of International Management*, 7(3), 173–89.

Helm, R., Mauroner, O., and Pöhlmann, K. (2017). Gazelles versus mice: Understanding their characteristics and the specifics of growth as a performance measure for research-based spin-offs. *International Journal of Entrepreneurship and Innovation Management*, 21(4–5), 343–65.

Hsu, W-T., Chen, H-L., and Cheng, C-Y. (2013). Internationalisation and firm performance of SMEs: The moderating effects of CEO attributes. *Journal of World Business*, 48, 1–12.

Johanson, J., and Vahlne, J.E. (1977). The internationalisation process of the firm – a model of knowledge development and increasing foreign market commitments. *Journal of International Business Studies*, 8(1), 23–32.

Johanson, J., and Vahlne, J.E. (2009). The Uppsala internationalisation process model revisited: From liability of foreignness to liability of outsidership. *Journal of International Business Studies*, 40(9), 1411–31.

Knight, G. (2015). Born global firms: Evolution of a contemporary phenomenon. In *Entrepreneurship in International Marketing*. Bingley, UK: Emerald Group Publishing.

Knight, G.A., and Cavusgil, S.T. (2004). Innovation, organisational capabilities, and the born-global firm. *Journal of International Business Studies*, 35(2), 124–41.

Knight, G.A., and Liesch, P.W. (2016). Internationalisation: From incremental to born global. *Journal of World Business*, 51(1), 93–102.

Meuric, P-L., and Favre-Bonté, V. (2023). International high-growth of early internationalizing firms: A feedback loop experience. *Journal of Small Business Management* (forthcoming).

Meuric, P.-L., and Favre-Bonté, V. (2023). What makes early internationalising firms grow faster? *Management International Review*, 27(2) (forthcoming).

Romanello, R., and Chiarvesio, M. (2019). Early internationalising firms: 2004–2018. *Journal of International Entrepreneurship*, 17(2), 172–219.

Schueffel, P., Baldegger, R., and Amann, W. (2014). Behavioral patterns in born-again global firms: Towards a conceptual framework of the internationalisation activities of mature SMEs. *The Multinational Business Review*, 22(4), 418–41.

Sheppard, M., and McNaughton, R. (2012). Born global and born-again global firms: A comparison of internationalisation patterns. *Handbook of Research on Born Globals*, 46–56.

Steinhäuser, V.P.S., Paula, F.d., and de Macedo-Soares, T.D.L.v. (2021). Internationalization of SMEs: A systematic review of 20 years of research. *Journal of International Entrepreneurship*, 19, 164–95.

Weerawardena, J., Mort, G.S., and Liesch, P.W. (2019). Capabilities development and deployment activities in born global B-to-B firms for early entry into international markets. *Industrial Marketing Management*, 78, 122–36.

Zucchella, A. (2021). International entrepreneurship and the internationalisation phenomenon: taking stock, looking ahead. *International Business Review*, 30(2), 101800.

APPENDIX 3A

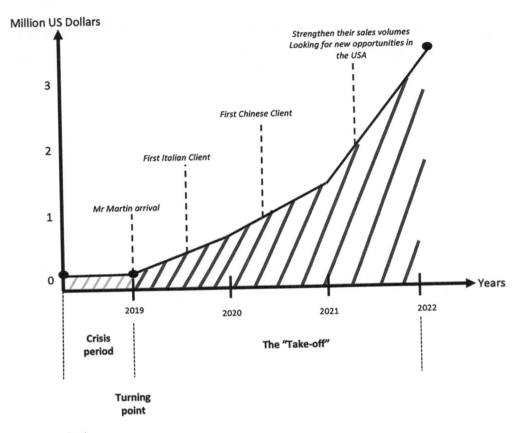

Source: Authors.

Figure 3A.1 Timeline

Table 3A.1 Competitors – key figures

	ABB	Siemens	Emerson
Year of creation	1988	1847	1890
Number of employees	110 000	303 000	87 500
Turnover (US dollars)	13.2 billion	62.3 billion	17.4 billion
Countries	UK, Germany, Norway, Canada, Japan	Brazil, China, India, Germany, US, Middle East	Canada, UAE, Singapore, Australia, Brazil, Germany

Table 3A.2   GASTECH – key figures

	N	N-1	N-2
Number of employees	25	25	25
Turnover (US dollars)	3.3 million	1.6 million	770 000
International sales	75%	75%	75%
Entry modes	Distributor – Subsidiaries	Subsidiaries	Subsidiaries
New market entries	–	1	1
Countries	–	China	Italy

4

CLOUDTECH, how to grow a Born Global firm

Pierre-Louis Meuric, Véronique Favre-Bonté and Charles Aymard

CASE SUMMARY

Born Global firms have seen their businesses as global since their inception and thus quickly internationalised. This case presents the story of CLOUDTECH, which has not experienced linear growth in its internationalisation. First, we will present the context to understand the sector and CLOUDTECH's business. Then, in the following sections, we will show how CLOUDTECH embraced its international growth and responded to its stagnation period. Throughout this case, we aim to discuss Born Globals' internationalisation. We want to stress the evolution of CLOUDTECH as a Born Global firm and show that small international firms do not necessarily follow linear growth and internationalisation. This case emphasises the role played by managerial decisions and their impacts on earlier internationalisation.

LEARNING OUTCOMES

The main learning outcome of this case study is to understand how Born Globals could achieve their growth after facing difficulties. The primary learning outcomes focus on three points about the path followed by Born Global firms. This case study shows that we can discern three phases. These phases demonstrate that internationalisation is not smooth sailing. Indeed, the internationalisation of Born Global firms is highly contingent on several factors. Some are external, such as market tendencies; others are internal, such as the Top Management Team's (TMT) managerial vision. In order to discuss the paths taken by Born Globals, we suggest analysing the three main phases experienced by CLOUDTECH. The case of the CLOUDTECH company teaches us that the internationalisation of Born Globals is not necessarily linear. Even if a company can quickly take itself internationally shortly after its creation, its presence abroad does not necessarily grow steadily. Thus, thanks to this case study, we think it is interesting to identify and thoroughly discuss the following main phases:

PHASE 1: A FAST GO-TO-MARKET STRATEGY

The first phase seems to be familiar to all Born Globals because this type of company takes a startup approach, both responsive and open to opportunities. Two characteristics of CLOUDTECH seem particularly interesting to illustrate the rapid departure of Born Globals:

- Seeking market opportunities
- Using first successes as an accelerator to grow.

PHASE 2: A STAGNATION PERIOD

The second phase of the internationalisation of Born Globals seems to be dependent on the evolution of the economic context. During the first phase, the company is reactive and knows how to seize opportunities to develop rapidly, but during the second phase, and to continue its rapid growth, the company must analyse more precisely the evolution of its environment.

- Slow down in the economic dynamic and the necessity to identify weak signals
- Difficulties in managing changes and new challenges.

PHASE 3: THE RENEWAL OF THE STRATEGY

The renewal of the strategy was carried out under the action and determination of the managers. Two main points were important for CLOUDTECH to make a renewal in its strategy:

1. The use of financial tools :

    - Entering the stock exchange
    - Using funds to buy rivals
    - Using these funds to exploit licenses.

2. Cross-cultural teams and new ways of managing:

    - Recruiting a team with different profiles
    - Adopting new methods (like the Agile method).

THE CONTEXT – INDUSTRY AND COUNTRY OR REGIONAL SETTING

CLOUDTECH[1] is a French firm based in the Auvergne Rhône-Alpes region[2] (AURA). The AURA region is the second largest economic region in France: 12 per cent of the French national wealth and GDP[3] are created in this region (INSEE, 2021). The AURA region has a strong and diversified industrial base. While sectors such as electronics/digital, energy, and biotechnologies are well represented, there are also more traditional sectors such as mechanics, plastics, and chemicals.

The software sector is exceptionally well represented in AURA firms, as seen in the Digital League.[4] The Digital League is made up of 500 firms that are involved in the software market. This cluster supports companies wishing to develop and extend their business. The software industry is a highly competitive market due to the large number of participants who have gained entry into this market since the entry price has been sharply reduced. If we look closer at these participants, we see that they use one of two business models: the SaaS business model (Software as a Service) and the Software Licensing Model. The SaaS business model bases its strategy on providing unlimited services to customers who pay monthly. The best and most famous example of this is Netflix. The Software Licensing Model involves marketing the software as a specific good or programme. When the software editors offer updates, the customers will have to pay for a new version if they want to take advantage of the latest 'groundbreaking' updates. The standard bearers of that industry are Microsoft and Oracle. Today, most software firms use a SaaS business model, which requires a high level of agility as the firms need to offer the latest update, which needs to be well implemented. Indeed, in that industry, customers are more demanding. If the firms do not meet their expectations, clients will subscribe to the firm's competitors.

Today CLOUDTECH is involved in an international market with just a few competitors, mostly North American companies like Coupa and Kofax as well as Basware, a firm from Scandinavia. There are also local competitors in the countries where CLOUDTECH is present, like Itesoft and Sidetrade in France. Thus, CLOUDTECH belongs to a dynamic and diversified ecosystem within the French economic landscape.

THE FIRM AND ITS COMPETITORS

CLOUDTECH is a French software firm located in the Auvergne Rhône-Alpes region. Established in 1989, the firm offers cloud technology services for companies. CLOUDTECH is one of the top software firms in France because it has developed a wide range of activities over the past 30 years. CLOUDTECH's product is a range of cloud services for management activities such as invoice management, customer order management, supplier invoice management, inventory and deposit management, etc. CLOUDTECH can be defined as a high-growth firm as its growth rate is around 20 per cent per year. Currently, CLOUDTECH is a medium-sized company: the organisation employs 800 people and has generated €118 million in revenue. CLOUDTECH is active in North America, Europe, and Asia. The firm has established 14 subsidiaries abroad in its 30 years. Thus, CLOUDTECH sees itself as a Born Global company due to its solid and early international high growth. We summarise this information and the CLOUDTECH evolution in Table 4A.1 in the Appendix.

CLOUDTECH has three main competitors, namely: Coupa, Kofax, and Basware. Coupa was founded in 2006. This company employed 2,615 employees and generated a 542 million USD turnover. Today Coupa is in 125 countries on all continents. The second main competitor is

Kofax. Kofax was created in 1985 and now has 1,900 employees. Nowadays, Kofax reaches a turnover of 400 million USD and is present in 31 countries in North America, the Middle East, Asia, Europe, and Oceania. The last main competitor is Basware. Basware was founded in 1985 and generated a turnover of 148 million USD. This firm employs 1,339 employees. Baseware is present in 14 countries in North America, Middle East, Asia, Europe, and Oceania. We summarise this information in Table 4A.2 in the Appendix.

A SHORT HISTORY OF THE FIRM, WITH A TIMELINE IN THE APPENDIX

The story of CLOUDTECH can be told in three phases: the beginnings, the stagnation period, and the resurgence period (new growth dynamic).

The beginning

CLOUDTECH was created by Mr Phillip and Mr John, two colleagues from the same computer science university. They were doing an internship in the same company when they realised they wanted to create their organisation. Many companies like Microsoft and Oracle were created during that period. Thus, Phillip and John wanted to take advantage of the entrepreneurial opportunities of software development and build a top international company. After their internship, they decided to create an IT consulting firm. They had few clients, and their company did not find market opportunities during its first years of life. CLOUDTECH would develop its business sometime later after a discussion with one of its clients looking for a 'terminal emulator'.[5] After trying to find solutions in the market, Phillip and John finally saw the opportunity they had been looking for. Indeed, they realised that no products existed in the market, and they could perhaps create their emulator to respond to their client's expectations.

> We found it within the framework of a mission by discussing with a customer; he had bought PCs because the PC had just appeared, the Internet did not exist … he had bought PCs, he used them to do word processing and spreadsheets, but at the same time, he had a central system that worked with Unix, and he wanted to connect them because these machines unique to the team had passive terminals, it is these green screens like we see in the airport or certain big stores … and he wanted to replace the passive terminals with the PCs, so it was necessary to add a program to the PCs so that they behaved like a terminal … It's a little technical … but it's a terminal emulator … and so I searched the market for products that could satisfy the customers' needs, but there was nothing satisfactory, and so we decided to develop it ourselves … (Phillip – CEO)

Thus, they created their first product, and it was a hit! Soon they received numerous propositions from other clients in France, and they saw the market opportunities of that emulator. As France's market was dynamic, they quickly turned their activities abroad. They began with neighbouring countries like Spain, Belgium, and Germany, where some clients were interested in those emulators. Quickly, then, CLOUDTECH turned its business toward the United States.

Nevertheless, soon after, they realised they were not financially strong enough to succeed in that market, which is bigger and more competitive than European markets. At that time, it was risky for a small firm like CLOUDTECH to enter that market. CLOUDTECH thus decided to go public on the stock market to raise funds and buy five of its competitors. The goal was to reach a specific critical size to gain legitimacy and survive in that market.

> So we looked for distributors, and it was much more complicated in the United States because there were competing products, which had a very good quality, which had already taken place. They had not had time to cross the Atlantic … but for us it was a problem because we could not find good distribution channels … So for a long time we had a subsidiary in the United States that was losing money, that was making a little bit of money, but was losing as much … It was a big problem … and so at that time, we wanted to change our approach … we decided, in fact, as it was working very well in Europe, we decided to go public in 1997, to raise money, and to buy our American competitors … So we proceeded by acquisition … (Phillip – CEO)

In summary, just a few years after its inception in 2000, CLOUDTECH reached USD 31 million in turnover, mainly in Europe and North America. Its international turnover was around 65 per cent, the same as today. Indeed, even though CLOUDTECH kept the same proportion of sales abroad, the organisation nearly quadrupled its turnover.

A slight stagnation period

After growing abroad for nearly ten years, CLOUDTECH realised that its business had shrunk. Indeed, the market where it was active was slowly declining. CLOUDTECH was not selling enough emulators to sustain its activity as the market saturated. Therefore, during this period, the board decided to overcome these new challenges through technologies developed by a competitor they had acquired. Many of those technologies are related to fax, the cloud, and customer relationship management (CRM). Phillip and John were thus able to enter the file digitisation market gradually. They wanted to provide software that would allow organisations to store their files on a cloud platform. Thus, for nearly eight years, CLOUDTECH worked to make its strategy effective and create its second product range (Cloud) to replace the first (Emulator).

> It evolved, abruptly … because in fact in 2000, the market … of the terminal emulators … after the year 2000… started to decline seriously … roughly in 2000, in 2001, in 2002 … in the end it collapsed … so it wasn't quite in line with our plans … and it turns out that in the acquisitions we had made in the United States, there were other products than this one … there was a product called the fax server … it was a product that allowed you to send and receive faxes … at the time it was no sexier than it is today … the fax was already dead … but at the same time, we realised that customers were using it to send and receive purchase orders, so that gave us the idea of providing additional data extraction and ERP integration

services, which we applied to everything like PDFs, email, etc ... and so in fact that allowed us to enter the market of document digitisation slowly ... (Phillip – CEO)

To summarise, at the end of this period, in 2009, CLOUDTECH had stagnated. When CLOUDTECH bought its US competitors in 1997, the firm generated around USD 21 million in turnover. From 2000 to 2003, the firm experienced a strong contraction and then stagnated between 2003 to 2009. Beginning in 2009, the company started to grow again.

No, there was a period of strong growth from 1989 to 2000, and then there were a few years of strong decline between 2000 and 2003, and then, to put it simply, from 2003 to 2009, we were on a plateau ... and it was only from 2009 onwards that we started to grow again ... now we have far exceeded where we were at the time in 2000, in 2000 we were at 31 million USD, and this year we are at 117, which means that we are more than four times higher than in 2000... (Phillip – CEO)

The resurgence (new growth period)

From that point, CLOUDTECH entered a new growth phase. Indeed, exploiting cloud technology during the 2000s was somewhat visionary as there were no competitors in the market. Actors like Oracle, Amazon, and Azure had not yet developed this part of their business. Therefore, applying a SaaS business model was a big step for CLOUDTECH. Indeed, companies were not used to paying for 'all-inclusive' digitised services at that time. CLOUDTECH started by creating services related to purchasing orders, invoices, supplier invoices, etc., and then developed all the services related to the client's activities and documentation. Moreover, the client did not have to purchase new equipment to make the software work. This approach was somewhat disruptive to the market.

Well, at the time, there wasn't even any cloud technology; people like Azure, Google, and Amazon didn't exist, so we developed our own server to support our infrastructure, and then it's only recently, since 2015, that we switched our development to Microsoft's AZURE, that keeps us from having to manage the hardware, the operating systems, they do that better than us, so ... The idea was to say to the customer, he buys a solution, he needs to buy the hardware and install the software, but he does not need to pay someone to manage the maintenance ... there is no hardware to buy ... he just pays a subscription ... at the time it was visionary, today it's normal ... the technology has matured ... but in the early 2000s it was visionary ... (Phillip – CEO)

Today, CLOUDTECH can automate all its clients' digitisation processes. It has developed all these technologies by adopting specific methodologies like the Agile method. This approach is due to market requirements linked to CLOUDTECH's SaaS business model. Indeed, SaaS business models require companies to update their software frequently. Thus, the engineers need to quickly understand customers' needs, competitors' new offers, new market regulations, etc. By setting up a flexible roadmap and specific product conception processes, the Agile method helps firms to quickly seize opportunities that have not been targeted and thus make the organisation more innovative. Therefore, CLOUDTECH successfully integrated technology into its offerings thanks to that methodology. The Agile method is in opposition to another methodology previously used by CLOUDTECH: the Waterfall method. CLOUDTECH dropped the Waterfall method because it required long and slow planning. This slow product conception process was ineffective in a dynamic and competitive environment like the software market.

> ... what counts in agility is what we have put in place because of, or thanks to, the cloud ... the cloud doesn't allow us to ... We can't afford to do an update every 18 months on the cloud like we used to do on traditional software ... because there are so many customers on a platform that we're sure we'll kill them for a week or two ... and make them mad because of the small problems, even big problems that can occur ... so the best solution is to have an incremental approach to the evolution of the product, hence the implementation of agility, which means that we release a version every 15 days ... and that allows us to very quickly integrate an idea, or a customer need, or a new technology, or a new concept, into the customer software ... In the past years, we have seen the appearance of the cell phone, social networks, online payment, many things that didn't exist ten years ago ... we were able to integrate them very quickly... (Phillip – CEO)

This methodology has been closely related to CLOUDTECH's internationalisation. Indeed, according to Phillip, the company needed to integrate international constraints and cultural and international market trends to make this product conception process effective. To apply that complex form of 'gymnastics' to the whole team, the firm needed to not 'turn international' but 'be international'. To do so, organisations need to be internationally focused and not create distinctions between the 'domestic market' and the 'international market'. The firm's culture is perhaps the first success factor.

Moreover, CLOUDTECH set up cross-cultural teams (18 nationalities inside CLOUDTECH teams) and discussions with local consultants and institutions abroad and mastered foreign languages. Thanks to these intercultural teams, CLOUDTECH can effectively enhance its Agile process and improve discussions with culturally distant clients with different behaviours and expectations and thus apply brand new technology to their products. Therefore, CLOUDTECH is not constrained by cultural or geographical distance.

Phillip (CEO) about the feedback generated by clients:

> Clearly, because we try to collect feedback from all over the world ... the markets are not always at the same level, we generally follow the most advanced market on certain features; in Europe, we are ahead on everything that is economic fluctuation, but not in the US ... On the other hand, in the US, they are very strong in payment, invoicing and discount management ... so I don't know if this speaks to you ... they are ahead on other aspects ... so it allows us to capitalise on very advanced customer needs, and to offer this to customers all over the world, and sooner or later, they end up using it ...

Phillip (CEO) on his vision of Born Global firms:

Well, from the moment you decide to go international, it's not about adding a feature to a product … it's clearly, you have to expect that it will shift the lines in the company … It's not a little extra that we're going to pick up left and right in Europe; no, it's global … it's a transformation of the company …

Regarding internationalisation, CLOUDTECH developed its business in the same countries as before. Phillip and John did not change their international strategy. Today, they mainly focus their international development on Europe, targeting some opportunities in Germany and Benelux. Indeed, as a big firm, they do not expect to extend their business geographically but rather exploit current market opportunities. According to Phillip, there is still room for improvement. To do so, they support their strategy through resource deployment. They decided to set up subsidiaries, hire local agents, etc. In brief, they aim to strengthen their commercial capabilities in those places.

Then from a geographical point of view, there is no urgency to do more, because there is France, which represents 35% of the whole, so that means that 65% is already done internationally … So there are areas that we would like to strengthen, such as Germany, which has greater potential than we have … after that, we are very opportunistic … that is to say, if we feel that in a market that has demand … for example, Benelux, which we serve from Germany and France … we realise that there is a lot of business, in this case, we will create an office, but it is already the case, there is no office, there is no company, there are already four people at CLOUDTECH working full time on the Benelux area … We have the same thing … we created a subsidiary in Canada because of demand, and then we did the same thing in Latin America, but it's not really part of a well-thought-out strategy … it's more of an opportunity… (Phillip – CEO)

Figure 4.1 illustrates CLOUDTECH's broad perception of growth.

THE PROBLEMS TO BE DISCUSSED – MARKETING, SALES, MANAGEMENT, R&D, SOURCING, ETC. – WITH A FOCUS ON THE TASK FOR STUDENTS AND READERS

Throughout this case, we aim to discuss how the vision of the entrepreneurial team, listening to customers and seizing opportunities help a Born Global firm take off at the international scale.

To analyse this case, we propose the following scenario. You are a member of a consulting firm whose mandate is to support young companies in their international development. Given the contextual elements presented above, you are asked to formulate an audit around the questions asked by your clients. In order to make recommendations to enlighten business leaders on the resumption of the internationalisation process, you will focus on coherence between the practical and theoretical elements.

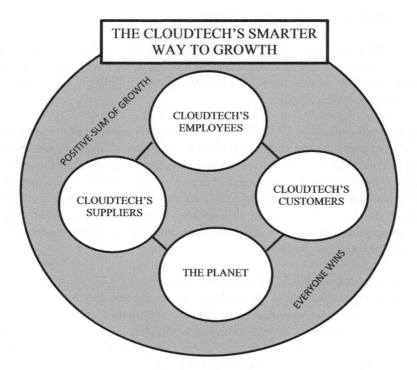

Source: Authors, inspired by CLOUDTECH's website.

Figure 4.1   A smarter way to grow

Four main issues could be discussed in this case:

- Vision & international mindset:
  - International vision of the Top Management Team (TMT) and organisational culture (think and act globally; international product development);
  - Development of a global mindset for the whole firm, not only for the export manager/department.
- Seizing opportunities:
  - The importance of market scouting;
  - The choice between tools and methods used: Agile vs Waterfall;
  - Human Resources Management (scalability, flexibility, languages); specialists employed (PhDs and experienced managers).
- Initial Public Offering (IPO) for financing and structuring the firm's international expansion (e.g., acquisition of firms abroad).
- Market approach:
  - External growth, ability to seize new opportunities;
  - Eagerness to create new subsidiaries abroad.

Some questions arise in connection to the issues mentioned above. To answer these questions, you can rely both on the texts above and articles on international business.

1. Can you define the international strategy of CLOUDTECH at the beginning? Ten years later? Do you notice any changes?
2. What do you think has enabled CLOUDTECH to achieve scalability?
3. What is the role of Agile methods?
4. What is the role of cross-cultural teams?
5. What is the role of acquisition and IPO (Initial Public Offering)?

LEARNING OUTCOMES – WHAT THE READER WILL LEARN BY USING THE CASE STUDY

The primary learning outcomes are focused on three points explaining the international high growth of Born Global firms:

- Build a global vision: the importance of the TMT (characteristics and international vision). This vision is strengthened by the open-mindedness of the managers and their ability to conduct scouting activities and transform these weak signals into market opportunities. Moreover, the construction of this vision is shared with the teams through internal communication; by disseminating the vision, managers create trust and get ideas from employees.

- How to acquire resources to make success possible: the importance of financial resources, M&A and firm structure, emphasising the importance of financial resources in the internationalisation process. Internationalisation is costly for firms, and knowing how to find the financial resources for IPO, fundraising, and bank loans is relevant. We can then highlight the importance of external growth, which seems to be the essential outcome when firms cannot grow organically anymore.

- Being proactive: seizing market opportunities (via agility, listening to customers, etc.). Showing the firm's international development relies on market exploration and a range of processes. These processes allow early internationalising firms (EIFs) to seize opportunity quickly, reconfigure their resource sets and become more resilient. Firms can embrace and sustain their international growth thanks to these different processes. One specific focus can be on the Agile and Lean startup methods, which are currently popular and broadly applicable in high-technology sectors.

TARGET AUDIENCE

This case could be taught in international strategy, entrepreneurship, and small business management courses. This case is appropriate for Master's degree students.

SUGGESTED TEACHING STRATEGIES

We see three possible scenarios for using this case:

- Scenario 1: this case could be used during a course (3 hours);
- Scenario 2: a 2-hour exam;
- Scenario 3 (our preference): we think it is best to give the case as homework, allowing students one or two weeks to read the case and collect information about it (academic papers, internet research, etc.).

SUGGESTED ANSWERS TO DISCUSSION QUESTIONS

Q1 Could you define the international strategy of CLOUDTECH at the beginning? Ten years later? Do you notice any changes?

At the beginning: CLOUDTECH's strategy was built around identifying market segments neglected by the competition. By offering innovative services in the digital field, CLOUDTECH adopted a 'blue ocean' strategy to reach markets where the offer was growing (see Kim and Mauborgne, 2005 in the references to deepen the discussion). Following the creation of new digital companies (which were to become world leaders), CLOUDTECH wanted to participate in new, dynamic markets. This determined mindset allowed the company to launch its products internationally quickly.

Ten years later: Ten years later, CLOUDTECH was in a period of uncertainty during which the market was not growing. Noting the reduction in its business and the scarcity of development opportunities, CLOUDTECH managers decided to change their international development strategy. They opted for aggressive internationalisation by buying existing companies to revive the stagnant dynamic. The Top Management Team of CLOUDTECH tried to instil a new mindset by exploiting the licenses produced by companies that they had bought. Meanwhile, CLOUDTECH realised it had become more mature and thus needed to adopt new methods and management practices to conserve its agility and sustain its international growth.

Has it changed? The mindset of CLOUDTECH's leaders evolved between these two periods. They have gone from a vision of an international startup reacting to opportunities identified on the world markets to the vision of a multinational company that takes a deliberate and structured strategy on the acquisition of companies, the exploitation of innovations from acquisitions, and the adoption of intercultural management.

This question, Q1, makes it possible to emphasise the importance of the mindset and vision of the CEO during the management of international operations. The literature related to the individual characteristics of startup managers will support the answer and discuss the elements mentioned in the proposal.

Q2   What do you think has enabled CLOUDTECH to achieve scalability?

In addition to the seizing of opportunities, acquisitions, and fundraising carried out by CLOUDTECH to make the company scalable, it is interesting to discuss the fertile ground created by CLOUDTECH and how this allowed it to grow quickly and sustainably. Thus, a discussion can be conducted around Figure 4.1, 'A smarter way to grow'. Indeed, this figure shows the importance of aligning employees, environment (with its different actors), customers, and suppliers. Scalability is not only a matter of market, turnover, etc., but it is also a matter of anchored vision and values in the local and international field. Growth is thus the result of a much more upstream reflection that creates the conditions of this scalability.

This question, Q2, helps understand how scalability can be reached by managers who want to grow internationally after facing some difficulties (a stagnation period for CLOUDTECH, for example). Q2 shows that scalability may be a result of managers' willingness.

Q3   What is the role of the Agile method?

Adopting Agile methods has allowed CLOUDTECH leaders to refresh their perception of the international market while maintaining their original state of mind (during the first phase of growth). Indeed, Agile methods enabled the company to adopt a strategic road-map redefining its initial vision thanks to a finer-grained reading of the international environment. Unlike the previous method (Waterfall[6]), the Agile[7] method allowed managers greater adaptability and flexibility in defining their international strategy. By mixing analysis tools to build a real roadmap and a 'startup' mindset, the TMT of CLOUDTECH was able to relaunch its internationalisation. In conclusion, Agile methods have proven their effectiveness because they have constituted a synthesis between the necessary definition of a strategy and the agility of a 'startup' approach.

Interestingly, CLOUDTECH adopted a classic approach at the beginning before moving on to a second method that corresponds more to its environment. The two methods were used successively, and the change was made after the first difficulties of the company during its internationalisation. It would seem that neither of the two methods is preferable, but their use responds to the firm's context.

Q3 highlights management practices' role in driving Born Globals' internationalisation. Unlike gradual internationalisation, the internationalisation of Born Globals seems to be more conditioned by managerial choices (especially of methods and tools). The discussion could also use references such as Paul and Rosado-Serrano (2019) or Knight and Liesch (2016).

Q4   What is the role of cross-cultural teams?

The cross-cultural teams made it possible to lead the company to an international level and be a truly international company. The difference is notable because having multicultural teams is no longer a simple means but an end that makes it possible to change the very nature of the company. Going from a company that expands internationally by establishing itself in several countries to becoming a global company, the very nature of the firm is altered. Therefore, the recruitment of cross-cultural teams seems to be a valuable lever for initiating the company's transformation and leading the change.

Q4 highlights the importance of intercultural management in the international development of Born Globals. By emphasising the cross-cultural character of its teams, the CLOUDTECH company echoes the literature on the fit between the decided strategy and the teams that implement it. The reference Breuillot, Bocquet, and Favre-Bonté (2022) could help to continue the discussion on diversity in Born Globals. A discussion about hiring multicultural employees and managing them could be of interest.

Another discussion could take place on what multicultural, cross-cultural, and intercultural mean. For the distinction between the three, see, for example:

- What is the difference between multicultural, cross-cultural, and intercultural? While they all might be under the same roof, they describe entirely different rooms. The differences in the meanings have to do with the perspectives we take when interacting with people from other cultures.
- Multicultural refers to a society that contains several cultural or ethnic groups. People live alongside one another, but each cultural group does not necessarily have engaging interactions with each other.
- Cross-cultural deals with the comparison of different cultures. In cross-cultural communication, differences are understood and acknowledged, and can bring about individual change, but not collective transformations.
- Intercultural describes communities in which there is a deep understanding and respect for all cultures. Intercultural communication focuses on the mutual exchange of ideas and cultural norms and the development of deep relationships. (Source: https://springinstitute.org/whats-difference-multicultural-intercultural-cross -cultural-communication/)

Q5   What is the role of acquisition and IPO (Initial Public Offering)?

The CLOUDTECH IPO allowed the firm to develop abroad quickly in a highly competitive market (United States). Indeed, during CLOUDTECH's first attempt to enter that specific market, they suffered from their liabilities of newness and smallness as the US market size was not the same as the European Union. By raising a massive amount of money quickly, CLOUDTECH grew bigger by buying its competitors and thus capturing new knowledge and resources. This strategy allowed CLOUDTECH to grow and sustain itself in the long term.

A discussion about the necessity to grow fast and to have the financial means to do so could also be of interest: it is difficult for small companies to raise money, but most of the time, they need to take risks to do that in order to outperform their competitors and stake a place in the market.

Q5 emphasises the financial aspects of Born Globals' internationalisation. Most of the time, young firms and startups need vast amounts of money to develop their projects. To do so, using financial leverage, as CLOUDTECH did for its strategy, is essential.

NOTES

1. For confidential reasons, the name has been changed.
2. https://www.auvergnerhonealpes.fr/ (accessed 2021).
3. Gross Domestic Product (GDP) is a monetary measure of the market value of all the final goods and services produced in a specific time period by countries.
4. https://www.digital-league.org/ (accessed 2021).
5. A terminal emulator or terminal application is a computer program that emulates a video terminal within some other display architecture. This program enables one computer system (called the *host*) to behave like another computer system (called the *guest*).
6. The Waterfall method is based on the idea that as soon as one stage of the project is completed, the team moves on to the next stage; there is no (or little) turning back. The idea is to move forward naturally, step by step, until you reach the final goal following a clear and precise direction.
7. The Agile methodology is based on a simple idea. Planning an entire project down to the smallest detail before developing it is counterproductive. The Agile method recommends setting short-term goals. The project is therefore divided into several sub-projects. Once the objective is achieved, firms move on to the next one, until the final objective is achieved.

SUPPLEMENTARY INFORMATION NEEDED TO ANSWER THE CASE QUESTIONS

Below are key references to scientific papers and suggestions for reading that can be used in the discussion.

Breuillot, A., Bocquet, R., & Favre-Bonté, V. (2022). Navigating the internationalisation process: Strategic resources for early internationalising firms. *Journal of International Entrepreneurship, 20*, 1–34.

Cavusgil, S.T., & Knight, G. (2015). The born global firm: An entrepreneurial and capabilities perspective on early and rapid internationalisation. *Journal of International Business Studies, 46*(1), 3–16.

INSEE. (2021). L'essentiel sur… Auvergne-Rhône-Alpes. https://www.insee.fr/fr/statistiques/4479805.

Kim, W.C., & Mauborgne, R. (2005). *Blue Ocean Strategy*. Boston, MA: Harvard Business School Press.

Knight, G.A., & Liesch, P.W. (2016). Internationalisation: From incremental to born global. *Journal of World Business, 51*(1), 93–102.

Masango, S.G., & Lassalle, P. (2020), What entrepreneurs do? Entrepreneurial action guided by entrepreneurial opportunities and entrepreneurial learning in early internationalising firms. *International Marketing Review, 37*(6), 1083–119. https://doi.org/10.1108/IMR-10-2018-0273.

Meuric, P.-L., and Favre-Bonté, V. (2023). International High-growth of early internationalizing firms: A feedback loop experience. *Journal of Small Business Management* (forthcoming).

Meuric, P.-L. and Favre-Bonté, V. (2023). What makes early internationalising firms grow faster? *Management International Review, 27*(2) (forthcoming).

Paul, J. & Rosado-Serrano, A. (2019), Gradual Internationalization vs Born-Global/International new venture models: A review and research agenda. *International Marketing Review, 36*(6), 830–58.

Pawęta, E. (2015). Entrepreneur-related constructs explaining the emergence of born global firms: A systematic literature review. *Entrepreneurial Business and Economics Review, 3*(4), 11–36.

Rasmussen, E.S., & Tanev, S. (2015). The emergence of the lean global startup as a new type of firm. *Technology Innovation Management Review, 5*(11), 12–19.

Romanello, R., & Chiarvesio, M. (2019). Early internationalising firms: 2004–2018. *Journal of International Entrepreneurship, 17*(2), 172–219.

APPENDIX 4A

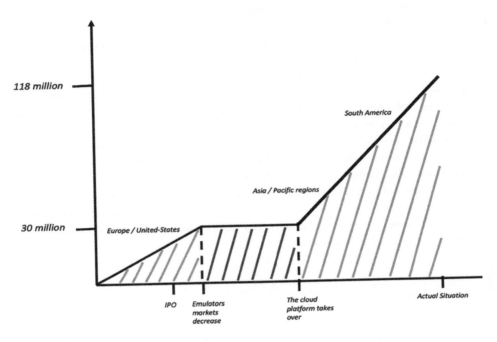

Source: Authors.

Figure 4A.1   Timeline

Table 4A.1   CLOUDTECH – key figures

	1997	2000	2009	2021
Number of employees	140	250	250	764
Turnover (USD)	21 million	31 million	31 million	117 million
International sale	65%	65%	65%	65%
	Distributors	Distributors, subsidiaries & acquisitions	Distributors, subsidiaries & acquisitions	Distributors, subsidiaries & acquisitions
New market entries	1	–	3	2
	United-States	–	Singapore, Kuala Lumpur, and Hong Kong	Australia, Argentina

Table 4A.2 CLOUDTECH's main competitors – key figures

	Coupa[1]	Kofax[2]	Basware[3]
Year of creation	2006	1985	1985
Number of employees	2,615	1,900	1,339
Turnover (USD)	542 million	400 million	148 million
Countries	125: all continents	31: North America, Middle East, Asia, Europe, Oceania	14: North America, Middle East, Asia, Europe, Oceania

Notes:

[1] https://www.coupa.com/ (accessed 2021).

[2] https://www.kofax.com/ (accessed 2021).

[3] https://www.basware.com/en-en/home/ (accessed 2021).

5

A decacorn in on-demand delivery: the case of Getir from Turkey

Rifat Kamasak, Deniz Palalar Alkan, Berk Kucukaltan and Mustafa F. Özbilgin

CASE SUMMARY

Social movements and technological innovations have transformed how we think, live and work. For instance, the Covid-19 pandemic has radically changed our purchasing behaviours and the preferred shopping mediums, sparking the exponential growth of online on-demand platforms. Under strict social and healthcare policy measures of the Covid-19 pandemic, technological innovation through e-commerce platforms became the main route through which public demand for goods and services has been met. The chapter is set in this context to examine on-demand platforms in the e-commerce field and explore the online grocery delivery system through an illustrative case study. Getir, an international e-commerce company headquartered in Turkey, provides an illustrative case for Born Globals. The chapter explores digitalisation and its impact on business and the unprecedented growth of the platform economy through a case study from a developing country.

LEARNING OUTCOMES

The main learning outcomes of this case study are:

- To increase learners' academic performance and engagement with e-commerce
- To benchmark offline and online markets in the international trade
- To develop critical thinking skills for entrepreneurship and develop a proactive entrepreneurship environment through enhanced entrepreneurial motivation
- To promote the implementation of on-demand business models.

THE IMPACT OF DIGITALISATION ON BUSINESS AT A GLANCE

Emerging internet-based technologies have created a new industrial landscape affecting our lives and work. New technologies lead to disruptive innovations in business models and functions of organisations (Walton and Nayak, 2021). Technological innovation also radicalised individual experiences of consumption and work as individuals sought effective solutions to the challenges that they were facing (Kucukaltan, 2020). Technological innovation allowed organisations to address the emergent needs of individuals in this new landscape.

Opportunities for growth and expansion in business markets allured many individuals with entrepreneurial mindsets and resources to invest in internet-based technologies that radically transformed business and economy models. Bălan (2016) emphasised that collaborative platforms and smartphone applications significantly shape new business models. Further, the services provided by smartphone applications connect people across fault lines and remote locations (Ercoskun and Ocalir, 2018). Technological innovations also shape social relations and habits, catering to individual needs. Individualisation of service provision sets this digital era from previous periods where market provisions captured and aggregated the needs of large groups of people.

In parallel, digitalisation and individualisation have fostered the development of on-demand services in various industries (Zeier Röschmann et al., 2022). In other words, services provided by on-demand platforms, also known as e-commerce platforms, have come with more accessible, practical and sustainable provisions to meet individual needs. Therefore, as Kumar et al. (2022) highlighted, internet-based platforms and mobile applications have fostered the digital revolution, especially in the service industry. As a result, smart devices are used extensively to fulfil the daily requirements of individuals in convenient ways. A report by Technavio Research (2021) underlines the distinctive potential growth in the online on-demand economy and forecasts. According to the report, the online on-demand home services market will grow by $ 4,730 billion during 2021–25.

The report adds that between 2021 and 2025, the market growth of the global online on-demand home services market is expected to increase by over 70 per cent, and over one-third of the growth is contributed by the Asia-Pacific (APAC) region countries. In this sense, it is of critical importance to examine the countries in the APAC region and similar emerging markets such as Turkey.

Speaking of the features of on-demand platforms, it is worthwhile to note that there are a number of advantages and shortcomings of on-demand services. According to Benjaafar and Hu (2020), the distinctive characteristics of on-demand platforms compared to traditional service platforms are the interplay between capacity and demand. The characteristics of on-demand service platforms differ from the traditional service platforms since 'capacity affects demand, and vice versa, capacity can be controlled only indirectly via wages and prices, and capacity and demand vary temporally and spatially' (Benjaafar and Hu, 2020, p. 94) in on-demand service platforms. Given these features, it becomes apparent that on-demand services offer a connection between organisations, as a proxy of the capacity, and individuals, as a proxy of the demand for services (Mitchell and Strader, 2018). Furthermore, using digital technologies in on-demand services also reduces costs and lowers barriers to entry (Walton and Nayak, 2021).

On the other hand, potential backlashes against on-demand platforms are about data ownership and reward (Walton and Nayak, 2021) and consumer trust (Kamasak et al., 2023; Kumar et al., 2022). Companies that utilise the advantages of on-demand platforms with a rapid response reduce the inherent shortcomings in their services, becoming more competitive. Regarding academic discourses on the business model concept, there is much focus on problems in the e-commerce domain. Agility and variety in products and services render e-commerce platforms pivotal in meeting exploding expectations of different customer groups, particularly in omnichannel experiences. The prominent motivations for using the on-demand business models in the e-commerce market, such as speed of delivery, product variety, convenience and time-saving, are widely discussed (Eken and Gezmen, 2020; Kumar et al., 2022; Walton and Nayak, 2021).

Despite the plethora of studies on the subject, problems occurring in on-demand platforms and in the e-commerce field have been increasing globally. Academic research on solutions to these problems has received limited attention. Several operational concepts, such as understanding service quality (Sharma and Lijuan, 2015), exploring purchase intentions (e.g. Wagner Mainardes et al., 2019), and focusing on technical IT-based concerns, such as cloud and SaaS (Software as a Service) (Malik et al., 2021; van der Burg, 2019) are widely discussed in the literature. However, in addressing these problems, as pointed out by Kranz et al. (2016), a vast majority of the prior academic work tackles the constant change and the necessity of adapting to these changes for businesses rather than reflecting how and why organisations change their business models over time. This chapter addresses this research gap by exploring the development of an on-demand platform and an illustrative case study.

E-COMMERCE IN THE WORLD AND TURKEY

The use of online shopping applications has shown a dramatic increase during the Covid-19 pandemic when governments forced the public to stay home and later avoid crowded public spaces and purchase online. With soaring growth since 2015, the on-demand economy is expected to reach US$335 billion by 2025 (Peerbits, 2021). The on-demand economy includes digital platforms that link consumers to a service through a mobile application or website. Globally, the increase in online shopping is associated with the everyday use of mobile devices for shopping. Coppola (2022) argued that such rapid adoption of mobile devices is especially evident across Asia. In particular, the majority of online transaction volumes are created by mobile ways. This being the case, South Korea is shown among the major players in the e-commerce markets worldwide.

Similarly, in another leading country in the e-commerce domain, the USA, according to the Census Bureau's Annual Retail Trade Survey in 2020, e-commerce sales grew 43 per cent in 2020, the first year of the pandemic, compared to 2019 (Census, 2022). In another country with a mature e-commerce market, the UK, e-commerce shares soared by 31.3 per cent (Chevalier, 2021). In an emerging economy listed among the West Asia countries by the United Nations

Conference on Trade and Development (UNCTAD), Turkey ranks among the top ten developing and transition economies in the UNCTAD B2C E-commerce Index in 2020 (UNCTAD, 2021). Customers' purchasing behaviour has shifted to online shopping for nearly all products and services after Covid-19. This shift is quite evident in grocery products, as seen in Figure 5.1. For example, while the projected shares of online shopping in grocery are 10.7 per cent in 2024 and 13.5 per cent in 2025 before Covid-19, the figures are revised to 19.1 per cent in 2024 and 21.5 per cent in 2025.

CAGR for Online Grocery

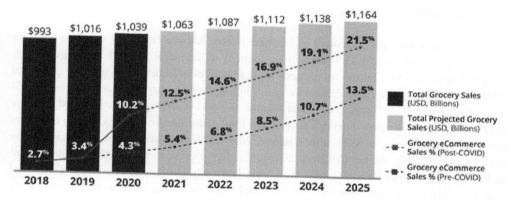

Source: Supermarket News.

Figure 5.1   The shares of actual and projected online sales in the grocery market between 2018 and 2025

As presented in Figure 5.1, online sales in grocery markets have exponentially increased with the strong effect of the pandemic in particular. The sales gaps for the years between 2021 and 2025, the impetus of the pandemic period expansion, are set to continue. Accordingly, depending on these projections, focusing on e-commerce sales of grocery items is critical for elucidating and forecasting future growth.

In the Turkish context, the share of e-commerce to general commerce was 17.7 per cent in 2021, when the share of e-commerce in the GDP increased by 1 per cent from 2020, the e-commerce expenditure per capita rose by around 0.70 per cent, and the major two sectors for the high volume of e-commerce activities were food and supermarket industries (eticaret, 2022). In line with the Turkish customers' purchasing behaviour that offers a promising growth in e-commerce, many startups are engaged in developing unique mobile applications. Coupled with funding from investors, some of these startups became unicorns or even decacorns. The global success history of Turkish startups traces back to the mobile gaming startup Peak Games. After the startup acquisition by the US-based gaming giant Zynga in a $1.8 billion deal, Peak Games, established in 2010, became Turkey's first-ever unicorn in 2020 (Daily

Sabah, 2022). Although Peak Games was granted the title of the first Turkish unicorn, the first Turkish decacorn title was obtained by the online shopping startup, Trendyol. Founded in 2010, Trendyol created its first strategic interest in Chinese online giant Alibaba Group that bought an initial 75 per cent stake amounting to $750 million in June 2018 (Webrazzi, 2018). The president of Alibaba Group, Michael Evans, pointed to the potential of Turkey in digital markets as:

> Turkey is an exciting and important market as we assess the development and proliferation of digital economies in the region and around the world, and we will continue to support Turkish brands, merchants and manufacturers in their journey to become truly global. (Alizila – news from Alibaba, 2018)

Only three years after the statement of Michael Evans, Alibaba raised its stakes to 86.5 per cent through an additional $330 million investment in Trendyol in 2021. In August 2021, Trendyol secured a $1.5 billion investment from a number of high-profile investors, General Atlantic and Japanese SoftBank Vision Fund 2, valuing the company at $16.5 billion and labelling it a decacorn (U.S. News, 2022). The success of Turkish startups has continued with the acquisition of Yemeksepeti, Turkey's first online food ordering site, by the German company Delivery Hero at a value of $589 million in May 2015, the biggest acquisition ever made in the online food ordering market (Milliyet, 2015). Another success story was the Istanbul-based mobile gaming startup Dream Games, which marked a massive leap after collecting a total of $207.5 million in funding between 2020 and 2021 from investors, valuing the business at $1 billion and granting it the title of Turkey's fastest unicorn startup in 2021 (Doing Business in Turkey, 2021). The dynamic Turkish startup ecosystem is not limited to the aforementioned companies. As of October 2021, Turkey hosts five unicorns, Peak Games, Getir, Dream Games, Hepsiburada and Insider, and one decacorn, Trendyol (World Economic Forum, 2022). However, Getir became the second decacorn of the country in March 2022 after having a considerable amount of investment from a venture capitalist. The startup journey of Turkey between 2011 and 2021 is summarised in Figure 5.2.

Although the online shopping trend has risen in almost every business sector, this trend has been apparent particularly in the grocery and food industry due to the Covid-19 effect. Online grocery shopping and delivery have become popular in Turkey, and many startups and supermarkets have focused on this business. The Turkish online grocery and food market that hosts nearly 75 online startups are competitive (Tracxn Report, 2022). However, the market has been dominated by some major players. The major players of the Turkish online food and grocery market are shown in Figure 5.3. These companies originated from Turkey as startups but achieved remarkable growth rates afterwards and obtained a considerable amount of investment from venture capitalists and/or angel investors worldwide. The food and supermarket industry in the Turkish e-commerce field is placed at the focal point. Among the major players, Getir's international expansion strategy and its achievement on the way of becoming a global firm and among the most popular rapid delivery platforms in Europe with a potential of accounting for over 40 per cent of the market in the third quarter of 2022 (*Financial Times*, 2022) is noteworthy.

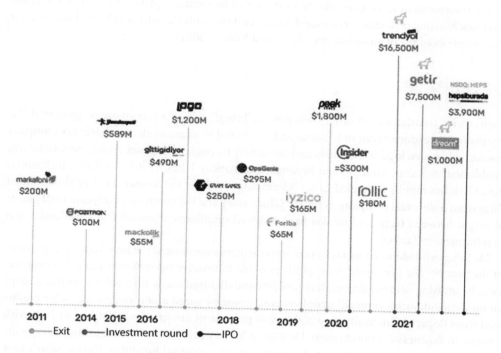

Source: ScaleX Ventures (2022).

Figure 5.2   Turkish startup ecosystem between 2011 and 2021 at a glance here

Source: Authors.

Figure 5.3   The major players in the online food and grocery market in Turkey

At the international level, preliminary examples of on-demand platforms include Craigslist and Couchsurfing provided services and, in the Turkish context, Getir is indicated as a popular and unique example of an online app (Barış and Yılmaz, 2021).

GETIR CASE

Getir, which translates as an order form phrase: 'bring!' in Turkish, is an online grocery delivery platform headquartered in Istanbul and is referred to as an on-demand delivery company operating between local warehouses and customers through its internet application. Getir was established by Nazım Salur, Serkan Borançılı and Tuncay Tütek in 2015, and after its foundation, Getir has rapidly expanded. Since Nazim Salur is one of the co-owners, they also founded Bitaksi, an online taxi company. Both Mr Salur's story and the common entrepreneurial points of origin between Getir and Bitaksi have received significant attention from academics and practitioners in Turkey.

Mr Salur, who identifies as a serial entrepreneur, was nominated the Best Male Entrepreneur of the year by *The Economist*; he exploits possible innovative opportunities in delivering services by utilising communication technologies and digitised marketing. Salur's ventures adopt an on-demand business model mainly characterised by speed and convenience. Salur graduated from Boğaziçi University, one of the most prominent universities in Turkey, in 1986 with a major in Business Administration. He started his business career by establishing intermediary companies that sell companies that manufacture industrial furniture. Nazim Salur's first technological investment was in 2013, as he developed an application called Bitaksi. Bitaksi services residents of Istanbul, the largest metropolitan city in Turkey, aimed at delivering taxi service to users within three minutes. In an interview, Salur stated:

> I wanted to invest in the technology field. It was the year 2012, the year that smartphones were introduced into our lives, and 20% of the population has smartphones. Therefore, I believed that mobile applications would be the biggest medium doing business in the future, and I took the opportunity.

Although Bitaksi was not an original idea at the time of the venture, Salur was the pioneer in delivering the service to consumers in Turkey. Salur, who replicated the idea after observing the taxi service applications provided in developed countries like the UK, the US and Germany, stated that cloning an idea has become a norm in the economy. In a meeting, he commented that even in the automobile industry, it was first manufactured in the US; however, Germany, the UK, Italy and even Japan manufacture automobiles.

The idea of Getir was modelled by the Bitaksi venture (Eken and Gezmen, 2020), and this togetherness has witnessed a hackathon project known as Getir Hackathon. Due to its financial status, Getir is referred to as a decacorn and, thereby, it has become Turkey's most valuable startup company (Bloomberg, 2021). This being the case, a closer look into its business model revealed that selling online products (predominantly foods) and delivery-related fees are the primary revenue streams of Getir. Regarding its operational and organisational ambidexterity,

Table 5.1   Getir annual users and cumulative downloads 2019 to 2021 (mm)

Year	Users (million)	Downloads (million)
2019	0.3	3.5
2020	1.3	8.7
2021	3.5	34

Note: Cumulative downloads; taken at the start of each year.
Source: AppFigures – Food Delivery App Report (2022).

Getir offers 7/24 fast service (delivers products to consumers within ten minutes) with higher availability and coverage (delivering to various locations in Turkey and foreign markets). One of its distinctions from its rivals (e.g. Deliveroo) is that Getir has its own riders who are not self-employed, while other platform-based businesses, that is, Uber and DoorDash, mainly work with independent contractors. A report by the *Financial Times* (2022) stated that Getir would have 32,000 employees globally in 2022. The main strength of Getir can be considered as trustworthiness, convenience and the variety of food choices, whilst major weaknesses are higher prices than other businesses in the Turkish context (e.g. Yemeksepeti Banabi and Migros), the system failure for out-of-stock products, and the difficulty of reaching customer services (Barış and Yılmaz, 2021).

Getir achieved its most conspicuous growth at the beginning of the Covid-19 pandemic in Turkey in March 2020. According to Salur (Milliyet, Economy News, 2020), downloading numbers of the mobile application increased by 60 per cent, reaching nearly 2 million active users. The average age of the users also increased from 18–45 to 65 and even 70s. The user and cumulative download number are significant indicators to assess the market penetration rate for firms that use online apps. While Getir increased its users from 1.3 million in 2020 to 3.5 million in 2021 (Table 5.1), with a 169 per cent increase annually, its cumulative downloads reached 34 million by the end of 2021. In line with the sharp growth in user and cumulative download statistics, Getir's valuation increased rapidly to $12 billion in March 2022, granting it the second decacorn of Turkey.

The Covid-19 effect on online delivery

Covid-19 is far more than a health crisis impacting societies and economies. Societies have witnessed paradigm shifts during the outbreak, particularly in consumer purchasing behaviour patterns (Chanlat, 2020). For example, the Nielsen Company Study (2020) has yielded that Covid-19 has led to significant shifts in consumer behaviour focused on basic needs such as food, hygiene and cleaning products. Although it is expected that purchasing necessities takes precedence in emergency circumstances (Durante and Laran, 2016; Kemp et al., 2014; Larson and Shin, 2018), unprecedented events can alter the psychologies of individuals. For example, these novel events inevitably change purchasing behaviour due to elevated levels of anxiety that arise from ambiguity and the choice of purchasing channel (Alaimo et al., 2020). Furthermore, during crises, young consumers are inclined to purchase hygiene products and non-necessities products through online shopping (Di Crosta et al., 2021).

In Turkey, there are similar experiences in consumer purchasing habits during the pandemic, as the markets have seen a 125 per cent increase during the pandemic for e-commerce-based purchasing (McKinsey, 2020). Although online purchases of consumer goods were obtained through chain supermarket online shopping websites and applications, Getir was the consumers' choice. Prior to the pandemic, customers used the Getir application to purchase snack items like chocolate and crisps. However, during the pandemic, consumers' perception towards the Getir application has shifted, and Getir has become one of the marketplaces for various consumer goods as the download rate of the application increased by 60 per cent after the initial declaration of the pandemic nationwide. In addition, before the global pandemic, the users' average age varied between 18 and 45, yet it increased to 65–70 after the initial declaration (Milliyet, Economy News, 2020).

Along with an increase in the application's download rate, consumers' basket variety has also grown. 'Pandemic impact on online shopping' report by UNCTAD (2020) has shown consumers started to purchase products with long shelf life (foods like rice, bulgur, pasta, legumes and canned foods), along with flour and hygiene products through Getir. Mr Salur stated:

> The first three days of Covid-19, consumer demand for pasta has increased 22 times, and for staple goods, we had a 165% increase in sales compared to previous years. Also, for fruit and vegetable sales, we have grown 75% and cosmetic, personal care along with household products have increased by over 60 per cent. We used to be a company that came into the minds of consumers for certain goods during times of urgency, but Turkish people have made us a major player in the market. (Milliyet, Economy News, 2020)

One of the reasons Getir has become a significant player within the market is due to the government implementing emergency measures and amending shops and shopping malls to mandatory lockdowns. With imposed measures, Salur stated that Getir, as an on-demand business, has witnessed extraordinary growth and added:

> Consumers' demand was rapidly shifting due to the pandemic circumstances and its adverse effect on their psychologies. It was challenging at first to predict the demand volatility, but we have worked on how to effectively manage the value chain and continuously followed the progression in other countries to forecast the demand. (Milliyet, Economy News, 2020)

In the pandemic, the Turkish government imposed a curfew on people aged 65 and over and those with chronic illness. In order to help these elderly people and other people in need, Getir distributed 300,000 food parcels to Istanbul residents for six weeks between March and May 2020 under the organisation of the Governorship of Istanbul. The brand prepared and delivered an additional 10,000 parcels themselves (Marketing Türkiye, 2020). Similar socially responsible activities continued in the holy month of Muslims, Ramadan. All these efforts strengthened Getir's corporate prestige in the minds of society and local authorities. The founders' entrepreneurial mindset and experience, being vigilant for pursuing external trends and possessing strong network ties with government and local authorities have been critical success drivers for Getir in the entrepreneurial ecosystem. From this angle, it is apparent that

Getir aligns its internal capabilities with external changes and trends. Figure 5.4 indicates the interactive factors that led to the brand's growth in the market.

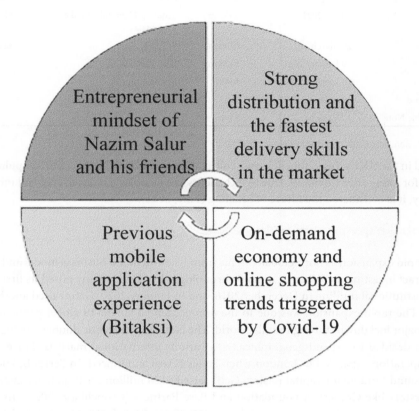

Figure 5.4   The growth ecosystem of Getir

After the initial expansion rate due to the pandemic, Getir has launched four additional services: Getir Food, Getir More, Getir Water and Getir Locals. Getir Food, akin to its major rival Yemeksepeti, known as 'food basket', is an online food delivery system that connects restaurant networks to individual consumers through an application. Like Hepsiburada and Trendyol applications, Getir More delivers various products at affordable prices, including meat and produce, home and personal care. In addition, Getir Water delivers bottled water to consumers on a 7/24 basis. Getir Water service is similar to BİSU, a thriving bottled water delivery venture aiming to service consumers in under 30 minutes. Getir Locals also aims to deliver products and services from local shops to its consumers within minutes.

Getir manages its vast web of on-demand delivery services via a managing network of dark stores. Dark stores, which used to be brick-and-mortar locations, were remodelled into a distribution hub exclusive for rapid delivery. The idea of the dark store concept, initially

Table 5.2   The fundraising rounds of Getir between 2017 and 2021 (million US dollars)

Fundraising History (Crunchbase)				
Round	Date	USD	Notable VCs	Value
Series D	4 June 2021	$555 m	Sequoia, Tiger, Silver Lake, Mubadala	$7.5 b
Series C	26 March 2021	$300 m	Sequoia, Tiger	$2.6 b
Series B	19 January 2021	$128 m	Base Partners	
Series A	16 January 2020	$38 m	Michael Moritz	
Seed Round	4 December 2018			
Convertible Note	1 December 2017	$4 m		

Sources: SandHill (2022) and IntelliNews (2021).

launched in the UK by Tesco for click-and-collect delivery in 2009, has become a popular retail channel for many after Covid-19. Due to its benefits like flexibility, reduced cost and increased efficiency, it is considered the future of retailing (Fine, 2021).

The global expansion of Getir

Getir's rapid expansion as born globally stems from its on-demand business model and capacity to attract investments. When examined chronologically, the company raised its first undisclosed institutional funding in December 2018, and in January 2020, Getir raised another $38 million. The rapid expansion was due to the unprecedented Covid-19 global pandemic that caused major lockdowns throughout the world. The company's revenue doubled in 2020 since the team decided to expand geographically to various international markets. For example, Getir's operation expanded to London when Series B was announced. In Series B, known as second round funding for capital raising, Getir raised $128 million on 19 January 2022, from lead investors like Crankstart Foundation and Base Partners (Crunchbase, 2021). In March 2021, in Series C, led by venture capital investors Tiger Global Management and Sequoia Capital, Getir raised $300 million additionally (FINMES, 2021). In Series E funding launched in 2022, led by Mubadala Investment Company with Abu Dhabi Growth, Alpha Wave Global, Tiger Global and Sequoia Capital, Getir reached an $11.8 billion valuation with an additional $768 million in funding (Dillet, 2022). Getir's fundraising rounds can be seen in Table 5.2.

The vast amount of investment that Getir attracted allowed the brand to become one of the dominant players in the marketplace operating in 81 cities in Turkey and 56 cities in eight other countries, which are the UK, Germany, France, Italy, Spain, the Netherlands, Portugal and the US as of September 2022. Getir, prior to its additional services like Getir More, Getir Water and Getir Local, has attained revenue through various revenue streams. The initial Getir business model attained its revenue through selling groceries at marked-up prices (approximately 10 per cent) along with delivery and other related fees. Getir has lower operating margins than conventional supermarkets since the company has created partnerships with warehouse owner franchisees and manages dark stores in affordable urban areas. There are advanced features of the Getir application, which can match individual customer experience and increase recurring purchases. For example, Getir uses push notifications to customers similar to their previous purchases and creates tailored content for the individual user. In addition, Getir provides its customers with real-time tracking of the drivers.

Things may not always go well!

What makes Getir different from its competitors is its speed of delivery. With online grocery deliveries taking up to hours and sometimes even days, the founders established the company's competitive strategy on delivery within ten minutes. Previous research has highlighted precarity (Kamasak et al., 2020a, 2020b) and accident risk (Özbilgin and Erbil, 2021) that the tight delivery deadlines in Turkey expose the food and grocery delivery drivers to. Despite the significant cost to the environment and worker safety, the general manager of Getir, Berker Yağcı, noted the significance of this strategy for the company in an interview:

> Delivering within 10 minutes is significant for customers because 10 minutes means right now. If we can achieve delivery within 10 minutes, we can retain our competitive advantage even when other players come into play. (McKinsey Podcast, 17 August 2022)

The competitive strategy of the brand could only be achieved through an efficient supply chain and information technologies (Kucukaltan et al., 2022) system that integrates all elements, that is, taking and tracking orders, optimising stocks, communicating with deliverers, managing customer services etc. in the whole distribution process (Kamasak, 2015, 2017). One of the most significant elements for the achievement of this strategy is the locations of the dark stores from where the deliveries are done. Getir operates 400 dark stores across 30 cities in Turkey and 54 in the UK (Staple, 2021). Although dark stores provide various advantages to consumers and retailers, there are growing protests from local communities and city authorities in European cities against operating dark stores. President Emmanuel Macron's government has mandated that dark stores be categorised as warehouses. If the decree is finalised, dark stores will be forced to close in Paris and other cities like Lyon, Nice and Montpellier (BBC, 2022). Aside from political and legal pressures, since dark stores have become a core strategy to solve supply chain vulnerability, volatility in the economic landscape, like the fear of forthcoming recession, constrains the growth of on-demand delivery companies.

Furthermore, Dutch and British citizens have filed similar complaints against having dark stores within the city centres. Although the European general manager of Getir Berker Yağcı stated that Getir has created 1,500 Dutch workforces and anticipates generating even more, the city officials amended a 'one-year freeze' for dark stores in Rotterdam and Amsterdam. This decision will cause significant disruptions in delivering services embedded in the fast-delivery business model (Reuters, 2022a). Amsterdam deputy mayor Marieke van Doornick disclosed that the one-year freeze decision is not unique to the cities of Amsterdam and Rotterdam; it is an overall verdict for most of the European cities (Reuters, 2022b). London's Islington and Berlin's Kreuzberg neighbourhoods also filed complaints due to 24-hour restocking and delivery of the merchandise and traffic hazards caused by rushing scooters around the city. Operating through dark stores allows on-demand companies to deliver services quickly, and despite the pressures from local communities, there is a surge of expansion of these hubs. According to Interact Analyses, there are currently 6,000 dark stores globally, which is expected to grow to 45,000 in eight years (The Grocer, 2022). However, besides the pressures of city officials and residents on dark store operations, on-demand businesses also face growing tension from other established grocery retailers. For example, in New York, the founder of the Bodega and Small Business Association and the United Bodegas of America pushed city officials to enforce zoning regulations to limit the expansion of on-demand establishments (CNBC, 2022).

There is no doubt that the company received a considerable amount of funding in six rounds of investment which supported its growth and international expansion. However, considering that Getir entered its overseas operations through big promotions and advertising campaigns, some cost and profitability-related challenges came to the fore. While the dark store problem became more complicated, the weak economic activities and the emerging recession due to tightening economic policies after the quantitative easing and excessive money printing by the European Union countries and the US during the pandemic period led to a slowdown in Getir's financial performance in 2022.

Getir works with a franchising system. Each franchisee is responsible for the deliveries in a defined region with a warehouse (dark store). Getir warehouses employ motor couriers with an hourly package limit. After the pandemic, Getir warehouses raised wages, yet the workers complained that it was not a raise but gum. Some workers announced they would not work until their wage request was accepted, but the franchisees dismissed them. Many workers across Turkey reacted to this decision, and protests started. A worker states:

> We try to fulfil orders at the expense of our lives, and due to time pressure on us the work-related accidents increase. This working model puts all the boss's responsibilities on occupational safety and labour rights on us. Our working conditions worsen every day; we work day and night under mobbing. (Sendika.org, 27 July 2022)

The requirements of workers for better conditions seem to be a challenge for warehouses. Against a successful business, some problems exist for the brand. The structural and social changes occurring in the external environment have revealed various business opportunities and threats. As experienced in the Covid-19 pandemic, purchase behaviours and the preferred tools or mediums in shopping activities have caused dramatic changes in individuals' habits and offerings of organisations. In line with these, various and increasing demands of people have triggered businesses to focus more on networking capabilities and providing innovative solutions on online platforms. In this regard, since physiological (food and clothing) needs are the first priority for individuals, especially when there are some restrictions and measures due to health conditions, the on-demand online grocery market has increased globally. This being the case, on-demand platforms operating in the e-commerce domain have become the focal point of studies and practical endeavours. Accordingly, this chapter initially discussed the concept of an on-demand platform and then presented an illustrative case study from the online grocery delivery platform, Getir, in Turkey since the case company is shown as a popular Turkish decacorn and the country is indicated as one of the top ten developing and transition economies in the B2C E-commerce Index. Thus, the discourses pointed out for online on-demand platforms and the arguments shared in the Getir case can be a reference point to investigate and understand the dynamics of these platforms in detail.

Further, e-commerce has generated a context in which the owner entrepreneurs accrue more benefits than anyone else involved, that is, drivers and customers, from the expansion of the platform economy. This ownership structure has polarised income distribution between platform economy workers stuck in precarious conditions of work and owner entrepreneurs, whose wealth accumulation has reached historical heights (Özbilgin and Erbil, 2022). Future research should examine how the polarisation of income distribution between stakeholders in the platform economy could be addressed.

TEACHING NOTES

LEARNING OUTCOMES

Upon completion of the chapter, the learner is expected to:

1. explain the e-commerce environment in the world;
2. elucidate online on-demand home services market within the e-commerce field;
3. address fundamental entrepreneurship questions;
4. apply principles of the on-demand business models.

TARGET AUDIENCE

The target audience of this chapter varies by interest in the e-commerce domain. In this sense, someone who wants to successfully establish an online business and/or manage online, especially on-demand, business models to grow their entrepreneurial venture is a potential audience of this chapter. This person is preferably someone over 20 since there needs to be some savings to invest, an understanding of the business management or experience in the business area and a willingness to improve themselves so that they can easily apply principles of online business models and capture business opportunities.

SUGGESTED TEACHING STRATEGIES

*   Problem-based teaching including a comparative approach can be used as an initial strategy to explain and benchmark offline and online markets in international trade.
*   Case-based teaching strategy as a follow-up strategy to explore various real-life examples and practices in the commercial market.
*   Project-based teaching strategy can also be used as another follow-up strategy to design a prototype and apply principles of entrepreneurship. In this strategy, after analysing different cases, learners can establish their own businesses by completing a business plan draft. At the end of this strategy, the presentation method can be utilised to deliver effective written and verbal communication.

REFERENCES

Alaimo, L.S., Fiore, M., & Galati, A. (2020). How the Covid-19 pandemic is changing online food shopping human behaviour in Italy. *Sustainability*, *12*(22), 9594. MDPI AG. http://dx.doi.org/10.3390/su12229594

alizila – news from Alibaba (2018). AliDay 2018: This is Alibaba. https://www.alizila.com/aliday-2018-this-is-alibaba/(accessed 2 November 2022).

AppFigures (2022). Getir revenue and usage statistics (2022), 13 September. https://www.businessofapps.com/marketplace/appfigures/

Bălan, C. (2016). Ride-sharing and car-sharing in Romania: What choices do potential users have? *International Conference of the Institute for Business Administration in Bucharest*, 2016, 103–12.

Barış, A., & Yılmaz, T. (2021). Consumers' perceptions of online grocery applications: 'Getir' a case study in Turkey. *Maltepe Üniversitesi İletişim Fakültesi Dergisi*, 8(2), 206–28.

BBC (2022). France clamps down on delivery depot 'dark stores'. https://www.bbc.com/news/world-europe-62838667 (accessed 21 October 2022).

Benjaafar, S., & Hu, M. (2020). Operations management in the age of the sharing economy: What is old and what is new? *Manufacturing & Service Operations Management*, *22*(1), 93–101.

Bloomberg (2021). https://www.bloomberg.com/news/articles/2021-03-26/getir-takes-turkish-unicorn-top-spot-on-2-6-billion-valuation, 26 March (accessed 5 October 2022).

Census (2022). https://www.census.gov/library/stories/2022/04/ecommerce-sales-surged-during-pandemic.html, 27 April (accessed 8 October 2022).

Chanlat J-F. (2020) La catastrophe sanitaire actuelle: un fait social total. *Le Libellio d'AEGIS* 2020, *16*, 3–30.

Chevalier, S. (2021). Development of e-commerce shares pre and post Covid-19, by country. https://www.statista.com/statistics/1228660/e-commerce-shares-development-during-pandemic/ (accessed 3 December 2021).

CNBC (2022). Bodegas are looking to zoning laws to defend their turf against instant delivery start-ups. https://www.cnbc.com/2022/02/04 /bodegas-look-to-zoning-to-defend-against-instant-delivery-rivals.html (accessed 21 October 2022).

Coppola, D. (2022). E-commerce worldwide. https://www.statista.com/topics/871/online-shopping/, 27 September (accessed 8 October 2022).

Crunchbase (2021). Series B- Getir. https://www.crunchbase.com/funding_round/getir-series-b--47b41675 (accessed 21 October 2022).

Daily Sabah (2022). 'Peak Mafia': Turkey's 1st billion-dollar startup fires up ecosystem, 29 July. https://www.dailysabah.com/business/tech/peak-mafia-turkeys-1st-billion-dollar-startup-fires-up-ecosystem

Di Crosta, A., Ceccato, I., Marchetti, D., La Malva, P., Maiella, R., & Cannito, L. (2021). Psychological factors and consumer behavior during the COVID-19 pandemic. *PLoS One*, *16*(8), e0256095. https://doi.org/10.1371/journal.pone.0256095

Digitalage (2020). Online market alışverişlerine koronavirüs etkisi. https://digitalage.com.tr/online-market-alisverislerine-koronavirus-etkisi/ (accessed 14 October 2022).

Dillet, R. (2022). Getir is now worth nearly $12 billion after raising another $768 million. https://techcrunch.com/2022/03/17/getir-is-now-worth-nearly-12-billion-after-raising-another-768-million/ (accessed 21 October 2022).

Doing Business in Turkey.com (2021). Dream Games become Turkey's new 'unicorn', 7 July. https://doingbusinessinturkey.com/dream-games-becomes-turkeys-new-unicorn/

Durante K.M. & Laran J. (2016). The effect of stress on consumer saving and spending. *Journal of Marketing Research*, *53*, 814–28.

Eken, I., & Gezmen, B. (2020). E-retailing practices in mobile marketing: The case of Getir application. In *Tools and Techniques for Implementing International E-trading Tactics for Competitive Advantage* (pp. 156–83). Hershey, PA: IGI Global.

Ercoskun, O.Y., & Ocalir, E. (2018). An urban tension about ridehailing: Uber experience in Istanbul. *Beiträge zu einer ökologisch und sozial verträglichen Verkehrsplanung*, *1/2018*, 131–46.

eticaret (2022). The Republic of Türkiye Ministry of Trade, E-Commerce Info Platform: Elektronik Ticaret Bilgi Sistemi (ETBİS) 2021 Yılı Verileri, 8 April. https://www.eticaret.gov.tr/dnnqthgzva

wtdxraybsaacxtymawm/content/FileManager/Dosyalar/2021%20Y%C4%B1l%C4%B1%20E-Ticaret%20B%C3%BClteni.pdf (accessed 8 October 2022).

Fast Company Türkiye (2021). https://fastcompany.com.tr/calisma-hayati/kar-eden-yok-rekabet-buyuk/, Issue 9 (accessed 8 October 2022).

Financial Times (2022). Getir valuation triples to $7.5bn as investors chase grocery app craze. https://www.ft.com/content/3acc197c-cd81-4b3b-a19b-32e58fc687e7 (accessed 20 October 2022).

Fine, T. (2021). Groceries at the speed of app: Trend or here to stay? https://www.nycfoodpolicy.org/groceries-at-the-speed-of-app-trend-or-here-to-stay/ (accessed 21 October 2022).

FINMES (2021). Getir closes $300m Series C funding; Valued at $2.6 billion. https://www.finsmes.com/2021/04/getir-closes-300m-series-c-funding-valued-at-2-6-billion.html (accessed 21 October 2022).

IntelliNews (2021). Turkey's Getir in partnership talks with local car rental app MOOV, 4 August. https://intellinews.com/turkey-s-getir-in-partnership-talks-with-local-car-rental-app-moov-217333/

Kamasak, R. (2015). Creation of firm performance through resource orchestration: The case of Ülker. *Competitiveness Review*, 25(2), 179–204.

Kamasak, R. (2017). The contribution of tangible and intangible resources, and capabilities to a firm's profitability and market performance. *European Journal of Management and Business Economics*, 26(2), 252–75.

Kamasak, R., Özbilgin, M.F., Yavuz, M., & Akalin, C. (2020a). Race discrimination at work in the U.K. In Vassilopoulou, J., Brabet, J., Kyriakidou, O., & Shovunmi, V. (eds), *Race Discrimination and the Management of Ethnic Diversity at Work: European Countries Perspective* (pp. 107–27). Bingley, UK: Emerald Publishing.

Kamasak, R., Özbilgin, M.F., & Yavuz, M. (2020b). Understanding intersectional analyses. In King, E., Roberson, Q., & Hebl, M. (eds), *Research on Social Issues in Management on Pushing Understanding of Diversity in Organizations* (pp. 93–115). Charlotte, NC: Information Age Publishing.

Kamasak, R., Palalar, A.D., & Yalcinkaya, B. (2023). Emerging trends of Industry 4.0 in equality, diversity and implementations. In Kucukaltan, B. (ed.), *Contemporary Approaches in Equality, Diversity and Inclusion: Strategic and Technological Perspectives* (pp. 129–48). Bingley, UK: Emerald Publishing.

Kemp, E., Kennett-Hensel, P.A., & Williams, K.H. (2014). The calm before the storm: Examining emotion regulation consumption in the face of an impending disaster. *Psychology & Marketing*, 31, 933–45.

Kranz, J., Hanelt, A., & Kolbe, L.M. (2016). Understanding the influence of absorptive capacity and ambidexterity on the process of business model change – the case of on-premise and cloud-computing software. *Information Systems Journal*, 26(5), 477–517.

Kucukaltan, B. (2020). Shifting towards technology-based on-demand transportation business models: A comparative research. *Afyon Kocatepe Üniversitesi Sosyal Bilimler Dergisi*, 22(4), 1035–45.

Kucukaltan, B., Kamasak, R., Yalcinkaya B., & Irani, Z. (2022). Investigating the themes in supply chain finance: The emergence of blockchain as a disruptive technology. *International Journal of Production Research*. https://doi.org/10.1080/00207543.2022.2118886

Kumar, P., Chauhan, S., & Jaiswal, M.P. (2022). An innovation resistance theory perspective on home service applications: The moderating role of country context. *International Journal of Consumer Studies*. https://doi.org/10.3389/fpsyg.2022.961589

Larson, L.R.L., & Shin, H. (2018). Fear During natural disaster: Its impact on perceptions of shopping convenience and shopping behavior. *Services Marketing Quarterly*, 39, 293–309.

Malik, S.R., Rafiq, M., & Kahloon, M.A. (2021). Cloud security in e-commerce applications. In *Research Anthology on E-commerce Adoption, Models, and Applications for Modern Business* (pp. 1720–32). Hershey, PA: IGI Global.

Marketing Türkiye (2020). Getir: 50 bin ihtiyaç sahibi büyüğümüze 6 hafta boyunca 300 bin gıda kolisi dağıtacağız, 27 March. https://www.marketingturkiye.com.tr/haberler/getir-50-bin-ihtiyac-sahibi-buyugumuze-6-hafta-boyunca-300-bin-gida-kolisi-dagitacagiz/

McKinsey (2020). Adapting to the next normal in retail: The customer experience imperative. https://www.mckinsey.com/industries/retail/our-insights/adapting-to-the-next-normal-in-retail-the-customer-experience-imperative (accessed 5 November 2022).

Milliyet (2015). Yemeksepeti 589 milyon dolara satıldı! https://www.milliyet.com.tr/yemek/bilgi/yemeksepeti-589-milyon-dolara-satildi-2054297

Milliyet, Economy News (2020). Çok Getir'di iyi kazandı! 19 May. https://www.milliyet.com.tr/ekonomi/cok-getirdi-iyi-kazandi-6215280

Mitchell, A., & Strader, T.J. (2018). Introduction to the special issue on 'Sharing economy and on-demand service business models'. *Information Systems and e-Business Management, 16,* 243–5.

Nielsen (2020). Key consumer behavior thresholds identified as the coronavirus outbreak evolves. https://www.nielsen.com/us/en/insights/article/2020/key-consumer-behavior-thresholds-identified -as-the-coronavirus-outbreak-evolves/?utm_source=sfmc&utm_medium=email&utm_campaign= newswire&utm_content=3-18-2020 (accessed 14 October 2022).

Özbilgin, M., & Erbil, C. (2021). Post-hümanist İnovasyon: Gig Ekonomi Özelinde Moto Kuryeli Teslimat Sektörü Örneklemi. *Sosyal Mucit Academic Review, 2*(1), 22–41.

Özbilgin, M. & Erbil, C. (2022). Robot Emeği ve İnsan-Doğa-Teknoloji İlişkisinde Robot Emeğine Yeni Bir Yaklaşım. In Cengiz, A.A. & Uçkan Hekimler, B. (eds), *Emeğin Hallerine Dair* (pp. 1–16). Yeniinsan Yayınevi.

Peerbits (2021). 8 service industries that drive the on-demand economy. https://www.peerbits.com/blog/ service-industries-that-drive-the-on-demand-economy.html (accessed 27 October 2022).

Reuters (2022a). European fast grocery hits speed bump with Dutch halt on new 'dark stores'. https:// euronews.com/next/2022/02/11/netherlands-dark-stores (accessed 21 October 2022).

Reuters (2022b). Rotterdam joins Amsterdam in freezing new 'dark stores'. https://www.reuters .com/business/retail-consumer/rotterdam-joins-amsterdam- freezing-new-dark-stores-2022-02-03 (accessed 21 October 2022).

Saif Benjaafar, Ming Hu (2020). Operations management in the age of the sharing economy: What is old and what is new? *Manufacturing & Service Operations Management, 22*(1), 93–101.

SandHill.io (2022). Getir – grocery delivery service, 25 February. https://teardowns.sandhill.io/p/getir ?utm_source=profile&utm_medium=reader2

ScaleX Ventures (2022). Trends Deep Dive (Part 3) – Turkey ecosystem at a glance. https://www .scalexventures.com/content/turkey-ecosystem-at-a-glance

Sendika.org (2022). Ankara'da Getir kuryeleri kontak kapattı: Saatlik ücretimize 1 TL zam yaptılar, kabul etmeyip eylem başlattık. https://sendika.org/2022/07/ankarada-getir-kuryeleri-kontak-kapatti-saatlik -ucretimize-1-tl-zam-yaptilar-kabul-etmeyip-eylem-baslattik-662311/

Sharma, G., & Lijuan, W. (2015). The effects of online service quality of e-commerce websites on user satisfaction. *The Electronic Library, 33*(3), 468–85.

Staple, K. (2021). Take a look inside a dark store. https://sifted.eu/articles/inside-dark-store/ (accessed 21 October 2022).

Technavio Research (2021). Online on-demand home services market by service and geography – forecast and analysis 2021–2025. https://www.prnewswire.com/news-releases/online-on-demand -home-services-market-to-grow-by--4-730-billion-during-2021-2025--insights-on-covid-19-impact -analysis-key-drivers-trends-and-products-offered-by-major-vendors--technavio-301249928.html

The Grocer (2022). Rapid grocery dark stores in UK set to number 1,500 by 2030. https://www.thegrocer .co.uk/online/rapid-grocery-dark-stores-in-uk-set-to-number-1500-by-2030/664831.article (accessed 17 September 2022).

Tracxn Report (2022). Online Grocery Startups in Turkey, 3 September. https://tracxn.com/explore/ Online-Grocery-Startups-in-Turkey

UNCTAD (2020). COVID-19 has changed online shopping forever, survey shows. https://unctad.org/ news/covid-19-has-changed-online-shopping-forever-survey-shows (accessed 26 October 2022).

UNCTAD (2021). 'Top 10 developing and transition economies in the UNCTAD B2C E-commerce Index 2020, by region, 17 February. https://unctad.org/news/switzerland-climbs-top-global-e-commerce -index (accessed 1 October 2022).

U.S. News (2022). Turkey's Trendyol plans dual IPO when revenue abroad is 30–35%, 19 January. https://www.usnews.com/news/technology/articles/2022-01-19/turkeys-trendyol-plans-dual-ipo -when-revenue-abroad-is-30-35

van der Burg, R.J., Ahaus, K., Wortmann, H., & Huitema, G.B. (2019). Investigating the on-demand service characteristics: An empirical study. *Journal of Service Management, 30*(6), 739–65.

Wagner Mainardes, E., de Almeida, C.M., & de-Oliveira, M. (2019). E-commerce: An analysis of the factors that antecede purchase intentions in an emerging market. *Journal of International Consumer Marketing, 31*(5), 447–68.

Walton, N., & Nayak, B.S. (2021). Rethinking of Marxist perspectives on big data, artificial intelligence (A.I.) and capitalist economic development. *Technological Forecasting and Social Change, 166,* 120576.

Webrazzi (2018). The long awaited answer about the amount of Alibaba's investment in Trendyol, 30 July. https://webrazzi.com/en/2018/07/30/the-long-awaited-answer-about-the-amount-of-alibabas-investment-in-trendyol/

World Economic Forum (2022). 4 Turkish unicorns on how to support digital transformation and the start-up ecosystem. https://www.weforum.org/agenda/2022/09/these-4-turkish-unicorns-divulge-how-to-support-digital-transformation-and-the-start-up-ecosystem/(accessed 28 October 2022).

Zeier Röschmann, A., Erny, M., & Wagner, J. (2022). On the (future) role of on-demand insurance: eMarket landscape, business model and customer perception. *The Geneva Papers on Risk and Insurance-Issues and Practice*, 1–40.

6
From dying SME to re-born global to multinational: Vendlet

Nicolaj Hannesbo Petersen

CASE SUMMARY

Born Global companies are unique because they can rapidly internationalise from their inception. However, most companies experience both temporality and speediness in growth affected by endogenous and exogenous factors and ups and downs in business cycles. In this case, we look at different periods of growth for a Danish wholesaler and manufacturing company. The company experienced different periods of gazelle growth, generational change, threatened bankruptcy, acquisitions and rapid global internationalisation. The Vendlet case is exciting and relevant to discuss because it questions our often-implicit understanding of the linearity of growth and perceived drivers of internationalisation. The company has been viable for more than 35 years, but the company was about to go bankrupt in 2010, and through acquisition, the new team and owner became re-born as a global gazelle. The new owner's vision, actions and business development are fundamental for transitioning from a dying SME to a re-born global gazelle. He made challenging and irreversible decisions resulting in ongoing business model innovation. The latest action was to sell the company to a Welsh conglomerate and thus transition to being part of a multinational.

LEARNING OUTCOMES

The primary learning outcomes of this case study are focused on three points explaining the international high growth of Born Global firms:

- The importance of owner-manager as an international entrepreneur, cultural gate-keeper and driver for Born Global's growth. How entrepreneurial vision and capabilities affect internationalisation through previous and new experience by associating, questioning, experimenting and networking with new opportunities, thus creating a firm culture for innovation and growth.
- From outsider to an insider within international markets: the role of relations and network positions, and their actor's motivation or vision for bonding, terminating,

bridging etc. Relations and networks are understood as learning opportunities and building trust and commitment.

- How to design a (successful) business model for rapid international growth: key decisions and configuration are needed regarding value creation, delivery and capture.
  - Value creation: business model innovation is related to value proposition or new offering, customers and markets, new channels, new customer relations etc.
  - Value delivery: business model innovation is related to new capabilities, new resources, new technology, new partnerships or networks, new processes etc.
  - Value capture: the business model is related to new revenue models and cost structures.

THE FIRM'S CONTEXT – MARKET NICHE, INDUSTRY AND KEY FIGURES

Vendlet[1] is a Danish manufacturer and wholesaler of assistive living aids and devices for the health and care sector. Vendlet develops and produces assisted living aids, including fully automatic patient transfer aid, support and bolstering cushions, mobility aids and incontinence bed pads. They operate globally as an assisted living technology company with distributors in Australia, England, Finland, France, New Zealand, Norway, Singapore and Sweden. They have an office in Denmark and the Netherlands, and their office in Denmark housed their headquarters in 2022.

Vendlet's product and market focus is characterised as a niche strategy. They operate in the market of assistive living aids and devices for the health and care sector. Vendlet specialises in accessories for beds and, therefore, niche-oriented instead of mass-market offerings within the industry. Their patient transfer aid system is advanced as it is fully automatic. They are branding themselves as the only fully automatic system using words like turn aid, an electric slide sheet and an electric turn sheet. Vendlet differs significantly from other competitors' mass-market product portfolio and manual patient transfer solutions, but in recent years, they have experienced increased competition in their business domain. The company Turnaid Aps, founded in 2014 is seen as a competitor by Vendlet on their core product. Peter Maindahl, CEO from 2010 to 2022, reflected in an interview on intensified competition from unforeseen places nearby:

Turnaid was sold on 1 July 2015; before that, there was something called *Dansk Pleje Teknik* which later developed a competing business and solution. We had a relationship with *Dansk Pleje Teknik* because they were a service partner for us. While we have trained them in Vendlet systems and technical fault solutions, problems, how to install, and everything else. They developed their Turnaid product without telling us anything and suddenly launched a product in direct competition with us.

When companies pioneer new markets and solutions with growth succes, imitators will often follow if it is perceived as attractive for them to become a competitor. This is an example of a competitive movement where the imitator is emergent from a previous collaboration. The industry association, Danish Care, carried out an analysis and report in 2017 on the Danish industry.[2] Key figures from the industry are disclosed in that report:

- The industry consists of over 300 dedicated welfare technology and assistive technology companies.
- A total of up to 1,000 companies deal with the area.
- The industry has DKK 5.1 billion in total revenue (2016).
- The industry delivers DKK 1.4 billion in total GDP contribution (2016).
- 3,600 people are employed directly in the industry's companies.
- The industry exports DKK 1.3 billion.
- There is a preponderance of small and medium-sized enterprises (SMEs) and Danish production companies in the industry.

THE FIRM, GROWTH AND TEMPORALITY OF OWNERSHIP AND VISION

In this next section, Vendlet's history and business development are described over four periods. The first period with prototype and firm development from 1970 to 1990, the second period with generational change from 1990 to 2010, the third period of re-born global growth from 2010 to 2022 and the fourth period of acquisition and joining a multinational corporation from 2022 to the present time. The reader should be attentive to differences in ownership, visions, innovation and development processes between the four periods.

Period of foundation and prototype development (1970–90)

In the 1970s, the Danish engineer, Christian Buus, faced a challenge. His disabled daughter was cared for at home, primarily by Christian's wife, and often had to be turned 3–5 times each night. As the daughter got older, the mother's back could no longer withstand the many turns and transfers. Christian Buus started solving the problem technically with multiple prototypes operated by hand with a V-belt. In searching for an operative mechanical solution to the problem, he invents the first automatic patient turning system, Vendlet. The powered Vendlet system has motors in the bars and is controlled by a control unit that stands by a bedside table. In 1981, the Vendlet system was awarded by the Muscular Dystrophy Foundation's idea competition, and the Vendlet system became patented. Christian experienced proof of concept in the coming years, and in 1985, the company was established under the name H.C. Equipment. The vision for H.C. Equipment stems from the owner-manager and founder's personal experience and challenge with his disabled daughter. Therefore, the company's development in these years is very much product-solution oriented with initial national and international commercial success.

Period of generational change, product and production innovation (1990–2010)

In 1990, a generation change was established with Flemming and Heine Buus. They are both Christian's sons; educationally, Flemming is an electrical engineer and Heine a blacksmith. The two sons continue the more technical-oriented vision for the company. In the following years, they improved and innovated the Vendlet system. The company now delivers two different models, HC-2 and V4, which can handle up to 200 kg as standard but can also be delivered in unique models, such as handling up to 400 kg. In addition, new products have been developed: Oplet, which is used for transfers to operating camps, and Sleep Tight, which reduces involuntary movements and creates good conditions for sleep, for example, for patients with Huntington's Chorea or dementia.

Heine Buus, CEO from 1990 to 2010, elaborates on the Vendlet system and its value for social workers, caregivers, nurses and patients/citizens. The focus is on product innovation for these users of the system. In addition, he also highlights commercial success within the Danish market and value proposition towards different segments (Magasinet Pleje, 27 April 2010):

> Nursing staff are among the most exposed to reported occupational injuries. Staff often experience a conflict between caring for citizens and focusing on their health during transfer tasks. The Vendlet manages the transfer of bedridden patients without physical strain on the staff while simultaneously turning the patient gently and uniformly. Operation is simple and only requires the assistance of a carer. It also requires fewer hands, and with the help of Vendlet, bedridden people are moved with ease and dignity. The citizen experiences a uniform and calm turning, which is comfortable, as the sheet supports the body at its entire length. The caregiver maintains an overview and can support the citizen's arms, legs or head as needed. It makes room for presence in the care and increases the carer's job satisfaction and the citizen's well-being.
>
> Across the country, 90 of Denmark's 98 municipalities have chosen Vendlet as a natural part of the daily care of the citizens. The director of H.C. Equipment, Heine Buus, expresses that Vendlet covers a significant need in the relief of staff. In residential care institutions and home care, we are experiencing an increasing interest in using the fully electric Vendlet V4 model. For care environments with limited space, the Vendlet V4 has significant advantages, as the operation does not require free space along the sides of the bed.

Period of Born Global growth, vision and business model innovation (2010–22)

Peter Maindal, at 44 years old, in October 2010 acquired H.C. Equipment. Flemming (age 59) and Heine Buus (age 61) continued in the company until the end of January 2011 as part of the transfer. As Peter says in a newspaper article from the period:

> H.C. Equipment has an inspiring product range, and I see great opportunities in the future, not least in the export markets. Within the care sector, there is an increasing focus on the

working environment and labour-saving technology, which means that Vendlet is particu-larly up-to-date, as the application provides both a better working environment, less strain on staff resources and better quality of care. (Magasinet Pleje, 24 September 2010)

Peter understands the value of the Vendlet system and the market potential from both pro-fessional expertise and industry experience. He is a trained physiotherapist with business experience in management and sales positions in rehabilitation. This combination of expertise and experience gives a strategic competence (vision) and a solid position to run and develop the company and product. However, it did not succeed immediately because H.C. Equipment and the organisation at Aalborg were commercially reactive. Furthermore, the company had a deficit of DKK 400,000 in 2010. It is challenging to grow a business when different mindsets, capabilities, values and goals drive it. Peter Maindahl reflects on this in an interview:

> Good people, Christian, Flemming and Heine, but they did not understand what they were doing and what world they were operating in. They were not business people, but the technology or concept they had developed and the patent with the first Vendlet that came out in around 1985 called HC2 was and is still very innovative. The principle of the product is an electro-mechanical sheet, for example, a motorised sheet where a citizen could be turned on. That principle was brilliant, which has enormous potential and was a bit funny because almost at the same time, there was a company called Guldman, V Guldman. Viggo Guldman started up in Aarhus at roughly the same time. He understood what he was dealing with and did understand the importance of making ceiling lifts a commercial success, the new best practice within the industry. Vendlet has changed the product, the principle, and the concept around it, but Guldman's ceiling lifting and tilting is an entirely natural thing or standard within the industry. The former owners have never, ever managed to do that. So, you can say Guldman has accelerated madly past them, where they have flown under the radar pretty much the whole time. So, I bought a company that was dying, a company that was 100% reaction oriented, that sat and waited for the phone to ring. No salespeople were employed, so it was not the company I bought, I bought the product. It was not because I bought a company that was super well organised, an organisation that was set up where it just kicked off and where the organisation knew what it had to do. So far from it, I would almost say that I bought the company in spite of the organisation or the company. It was about getting the technology.

Peter Maindahl had a vision of commercial success and a strong understanding of their value proposition. Still, Vendlet had to innovate incremental products, commercially tell the story and create awareness of its value proposition. More dramatically, the whole business model was re-innovated through critical decisions in firing the old employees, relocating their office, outsourcing production and international market development.

Incremental product innovation

Their core product is a fully automatic patient transfer aid. Their value or selling proposition is a fully automatic turning sheet that makes it possible to turn frail patients in their beds quickly and simply. The patient's sheet moves them from one position to another in the bed as gently as possible. This not only optimises time consumption and patient bed damage (prevention of pressure injuries), and thus costs for the customer, but also the working environment and potential course of injury due to, for example, poor lifting. The system was invented by an engineer in the 1970s–1980s but has innovated incrementally over the years. Notably, in 2012, the Vendlet system was updated and had a more modern design, and the models V5 and V5+ were launched. The new product launch won several innovation prizes, for example, by the 'Moving & Handling People' conference in London in 2013 and 2014. The patient turning system Vendlet V5 won the 'Best Product on Show' 2013 news award; in 2014, it won the 'Most Interesting Product' award. In a Danish context, their patient turning system and Vendlet have won the Danish physiotherapists' Innovation and entrepreneurship award 2015. Furthermore, in 2017 the Danish Industry Association gave an initiative award to Vendlet.

Radical business model innovation

In 2011, under the new CEO Peter Maindahl, Vendlet became re-born, he relocated the firm, and fired its employees. However, the company was under financial pressure, and he had to use his pension as capital to realise the internationalisation vision. He also outsourced production to focus on sales. As explained by himself in an interview:

> I was more than all in to make it work, so sales was critical and essential and something that probably still characterises the organisation. People have different perspectives, and I have noticed before that organisations can be built around different perspectives; if you are a person who is very administratively focused, for example, then organisations are often built around that. I am a sales-oriented person, I am an offensive-minded person concerning such things, I think sales, I think we have to deliver something, and then things are also built around that, to saying, well, how do we get something done, what works for the customers, how do we make it so that we can sell to our customers and how do we support the sales work. There were things like that and, for example, I have five consultants on the road now in Denmark, and two service technicians and I have an export man, for example, the people who make a living selling something, that is out of 20.

He was so committed to international sales and network development in the first years that he travelled 170 days a year. He hired a former colleague as responsible for sales in Denmark. He told him now you are responsible for Denmark and I am for the rest of the world. However, this was not easy because he experienced continued financial problems. As stated by himself:

> So it was about growing the company; it was about increasing it. Turn up the volume and move on. Then, unfortunately, it turned out that the due diligence that had been done at

the company. I had never done that before. It was absolute hell, so my life was seriously threatened. In other words, three months passed from when I added significant capital to the company, they were gone because it was rolling around with holes in the company I had bought, so it flowed out of the box simply to close holes, so I was very threatened. So it didn't take long, then I stopped taking a salary myself, and for the first year and a half, that is, I worked without pay, as it were, because I had no income. I had to sell everything I had of assets and values to create the capital needed or what I had left before buying the company. It was also very successful, so 2011 was the best year ever in the company's history at the time.

Since 2011 distributor agreements have been made around the globe. Australia and New Zealand are initial successful sales and network partners. In 2014, 2015 and 2016, the company experienced gazelle growth from international to global sales. In 2014, an export manager was employed to care for the European markets. In 2020, the profit doubled from DKK 937,275 to DKK 2.5 million before tax. It has done so despite the coronavirus pandemic.

'Because everything shut down, it started to go forward and strong in May. So had it not been for corona, we would have had the growth even more', Peter Maindahl points out in a newspaper article (Grubach, 2021) He views and understands his employed physiotherapists and occupational therapists as important salespeople, because they can brand Vendlet as a knowledge-driven company, but they also have Vendlet products with them that they can show off to customers. They are essential for giving free training to their customers, mainly the public sector in Denmark. They have developed bearing and support cushions and mattresses, making life and bed rest easier for the elderly, sick and carers. The customer group is perceived as growing because people are getting older, and more and more bedridden people can benefit from the technology. Moreover, there will be fewer and fewer people to care for the elderly, the sick and the weak. The biggest markets for Vendlet in 2020 exist in England and Norway in addition to the Netherlands, but Vendlet has completely abandoned the German market, although there is an immediate and immense customer potential. They tried to internationalise to Germany through a German subsidiary, but as reflected upon by Peter Maindahl in a newspaper article (Grubach, 18 November 2021), it was too complicated:

> There is an overly rigid system in Germany, which is not aimed at welfare technology at all. You must, therefore, first, have a so-called Hilfs model number. We have had the German subsidiary but gave it all up.

In 2020, Vendlet experienced a decline in the Netherlands, where they have a subsidiary with two employees but are understood by themselves as having a solid position in the market. They had been experiencing high growth in Australia, but Covid-19 generally affected that and they had to postpone activities and could not participate in fairs during the pandemic. Peter Maindahl argues they could have sold a lot more if it had not been a global pandemic.

Period of acquisition and joining a multinational corporation (2022–)

On 31 January 2022, Vendlet was sold to the Welsh conglomerate Direct Healthcare Group, which has an annual turnover of DKK 774 million and over 600 employees and subsidiaries in six European countries, including Denmark. Furthermore, Direct Healthcare Group has distributors in 35 countries globally, including the United States, Japan, Australia, France and Germany. Peter Maindahl states that the company is selling because it requires significantly more resources and competencies to internationalise and capture these opportunities than it has at its current disposal. Despite 20 productive employees and a well-trimmed business, which in 2020 gave a gross profit of DKK 12.7 million, a profit of just over DKK 2 million and an equity capital of nearly DKK 7 million, the international expansion requires more resources. Furthermore, selling Vendlet's products on the home market in Denmark has become more challenging, since changes have been made to national purchase agreements (SKI) for health-care sectors, which gather the purchases of most public organisations in Denmark. This is the right time and match, according to Peter Maindahl. A match, as elaborated by Peter Maindahl, because both companies work actively with professional education and knowledge sharing to (network) position themselves in the market. Direct Healthcare Group does it with a programme called Ethos. Furthermore, they value and focus on innovation and product development, which matches with Vendlet.

However, a key challenge within this new business setup can be to ensure continued progress from the previous owner. The reason is that the owner-manager is often a central gatekeeper and decision maker of culture, values and driver growth within SMEs. A new setup most likely changes this because Peter Maindahl does not continue in the company, Danish employees will be fired to some degree, and a new international CEO will be in charge. The purchase of Vendlet is the latest in Direct Healthcare Group's enduring period of growth and expansion and comes in the wake of the acquisitions of Talley Group and United Care in 2021 and the acquisitions of Gate Rehab and Handicare Patient Handling Eurowog Medimattress in 2020. Direct Healthcare Group is committed to quality – something Vendlet is similarly known for. Direct Healthcare Group works like Vendlet to create better quality and safety for patients and healthcare staff; therefore, they are the right buyer for Peter Maindahl.

DISCUSSION

A long-held discussion in international entrepreneurship and business is regarding the drivers of internationalisation. Born Global research has often positioned itself against inter-national business theories. For instance, the Uppsala model views internationalisation as a more step-by-step process driven through experience, market knowledge and commitment. However, Vahlne and Johanson (2017) recently elaborated on what has changed since they first introduced the Uppsala internationalisation model in 1977 in the *Journal of International Business Studies*. More dynamically, they view internationalisation as a web of relations connected through networks and positions. Thus, insidership in the relevant network(s) is necessary for successful internationalisation, and therefore barriers to internationalisation become a liability of outsidership. Relationships within these networks offer the potential for learning and building trust and commitment, which are similar preconditions for internationalisation. This corresponds to more dynamic network models of rapid internationalisation, such as International New Ventures or Born Global, which often overcome liabilities of smallness, newness and foreignness through their network and previous international experience (Freeman et al., 2006). Others have empirically validated founders' global vision, technology, capabilities and business model innovation as key drivers (Hennart et al., 2021). There is thus ongoing discussion of the driver of internationalisation as an entrepreneurial process, technology, network and business model innovation. If we look at the Vendlet case, what are their drivers of internationalisation, and do they differ in the four periods?

DISCUSSION QUESTIONS

Some questions arise in connection to the issues mentioned above. To answer these questions, you can rely on the case described above and articles on international business.

1. What are the CEO and top management's vision? Furthermore, what are their capabilities?
2. How do the different owner's visions and capabilities affect the growth of Vendlet if you compare the three first periods in the case description?
3. What is the role of knowledge and innovation (product, technology, branding) in developing a market (network) for Vendlet's growth (period 2010 to 2022)?
4. Identify critical changes and innovative actions to Vendlet's business model (period 2010 to 2022). Moreover, how does this affect their internationalisation process?
5. How does Vendlet continue its growth after joining a Welsh conglomerate, Direct Healthcare Group?
6. What would you do as a new owner-manager or CEO?

NOTES

1. https://www.vendlet.com/ (accessed 31 July 2023). A timeline of the company history of Vendlet may be found at https://www.vendlet.com/about-us/about-vendlet/company-history (accessed 31 July 2023).
2. https://www.danish.care/om-branchen/branchestatistik/ (accessed 31 July 2023).

SUPPLEMENTARY INFORMATION NEEDED TO ANSWER THE CASE QUESTIONS

Key references to scientific papers and suggestions for reading that can be used in the discussion.

Cavusgil, S.T., & Knight, G. (2015). The born global firm: An entrepreneurial and capabilities perspective on early and rapid internationalisation. *Journal of international Business Studies*, *46*(1), 3–16.
Dyer, J.H., Gregersen, H.B., & Christensen, C.M. (2009). The innovator's DNA. *Harvard Business Review*, *87*(12), 60–7.

Freeman, S., Edwards, R., & Schroder, B. (2006). How smaller born-global firms use networks and alliances to overcome constraints to rapid internationalisation. *Journal of International Marketing*, *14*(3), 33–63.

Grubach, Carsten B. (2021). Flere ældre giver øget vækst i velfærdsteknologi. *Erhverv+*, 18 November.

Hennart, J.F., Majocchi, A., & Hagen, B. (2021). What's so special about born globals, their entrepreneurs or their business model? *Journal of International Business Studies*, *52*(9), 1665–94.

Knight, G.A., & Liesch, P.W. (2016). Internationalisation: From incremental to born global. *Journal of World Business*, *51*(1), 93–102.

Magasinet Pleje (2010). Særlig risiko for personalet ved forflytning af sengeliggende. Section 1, Health & rehab. 27 April.

Magasinet Pleje (2010). H.C. Equipment på nye hænder. Section 1, Health & rehab. 14 September.

Vahlne, J.E., & Johanson, J. (2017). From internationalisation to evolution: The Uppsala model at 40 years. *Journal of International Business Studies*, *48*, 1087–102.

Vahlne, J.E., & Johanson, J. (2020). The Uppsala model: Networks and micro-foundations. *Journal of International Business Studies, 51*, 4–10.

7

Reinventing the footwear industry: the role of digital technologies in the market development strategy of an Italian Born Global firm

Giorgia Masili, Alessio Travasi and Fabio Musso

CASE SUMMARY

Design Italian Shoes is an agile fashion-luxury company combining the excellence of Italian craftsmanship with the most advanced digital technologies by providing a personalised shopping experience and operating the digitalisation of shoe production. The company's success is attributable to the entrepreneurial atmosphere typical of the territorial concentration in which it is localised, inside the Fermano-Maceratese industrial district in the Marche region in Italy. The case is an example of a small company that developed a disruptive business model by relying on digital technologies to reinvent the dynamics of the footwear sector. The company is identifiable as a Born Global as it started its internationalisation from its establishment. It developed an omnichannel marketing strategy and has demonstrated resilience during recent crises (e.g., the COVID-19 emergency). Based on the successful results, the company should evaluate which direction to take for further expansion in international markets.

LEARNING OUTCOMES

The main learning outcomes of this case study are to:

- Understand the internationalisation process of a Born Global company through a practical case.
- Understand the potential role of digital technologies in speeding up the internationalisation process of a company.
- Analyse and evaluate the development of an omnichannel marketing strategy complementing the online channel with physical stores.

- Understand the importance of a customer purchasing path characterised by highly interactive product customisation.
- Understand how to optimise the production process by exploiting the power of digital technologies.
- Develop experience in a decision-making scenario concerning the direction to pursue further international development.

THE ITALIAN PRODUCTION STRUCTURE AND THE FOOTWEAR INDUSTRY

The Italian production structure is mainly characterised by a larger population of small and medium enterprises (SMEs), and among them, micro-SMEs (MSMEs), that is, those with less than ten employees, represent the backbone of the Italian manufacturing system (OECD, 2020). Italian MSMEs are 99.9 per cent of the total Italian enterprises (European Commission, 2022), meaning approximately 3.6 million companies, most of which are micro-enterprises (3.4 million) (Statista, 2021). They are mainly part of traditional sectors that adopt low technology and human-capital intensity in production processes (OECD, 2020).

In the last three decades, the advent of globalisation and the evolution of ICT affected the competitive environment in which MSMEs operate. On the one hand, globalisation has helped in lowering communication barriers. On the other hand, small firms have faced higher barriers to accessing new technologies, being unable to respond promptly to environmental changes and having difficulties participating in global trade (OECD, 2020). However, it is also true that today, digital technologies are more accessible than in the past, and Italian SMEs are increasingly embracing a process of transformation (OECD, 2021). Indeed, in the last ten years, the Italian entrepreneurial environment has been stimulated with incentives that have accelerated the development of 'Innovative Start-ups' and 'Innovative SMEs' (European Commission, 2022) adopting new business models based on digital technologies that make them more competitive and oriented to international markets.

One of the essential traditional sectors of the Italian production system is footwear which represents an industry of excellence and one of the main pillars of the Italian fashion system (Assocalzaturifici, 2021). The success of the Italian footwear sector is attributable to the entrepreneurial atmosphere and the typical industrial structure, which is mainly composed of territorial concentrations of companies – also known as industrial districts and clusters (Becattini, 1990, 2002; Porter, 1998) – mainly localised inside seven Italian regions (Marche, Tuscany, Veneto, Campania, Lombardy, Apulia, and Emilia Romagna) which are highly specialised in the different activities of the footwear supply chain (Allianz Trade, 2022; Assocalzaturifici, 2021).

The Italian footwear industry's prime position in international markets is due to several factors, such as the superior quality of products that positively affect the ability of companies to be competitive as well as the ability to introduce innovation along the manufacturing process together with the high specialisation of shoemakers and their craftsmanship skills (Assocalzaturifici, 2021).

Italy is the leader in high-luxury fashion and the eighth-largest exporting country in the world (Allianz Trade, 2022). Italy is the first producer of shoes in the European Union, with 4,100 shoemakers and 72,000 employees, and it is in 13th place by the number of pairs produced worldwide (Allianz Trade, 2022) with a trade balance of €5.15 billion in 2021 (Assocalzaturifici, 2021). However, since the 1990s, the sector has suffered from a decrease in the number of companies and employees, with a significant impact on production (Eurispes, 2019).

The recent COVID-19 emergency impacted the footwear sector export, which suffered a contraction, and despite the recovery in 2021, the sector is still far from the pre-pandemic export level (Allianz Trade, 2022; Assocalzaturifici, 2021). The pandemic brought numerous shop closures by accelerating the transition to a more digital approach and online shopping while impacting online consumption habits (Braglia et al., 2022). Indeed, the impossibility of visiting shops due to the lockdown encouraged online shopping via social media and, especially in the luxury sector, several brands improved their connection with customers through the development of in-app shopping experiences (McKinsey and Company, 2022).

Moreover, with specific reference to the Marche region in Central Italy, the Fermano-Maceratese shoemaking area (provinces of Ascoli-Piceno, Fermo, and Macerata) is one of the most important industrial districts of the Italian territory inside which enterprises relate to one another by finding a balance between cooperation and competition (Becattini, 2002; Porter, 1998). The district has been the centre of excellence in Italian footwear production since the thirteenth century due to the passing down of artisans' know-how from generation to generation. The shoemaking tradition has survived the challenging conditions dictated by globalisation and digitalisation that affected consumers' behaviour and demand (Aureli et al., 2010; Eurispes, 2019). However, compared to the prominent international luxury leaders, the district enterprises are still suffering from the consequences of the pandemic and the emergence of new issues concerning the increased price of raw materials and energy costs (Assocalzaturifici, 2021).

In addition, the recent Ukrainian-Russian conflict has also impacted the exports of the sector in the Russian and Ukrainian markets, for which Italy is the leading supplier. Especially for the Fermano-Maceratese industrial district, the sanctions and restrictions have caused the block of production and delivery by threatening the survival of businesses in the district and the district itself (World Footwear, 2022).

THE CASE FIRM FEATURES AND ITS INTERNATIONAL-ISATION PROCESS

Design Italian Shoes (DIS) is an innovative Italian SME identifiable from a theoretical perspective as a Born Global firm (Kuivalainen et al., 2012) as it entered the international market from its inception in 2015 by selling its products in the USA, Germany, France, UK, Japan, South Korea, and China, reaching a percentage of export equal to 50 per cent within three years from its establishment (Table 7.1).

Table 7.1   DIS profile as BG company

Foundation	2015
Year of internationalisation	2015
First countries reached within three years from the foundation	USA, Germany, France, UK, Japan, South Korea, China
Countries in 2022	Albania, Austria, Canada, Croatia, Czech Republic, France, Germany, Greece, Ireland, Japan, Kazakhstan, Malaysia, Mongolia, Qatar, Slovakia, South Korea, Spain, Switzerland, UAE, UK, USA
% of foreign sales on total turnover within three years from inception	50%
% of foreign sales in 2022	90%

Source: Authors' elaboration.

The company was born from the idea of Andrea and Francesco Carpineti and Michele Luconi, three founders with expertise in different areas. The project's creator, Andrea Carpineti, has a PhD in Business Economics and a decade of work experience in various fields, including business strategy, HR organisation, and data analysis. As founder and CEO, he is in charge of coordinating all the company's operational activities. His brother, Francesco Carpineti, with ten-plus years' experience as a sales and e-commerce manager in the footwear sector, holds the company's product and sales manager role. The innovation manager in charge of research and development activities, including IT and mobile web development, is Michele Luconi, who has a background as a computer scientist with management experience within a well-known Italian technology consulting company in Marche.

DIS has its roots in the Fermano-Maceratese industrial district as an agile fashion-luxury company with customised footwear production combining the excellence of Italian craftsmanship with the most advanced digital technologies. It offers high-quality made-in-Italy handmade shoes to its customers by providing a shopping experience focused on personalisation. The typical DIS customer is a modern, informed, demanding, self-confident man who loves to stand out with a recognisable style to be flaunted. This customer wants to be the absolute protagonist of the creative process, driven by the desire for free expression. Consequently, the creation of his DIS shoes reflects his personality.

Moreover, as an agile company, DIS also digitised internal and external communication with customers and suppliers, starting the business exclusively through the company's e-commerce platform, reaching more than a thousand customers in 37 countries by the end of 2015, with a customer retention rate of 24.5 per cent.

In 2016, following a multichannel approach, the company decided to expand its distribution channels, forming partnerships with traditional physical shops, for example tailors and department stores, with the purpose of opening DIS-branded corners within these businesses. To find distributors and partners in specific markets such as Japan and South Korea, the company participated in trade fairs to facilitate the promotion of the brand and related products, favouring international expansion.

The following year, in 2017, the focus on offline channels was further strengthened to a total of 34 active corners in as many shops.

The decision to develop its own sales network was taken in 2018. It was carried out with the support of agents who facilitated the promotion of products and entry into international markets. In addition, new resources were hired to support sales and marketing, allowing customers to be reached in new countries such as Benelux, Qatar, Malaysia, Czech Republic, Switzerland, and Austria. However, the quick internationalisation is mainly due to the ability of the company to combine traditional and online channels to spread the brand and support foreign sales. Furthermore, a new technology-based corner was commissioned for partner shops in the same year. The corner includes an interactive touchscreen totem equipped with sensors for product recognition and a 3D scanner integrated with an innovative artificial intelligence algorithm developed to suggest the exact feet size. The renovated corner opens a new possibility for customer interaction and shifts the company's strategy from a multichannel to an omnichannel approach. This strategy allowed the company to increase revenues in both marketing channels: by 540 per cent offline and 30 per cent in online channels.

In 2020, the advent of the COVID-19 emergency encouraged the company to open its digital tailoring services to other brands (private labels) by signing up new partnerships between 2021 and 2022, also with non-footwear companies, by adapting the 3D configurator to different types of products besides shoes (hats, watches, and women's clothing). At the same time, in the B2B segment, four technology licensing agreements with four footwear and non-footwear brands were signed. Therefore, today, DIS boasts 39 business partners in 21 countries (see Appendix for the complete list).

As regards the company's target customer, the high customisation of products makes DIS-branded footwear a product for a medium-high market segment. Specifically, the target customer is made up of male individuals, professionally trained, with a career in the tertiary sector (banking/insurance) or a management position in any other industry, mainly sedentary in their free time, lovers of luxury and style, aged between 30 and 50, and with a net annual income of €33,000 or more.

THE OMNICHANNEL MARKETING STRATEGY FOR DIS' INTERNATIONAL EXPANSION

DIS is the brainchild of three partners who aimed to innovate the traditional handmade, made-in-Italy footwear sector. Their idea was to enhance the high-qualified Italian producers that do not have the resources and knowledge to expand in the international market, preserving the 'made-in-Italy' tradition while exploiting the power of technology.

Indeed, the inability of small Italian manufacturers in the footwear industry to develop innovative marketing strategies and to actively adapt to digital technologies for promoting their image and products in foreign markets makes them stay anchored to the local market or, at the most, expand to neighbouring markets, losing the opportunity to exploit their real potential.

Digital technologies are pervading all sectors, and social networks favour adequate visibility in international markets. Moreover, participation in trade fairs is no longer the only way to expand the contact network and reach new markets. The engagement of brands with social media is a common strategy in the globalisation era aiming at intensely involving consumers in company life (McKinsey and Company, 2022).

Accordingly, the consumer's shopping experience is constantly changing due to the possibility of resorting to online platforms or digital mobile applications to buy products. Their request for highly customised products is increasing; therefore, industry modernisation should follow a renewed marketing approach and even reconsider manufacturers' business models.

According to previous considerations, to support their idea, the founders developed a disruptive business model based on the digitalisation of the shoe production process in which the e-commerce platform developed by the company represents the point of contact between a network of local artisans and international customers. The company owes its global success mainly to the shoe customisation service based on a make-to-order (MTO) business model. The MTO is a corporate production strategy allowing consumers to purchase customised products based on their specifications. Specifically, by adopting the MTO model, DIS operates a manufacturing process in which the production of an item only starts after receiving a final order from the customer. To support the MTO system, the production chain has been entirely digitised, with real-time control over the order status, optimising the footwear's production time while respecting ancient manual construction techniques.

Such an approach makes it possible to dramatically reduce delivery times of products from the time of order (12 days), compared to traditional tailor-made crafted shoes, reducing – or even eliminating – both sales discounts and stocks of finished products, as well as better managing obsolescence. In other words, DIS produces what is sold, with materials of natural origin and raw material suppliers in an area of just 10 km, reducing carbon dioxide emissions by 30 per cent compared to a typical shoe manufacturing company. However, it is important to specify that for an MTO system to be successful, it must necessarily be associated with proactive demand management, taking care of the relationship with the prospective customer down to the smallest detail, from the first contact to the act of purchase (Hendry, 1998).

Reasoning in these terms, DIS aims to offer consumers a highly customised footwear service directly at home or in selected shops. Specifically, the online shopping experience DIS offers to its customers is based on using the 3D configurator (the company owns the registered patent). The consumer accesses the company's website, selects the preferred model, and begins customisation by clicking directly on the part of the shoe that they wish to modify (Figure 7.1). In this way, the customer can potentially vary every element of the shoe under consideration, from the type of material, the laces' colour, tongue and front and side masks. Thus, the consumer becomes the leading actor in a sustainable artisan production process, being able to choose the shoe model, customise it with more than 50 million combinations, and have it 'made-to-measure' in just ten days.

Moreover, to further support the consumer's purchasing process, DIS has developed a specific foot measurement mobile app which exploits access to the customer's smartphone camera to calculate the size of the sole previously framed. Such innovative tools make customers' online shopping experience as smooth and intuitive as possible.

A similar approach is also implemented inside the worldwide physical stores that sell the company's brand products. Indeed, the physical spaces within stores needed to be reinvented to offer a completely new shopping experience to customers who buy on-site instead of using

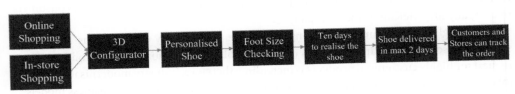

Source: Authors' elaboration on Andrea Carpineti's interview.

Figure 7.1   DIS digital and in-store purchasing experience

the platform. Therefore, DIS has recreated the physical space with an innovative concept that makes the most of all retail innovations, with an omnichannel system where the customer is at the centre of the shopping experience. The offline channel supports the online channel with two solutions: *tailor* (in tailor shops) and *corner* (in department stores). The *tailor* solution involves the display samples becoming interactive with the support of a tablet and a box set of leathers and soles. Whereas in the corner solution, the use of the touch screen totem amplifies the customisation experience, helping the salesperson to sell the shoe with a click thanks to its 'interactive shelf'. Such an organisation of offline channels allows the consumers to complete the transaction where and when they want. For example, they could decide to wait until the next day to revisit the shop, further evaluate the changes made so far from the comfort of their home, and then proceed to confirm the order.

In both solutions, the guidance of shop assistants is crucial in the order formation process; they act as style consultants helping the customer move through the collection. They suggest the footwear model that best suits the consumer's outfit, recommending leather and colour most suitable to the occasion. Using QR codes to select the model, the configurator for personalisation, and the DIS application to identify the perfect foot size, the salesperson gives the customer an innovative sartorial experience, reducing the time for taking the order to just a few minutes, transforming tradition into a unique experience.

This organisation goes in the well-established direction of reinventing the physical shop from a mere display space to an experiential meeting point (Alexander and Blazquez Cano, 2020; Fortuna et al., 2021), a trend that does not seem to see any signs of stopping despite the numerous lockdowns imposed throughout the pandemic between the years 2020 and 2021. Indeed, the online business model not only meets the changing needs of consumers' social shopping experiences according to the new trends in the footwear fashion industry (McKinsey and Company, 2022) but has been a lifeline during the worst period of the COVID-19 pandemic by allowing the company to be resilient in the face of market shocks that, on the contrary, have put pressure on companies not characterised by the same degree of digitisation (McKinsey and Company, 2021).

Once this point has been reached, the company, based on the successful results obtained, should decide in which direction to pursue its further international development, whether by strengthening online sales and using physical stores as flagship stores or whether to increase the network of physical stores, using the online platform as a support in an omnichannel approach. In other words, it is a question of understanding, as well as anticipating the future dynamics of the sector, if online sales will increasingly represent the predominant channel or if the type of product will allow an evolution of the retail channel, which is the only one that, given the current and near-future technologies, can exclusively guarantee the uniqueness of the shopping experience of which the tactile and olfactory, as well as visual, contact of the leather product is an essential part.

DISCUSSION QUESTIONS

1. What was the importance of the e-commerce platforms for the company's internationalisation process?
2. Which future channel strategy should be improved by the company between online sales and physical stores?
3. What other technologies could the company use to increase its presence in foreign markets?
4. If you were the company owner, what other marketing strategy would you use to boost the company's internationalisation?
5. Targeting customised purchasing paths is becoming increasingly important. Could you propose other activities that could be developed to offer a more personalised purchasing experience?
6. Mobile technology assumes a key role in developing applications (apps) that can enhance the customer shopping experience. What role could the development of mobile apps play in customers' shopping experience?

LEARNING OUTCOMES

Technology has now pervaded and is becoming accessible to almost everyone. This leads to redefining the business models of companies in many sectors at a time when the consumer purchasing process is enriched by elements both 'real' and 'virtual'.

The case of DIS is an example of a Born Global company which, through the development of a disruptive business model, was able to start and increase its internationalisation path by exploiting digital technologies. This happened on two fronts: on the consumer front, allowing a highly interactive product customisation process capable of overcoming, through the 3D scan of the foot size, the obstacle of measurement uncertainty that characterises online purchases; on the artisan producers front, by managing to optimise production processes and times, reducing stocks, accelerating delivery to customers, and ensuring step-by-step control of the entire make-to-order process.

The decision of the company to complement the online channel with physical stores is an example of how the omnichannel strategy can be expressed by pouring the features of virtual purchasing into the store and, at the same time, recovering those elements of physicality which in the act of purchasing products such as footwear always retain significant importance.

Looking ahead, the omnichannel strategy also requires an upgrade of supply chains and marketing channels, where companies like DIS see their identity melting between production and distribution. DIS does not physically produce footwear but relates to retailers as a manufacturing brand. It addresses both direct-to-customer e-commerce and retailer sales on the same online platform. This makes it possible to meet the growing expectations of consumers in terms of the shopping experience, personalisation, and speed while optimising costs of inventory, production, and delivery (Graf et al., 2021).

TEACHING NOTES

TARGET AUDIENCE

This case would be helpful for business students, preferably in the third year of their Bachelor studies and Master's students in Business Administration and Business Studies in courses of International Business Management and International Marketing and Strategic Management.

The audience has to have knowledge about the internationalisation processes or international management. Moreover, it is required to have a fundamental knowledge of marketing strategy and be familiar with the business model's definition. The students should also have a common understanding of SMEs' characteristics and digital technologies trends. The case is recommended for use as a functional case to introduce the role of digital technologies in speeding up the internationalisation path of a company and implementing marketing strategy, opening with reflections about the business model definition and innovation. Considering the moderate difficulty level of the case, it requires own research; however, supplementary information is provided and suggested literature is listed in the bibliography.

SUGGESTED TEACHING STRATEGIES

The questions at the end of the case reflect the key learning point of the case study and the potential direction to find solutions to further international development.

At the beginning of the class, it is crucial to introduce the case and guide the students in approaching it. Give the students the time to read and think about it. Then, to test whether students have understood the context, the companies' characteristics, as well as the strategy implemented, and the problem to be solved, they should be stimulated to answer preliminary questions (e.g., What are the characteristics of the company? What is the strategy adopted? What tools have been adopted to speed up the internationalisation?). These questions could be answered randomly to encourage students' participation.

Depending on the study course, the discussion could focus on different aspects of the situation, thus focusing more on specific questions than others. Therefore, considering adopting the case in a Bachelor or Master course, several activities could be developed to stimulate discussion and confrontation among students. Examples of activities include individual short essays and group discussions/group works.

Accordingly, the students could be invited to write a short essay to stimulate individual discussion. Each student should read and analyse the case and write their opinion giving a proposal about the best way to pursue a specific goal according to the assignment. To support the activity, the teacher should analyse the students' essays and discuss later the appropriate solution, the potential problems emerging from the solution identified, and answer the questions proposed at the end of the case to stimulate a general discussion with the whole class.

Alternatively, discussion in group work could be significant in stimulating reasoning and problem-solving activity. Students could be split into small groups, and according to the number of groups formed, each of them should be asked to answer one or two specific questions proposed at the end of the case. To ensure that all students are involved in the activity, they should be monitored and supported by indicating how to structure the discussion. The discussed aspects should be organised in a short PowerPoint presentation and supported by a report about conclusions. Such an approach will help students better structure their thoughts concerning the aspects they have learned by analysing the case and justifying the answers to the proposed questions. The presentation should be run in front of the whole class to open a broader discussion among students, stimulating and encouraging confrontation about the detailed reflections developed.

SUGGESTED ANSWERS TO DISCUSSION QUESTIONS

Q1 The students should answer the question by analysing the characteristics and advantages of an e-commerce platform to get a general idea of the opportunity given by an e-commerce strategy for export, speeding up the internationalisation process.

Q2 The answer requires the analysis of the industry trend in terms of channels to adopt in developing further expansion in international markets. The students should look at the industry's characteristics and the predominant channels adopted to deliver the products and the shopping experience offered to customers by motivating the adoption of the identified strategy.

Q3 The answer requires an analysis of digital technology's evolution and implementation to improve the company's performance in foreign markets. The students should analyse technology trends and identify potential implementation of emerging technology that can help to improve both the relationship with customers – by offering a better shopping experience – as well as the production system – by respecting the made-in-Italy and the values connected to the handmade production – aiming at expanding the company presence in international markets.

Q4 The answer requires identifying a potential marketing strategy to adopt to boost the internationalisation of the company according to the critical analysis and thoughts of the students. Therefore, the students should be able to define the action plan for achieving the company's objectives and good competitive positioning. Accordingly, the students should develop an analysis by following the steps that lead to identifying a marketing strategy that can increase international expansion. According to the availability of information provided by the company and the markets, the evaluation should include a SWOT analysis, brand positioning and objectives, marketing mix definition, and identification of key indicators for monitoring the progress against pre-fixed goals.

Q5 The answer requires an analysis of customer emerging needs and preferences connected to their shopping experience inside the footwear industry, especially in the luxury branch.

Q6 Mobile technology is assuming a predominant role in individual shopping experiences. The student should analyse the potential of mobile technology and the importance of the mobile application to understand better their benefits for improving customers' shopping experience and support the company's international expansion.

SUPPLEMENTARY INFORMATION NEEDED TO ANSWER THE CASE QUESTIONS

'Agile organisations – of any size and across industries – have five key elements in common' (2018). McKinsey: https://www.mckinsey.com/capabilities/people-and-organizational-performance/our-insights/the-five-trademarks-of-agile-organizations

Design Italian Shoes website: https://www.designitalianshoes.com/ (accessed 29 November 2022).

'How to create an agile organisation' (2017): https://www.mckinsey.com/capabilities/people-and-organizational-performance/our-insights/how-to-create-an-agile-organizationItalian Footwear sector: https://www.assocalzaturifici.it/en/home-en/ (accessed 29 November 2022).

'Internationalisation and igitalisation: Applying digital technologies to the internationalisation process of small and medium-sized enterprises': https://timreview.ca/article/1373.

McKinsey Technology Trends Outlook 2022 (2022): https://www.mckinsey.com/capabilities/mckinsey-digital/our-insights/the-top-trends-in-tech

Mobile Technology, IBM, https://www.ibm.com/topics/mobile-technology (accessed 29 November 2022).

The State of Fashion 2022, Report by McKinsey and Company: https://www.mckinsey.com/industries/retail/our-insights/state-of-fashion (accessed 29 November 2022).

BIBLIOGRAPHY

Alexander, B. and Blazquez Cano, M. (2020) Store of the future: Towards a (re)invention and (re)imagination of physical store space in an omnichannel context, *Journal of Retailing and Consumer Services*, 55, p. 101913. https://doi.org/10.1016/j.jretconser.2019.101913

Allianz Trade (2022) *Il settore Calzaturiero.* https://www.allianz-trade.com/it_IT/news-e-approfondimenti/studi-economici/thank-you-page-download/report-calzaturiero-2022-thank-you-download.html (accessed 10 November 2022).

Assocalzaturifici (2021) The Italian footwear sector 2021. Highlights & notes. https://www.assocalzaturifici.it/wp-content/uploads/2022/07/Highlights-2021-and-notes_EN.pdf (accessed 10 November 2022).

Aureli, S., Ciambotti, M. and Salvatori, F. (2010) Internationalisation of Italian shoemaking districts: Some empirical evidence from the Marche region. *Piccola Impresa/Small Business*, 2, pp. 97–121. https://doi.org/https://doi.org/10.14596/pisb.64

Becattini, G. (1990) The Marshallian Industrial District as a socio-economic notion. In Pyke, F., Becattini, G. and Sengenberger, W. (eds), *Industrial Districts and Inter-Firm Cooperation in Italy*, Geneva, International Institute for Labour St. pp. 37–51.

Becattini, G. (2002) From Marshall's to the Italian 'Industrial Districts'. A brief critical reconstruction. In Curzio, A.Q. and Fortis, M. (eds), *Complexity and Industrial Clusters. Contributions to Economics*. Physica-Verlag HD. https://doi.org/10.1007/978-3-642-50007-7_6

Braglia, M., Marrazzini, L. and Padellini, L. (2022) The impact of covid-19 on the Italian footwear supply chain of small and medium-sized enterprises (SMEs) – evaluation of two case studies. *Designs*, 6(2), p. 23. https://doi.org/10.3390/designs6020023

Eurispes (2019) *Strategie di difesa attiva del Made in Italy calzaturiero.* https://eurispes.eu/ricerca-rapporto/2019-2/strategie-di-difesa-attiva-del-made-in-italy-calzaturiero-2019/ (accessed 18 November 2022).

European Commission (2019) *2019 SBA Fact Sheet. Italy.* https://ec.europa.eu/docsroom/documents/38662/attachments/16/translations/en/renditions/native (accessed 18 November 2022).

European Commission (2022) *2022 SME Country Fact Sheet. Italy.* https://ec.europa.eu/docsroom/documents/50693/attachments/1/translations/en/renditions/native (accessed 18 November 2022).

Fortuna, F., Risso, M. and Musso, F. (2021) Omnichannelling and the predominance of big retailers in the post-covid era. *Symphonya. Emerging Issues in Management*, 2, pp. 142–57. https://doi.org/10.4468/2021.2.11fortuna.risso.musso

Graf, C., Lange, T., Seyfert, A. and van der Wijden, N. (2021) Into the fast lane: How to master the omnichannel supply chain. McKinsey & Company. https://www.mckinsey.com/industries/retail/our-insights/into-the-fast-lane-how-to-master-the-omnichannel-supply-chain (accessed 18 November 2022).

Hendry, L.C. (1998) Applying world class manufacturing to make-to-order companies: Problems and solutions. *International Journal of Operations & Production Management*, 18(11), pp. 1086–100. https://doi.org/10.1108/01443579810231679

Kuivalainen, O., Saarenketo, S. and Puumalainen, K. (2012) Start-up patterns of internationalisation: A framework and its application in the context of knowledge-intensive SMEs. *European Management Journal*, 30(4), pp. 372–85. https://doi.org/10.1016/j.emj.2012.01.001

McKinsey and Company (2021) The State of Fashion 2021. https://www.mckinsey.com/~/media/mckinsey/industries/retail/our%20insights/state%20of%20fashion/2021/the-state-of-fashion-2021-vf.pdf (accessed 18 November 2022).

McKinsey and Company (2022) The State of Fashion 2022. https://www.mckinsey.com/industries/retail/our-insights/state-of-fashion (accessed 18 November 2022).

OECD (2020) *OECD Insights on Productivity and Business Dynamics, Italy: Business Dynamics.* https://www.oecd.org/sti/ind/oecd-business-dynamics-insights-italy.pdf (accessed 28 November 2022).

OECD (2021) *OECD SME and Entrepreneurship Outlook 2021.* https://www.oecd.org/industry/smes/SME-Outlook-2021-Country-profiles.pdf (accessed 14 November 2022).

Porter, M.E. (1998) Clusters and the new economics of competition, *Harvard Business Review*, 76(November/December), pp. 77–90. https://hbr.org/1998/11/clusters-and-the-new-economics-of-competition

Statista (2021) Number of small and medium enterprises (SMEs) in Italy in 2020, by size. https://www.statista.com/statistics/1020211/number-of-smes-per-thousand-inhabitants-by-size-in-italy/ (accessed 10 November 2022).

World Footwear (2022) Italian footwear industry concerned over conflict in Ukraine. https://www.worldfootwear.com/news/italian-footwear-industry-concerned-over-conflict-in-ukraine/7583.html (accessed 10 November 2022).

APPENDIX 7A

Table 7A.1   Design Italian Shoes timeline

2015	Foundation: sales are initiated exclusively through the e-commerce platform and the adoption of technologies such as a 3D configurator, Order Management System (OMS), and Enterprise Resource Planning (ERP). First sales occur in the USA, Germany, France, and the UK.
2016	Online and offline selling strategies are integrated, with the aim of pursuing a B2C multichannel approach. New markets, such as Japan, South Korea, and China, are reached.
2017	The focus is on offline channels to increase the number of traditional shops (tailoring and department stores) in which to sell the products. Thirty-four corners open in as many physical stores.
2018	Initiation of a sales and agent network and employment of new internal resources to support the commercial area. Design of a new technological corner for the physical partner shops, equipped with an interactive Touch Screen Totem, sensors for product recognition, and a 3D scanner integrated with an innovative artificial intelligence algorithm developed to suggest the exact shoe's size automatically. The renovated corner opens up a new possibility for customer interaction, shifting the company's strategy from a multichannel to an omnichannel approach. New markets are reached via agents or by concluding distribution agreements such as Benelux, Northern Europe, Germany, North America, Malaysia and Southeast Pacific, the Middle East, the Czech Republic, France, Switzerland, Austria, Qatar, and the USA.
2019	Offline channels' revenue growth in 2017–19 (+540 per cent) is more significant than the online counterpart (+30 per cent).
2020	The COVID-19 pandemic hardly hit the omnichannel B2C business model of the company. The firm's tailoring services are open to other brands (private labels), and an innovative foot measurement app (FMA) has been released. A partnership is established with two footwear brands, to which DIS's leading technology tools are licensed: the 3D configurator and the MTOSuite module (OMS and ERP).
2021	The company's new business model focuses on the B2C omnichannel approach, which is complemented by the new B2B omnichannel approach. Partnerships are extended to four non-footwear brands. The 3D configurator is adapted to other product types (hats, watches, and women's suits).
2022	Online (e-commerce) and offline (corner store) presence in Albania, Austria, Canada, Croatia, Czech Republic, France, Germany, Greece, Ireland, Japan, Kazakhstan, Malaysia, Mongolia, Qatar, Slovakia, South Korea, Spain, Switzerland, United Arab Emirates, UK, USA. In the B2B segment, two partnerships concluded in previous years came to an end. In total, licensing agreements of DIS technology remain active with four brands, footwear and non-footwear.

8

The digitalisation of internationalisation activities: is social media the next international entrepreneurial opportunity recognition tool for Born Globals?

Emmanuel Kusi Appiah

CASE SUMMARY

Research articles on entrepreneurial opportunity are an emergent force in internationalisation research, and digitalisation also attracts significant attention. This chapter presents a business case integrating perspectives on entrepreneurial opportunity recognition and digitalisation in the internationalisation of a Finnish-born global company operating in the cleantech sector. The case provides a general overview of the company and its use of social media in international activities. The author poses thought-provoking questions associated with the reference materials and suggests solutions that challenge the reader to think outside the box. This case is suitable for students in universities and other institutions for higher education and a secondary audience, researchers in the field of international business and international entrepreneurship. It contributes to the call for more studies on the impact of digital technology on internationalisation in the international business field.

LEARNING OUTCOMES

The case covers international business issues such as (1) the international expansion of a Born Global firm and (2) social media usage in the context of a Born Global firm. Having studied this case, readers should:

- Be aware of useful concepts related to firm internationalisation and entrepreneurial opportunity recognition in the social media context.
- Have gained an understanding of the importance of social media in the international activities of Born Globals.

- Understand why and how Born global firms implement social media.
- Be aware of the current challenges associated with social media usage and how Born Globals can mitigate them.

INTRODUCTION

Digitalisation is the use of digital technology in the activities of firms (Autio et al., 2021). Among internationalising firms, such activities include communication, the development of new business models, distribution, and business relationship management. Autio et al. (2021) divide digital technologies into two forms: digital communication and digital technologies in situ. Digital communication technologies like social media include internet-enabled technologies that enable cross-border operations. Digital in situ technologies include technologies used in production processes, such as additive manufacturing, artificial intelligence, robotics, and big-data analytics (Autio et al., 2021). According to Manyika et al. (2016), 50 per cent of global trade in services is already digitised, approximately 12 per cent of the global goods trade is conducted via international e-commerce, and cross-border Skype calls constitute 46 per cent of the total of traditional international calls. Across 18 countries analysed by eBay, 88 to 100 per cent of the small and medium-sized enterprises (SMEs) using its platform are exporters (Manyika et al., 2016). Digital platforms such as eBay, Amazon, Facebook, and Alibaba have provided opportunities for small firms to become Born Globals. A Born Global is a firm that makes an early leap into international markets shortly after its foundation through export or any other entry mode to derive a significant competitive advantage from using resources and selling output in multiple countries. That advantage is operationalised as foreign sales comprising at least 25 per cent of total sales within three years of foundation (Knight and Cavusgil, 2004; Knight and Liesch, 2016; Oviatt and McDougall, 1994, 1997). More so, the accessibility of the internet has made the usage of digital platforms such as social media appealing to Born Globals (Jean et al., 2020).

Social media is a group of mobile and web applications that build on the ideological and technological foundations of Web 2.0 and allow users, such as individuals and communities, to create, share, collaborate, discuss, and modify user-generated content (Kaplan and Haenlein, 2010). Kaplan and Haenlein (2010) categorise social media in terms of social presence/media richness and self-presentation/self-disclosure (Table 8.1). Social media/media richness determines the level of ambiguities and uncertainties of information channelled through a particular medium (Jagongo and Kinyua, 2013; Kaplan and Haenlein, 2010). Social self-presentation/self-disclosure encompasses a user's unconscious and conscious actions to create an image consistent with their personality (Kaplan and Haenlein, 2010). Kietzmann et al. (2011) have also introduced the honeycomb framework of social media to categorise its use into seven functional building blocks, which include (1) Identity, (2) Presence, (3) Sharing, (4) Relationships, (5) Conversations, (6) Reputation, and (7) Groups (Figure 8.1).

The emergence of entrepreneurial opportunity represents a central concept in entrepreneurship research (Short et al., 2010). Considering how appealing digital technologies are to Born Globals, the central question is: Is social media the next international entrepreneurial

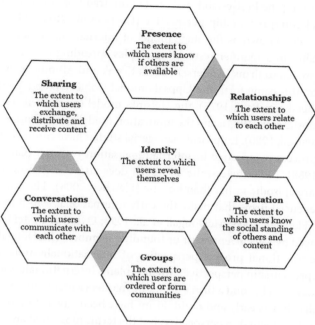

Source: Kietzmann et al. (2011, p. 243).

Figure 8.1 Honeycomb framework of social media

opportunity recognition tool for Born Globals? The next section examines the concepts of Born Globals and entrepreneurial opportunity.

THE BORN GLOBAL

Calof and Beamish (1995, p. 116) defined the internationalisation of a firm as 'the process of adapting firms' operations (strategy, structure, resources, etc.) to international environments'. Scholars have adopted a plethora of theoretical perspectives to explain the internationalisation

Table 8.1 Classification of social media

	Social presence/Media richness		
	Low	Medium	High
High (Self-presentation/ Self-disclosure)	Blogs Collaborative projects	Social networking sites (e.g., Facebook, Twitter, Flickr, LinkedIn, Skype, Pinterest, Instagram) Content communities	Virtual social worlds (e.g., Second Life) Virtual game worlds
Low (Self-presentation/ Self-disclosure)	(e.g., Wikipedia)	(e.g., YouTube)	(e.g., World of Warcraft)

Source: Adapted from Kaplan and Haenlein (2010).

process of firms. Among the best-established are (1) the traditional process perspective and (2) the international entrepreneurship perspective (Costa et al., 2017). First, the traditional process perspective, also known as the stage model of internationalisation, holds that firms should internationalise in a manner resembling ripples spreading on water. It is rooted in the behavioural approach to firms (Andersen, 1993; Kocak and Abimbola, 2009; Madsen and Servais, 1997). Upon this came forth the Uppsala model (Johanson and Vahlne, 1977, 2009; Johanson and Wiedersheim-Paul, 1975), the Helsinki model (Korhonen, 1999; Luostarinen, 1979; Welch and Luostarinen, 1993), and the innovation model of internationalisation (Bilkey and Tesar, 1977; Cavusgil, 1980). Empirical managerial studies have confirmed the importance of the traditional process perspective in internationalisation research (Chetty, 1999; Welch and Luostarinen, 1988). Nevertheless, the approach does attract criticism. Critics state that the process stages are episodic rather than holistic (Fletcher, 2008). The reason is that it fails to explain entrepreneurial firms that make the early international leap into foreign markets (Autio et al., 2000; Fletcher, 2008; McDougall et al., 1994; Oviatt and McDougall, 1997) and ignores the role played by the entrepreneur or founding members (McDougall et al., 1994).

Criticism of the traditional process perspective of internationalisation has spawned the international entrepreneurship perspective, which explains internationalisation as the process of opportunity recognition beyond a firm's domestic market (Knight and Liesch, 2016). It also views internationalisation as early and rapid. Firms have been labelled in different ways from the international entrepreneurship perspective, but the terms most used are international new ventures (INVs) (Oviatt and McDougall, 1994) and Born Globals (Knight and Cavusgil, 1996; Rennie, 1993). The INV term first appeared in McDougall's 1989 paper that compared domestic firms with INVs (Andersson et al., 2014), while the Born Global term was first adopted by McKinsey & Company when reporting on early internationalisation among Australian manufacturing firms that had expanded rapidly into global markets without having an established domestic base (McKinsey and Company, 1993; Rennie, 1993). Cavusgil (1994) highlighted the results of this study in the first scholarly article about Born Globals published in *Marketing News Journal*. Scholars describe similarities between INVs and Born Globals (Cavusgil and Knight, 2015; Crick, 2009) but also their differences. Research reports that both INVs and Born Globals are young firms, but Born Globals have a more global focus than INVs, which have a more regional focus. Born Globals 'view the world as their marketplace from the outset and see the domestic market as a support for their international business' (McKinsey and Company, 1993, p. 9). They embark on foreign direct investment in important markets with a global vision and strategy from inception (Crick, 2009). Other scholars have used the terms Born Global and INV interchangeably, but in this chapter, we use the Born Global term alone for theoretical parsimony and consistency.

ENTREPRENEURIAL THEORY ON OPPORTUNITY RECOGNITION

Holm et al. (2015, p. 339) define entrepreneurial opportunity as a 'desirable but uncertain situation present in foreign markets, which allows firms to benefit from engaging in new cross-border business activities that provide economic value for the firm'. It can also be described as an opportunity to engage in entrepreneurial activities, such as introducing services, organising activities, and networking to produce economic value (McMullen et al., 2007). Scholars offer different opinions on the conceptualisation of entrepreneurial opportunity (Ardichvili et al., 2003; Kirzner, 1973; Mainela et al., 2014; Schumpeter, 1934; Shane and Venkataraman, 2000). The most common conceptualisations are associated with discovering and creating entrepreneurial opportunities (Ardichvili et al., 2003; Shane and Venkataraman, 2000) in the international market. The discovery perspective assumes that entrepreneurial opportunity exists within the environment, waiting to be discovered and exploited (Kirzner, 1973). In contrast, the creation perspective assumes that entrepreneurial opportunity is created. Thus, the firm or entrepreneur influences the development of entrepreneurial opportunities (Mainela et al., 2014; Schumpeter, 1934). Entrepreneurial opportunity research frequently mentions these two opposing positions (Johanson and Vahlne, 2009). Below, I present an overview of a case focusing on how social media can serve as an entrepreneurial opportunity in Born Global firms using a single case from the Finnish cleantech sector.

CASE STUDY

Context

A context refers to 'situational opportunities and constraints that affect the occurrence and meaning of organisational behaviour as well as functional relationships between variables' (Johns, 2006, p. 386). The context for this case is the cleantech sector of Finland, which is a small-sized open economy with a tradition of firm internationalisation; a majority of its SMEs operate in foreign markets (Knight and Liesch, 2016; Luostarinen, 1994). According to Statistics Finland's database, Finnish enterprises had business activity in 5,430 affiliates located in 139 countries in 2018, with most investments concentrated in the European Union area compared with the previous years (Official Statistics Finland, 2020). Second, Finland has embraced the concept of a digital economy. According to Digibarometer[1] survey results (Figure 8.2), Finland ranked second in the degree of digitalisation for two consecutive years (i.e., 2020 and 2021).

Finland is also a leading country in finding solutions for climate change and sustainability issues in the cleantech sector (Cleantech Finland, 2022). The Finnish cleantech sector is an important sector that fosters innovation ecosystems in energy and sustainable manufacturing, connecting startups, large enterprises, research organisations, and the public sector (Business Finland, 2022). The cleantech sector encapsulates firms that produce products and services that are unharmful to the environment (Souza et al., 2019). The country offers a unique platform for companies to develop and commercialise energy and manufacturing technologies based on clean solutions. The Finnish cleantech companies' unique contribution to sustainability has been recognised globally. According to a 2019 Information Technology & Innovation Foundation survey, Finland is the second-most significant contributor to clean-energy innovations relative to GDP (Cunliff and Hart, 2019). Fourdeg, Solar Water Solutions, Altum

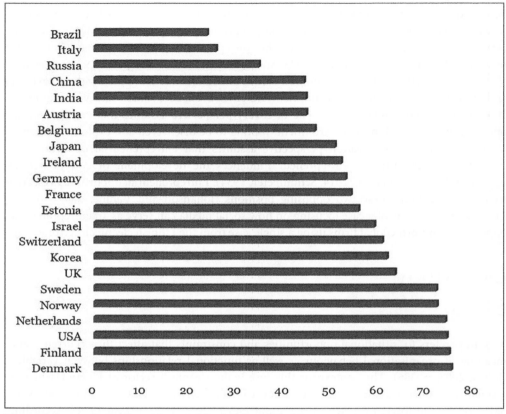

Figure 8.2 Overall ranking of digitalisation utilisation among countries

Technologies, and Solved are among the major cleantech firms that have attracted global recognition (O'Sullivan, 2020). Among these firms, I base my case on Altum Technologies.

Firm: Altum Technologies and social media

Two partners were importing cleantech based on ultrasound into Finland. They were trying to solve industrial issues with those applications and found that customers wanted applications with more sustainable attributes. The partners were not satisfied with the sustainability credentials of what was on the market. The partners contacted a professor at the University of Helsinki, an expert in ultrasound technology, and came up with ultrasound technology for use in industrial facilities in 2015. The firm's offerings use ultrasound to clean industrial equipment in the energy, heating, and power-generating; pulp and paper; food and beverage; oil and gas; and chemical and water sectors. Instead of using mechanical tools or hazardous chemicals to remove ingrained dirt (known as 'fouling') in industrial processes and heat exchangers, Altum Technologies adopts ultrasound technology. As the CEO reported: 'With our system, all you need is our externally attached power ultrasound device ... It emits high-power ultrasonic waves into the machinery, which break up fouling without any production stoppages.' The firm began effective foreign operations in 2016 and won the best energy startup award in 2016 and the Slush 100 Award[2] in 2017. The firm's headquarters are in Helsinki, Finland, and it now employs 14 professionals with diverse skills in R&D, industrial and mechanical engineering, artificial intelligence, electronics, and marketing. It collaborates with foreign firms, teams of people, and small organisations from Japan, the USA, the Netherlands, Chile, and Norway. The collaborations have broadened the firm's aim to see the bigger picture of its solutions. The firm has co-developed new technologies with partners to solve new issues related to ultrasound technology. In January 2022, Altum Technologies began a collaboration with Nippon Steel Engineering Co., Ltd. to launch a new smart cleaning service permitting process manufacturers to clean and prevent fouling from industrial equipment and piping using software-guided ultrasonic technology. Altum's social media platforms (LinkedIn, Facebook, and Twitter) reported that the collaboration will make Altum's Smart Cleaning Service available throughout Japan across different industries like energy, petrochemicals, paper manufacturing, food, and beverage companies. Altum Technologies is the first company in the world to use ultrasound technology to clean fouling from industrial equipment without stopping production. So far, it has provided its services in Thailand, Japan, the Netherlands, Switzerland, Spain, Sweden, and the USA. Currently, it is negotiating with countries like Canada, Thailand, and Brazil to establish operations. In August 2018, the firm announced its first expansion in the form of a permanent office in Las Vegas, in the United States.

The bulk of Altum's sales were to Finnish enterprises when it began operations, but three years after inception, around 80 per cent of its sales revenue was from overseas sales. The marketing manager reported, 'We are expanding globally, not focusing on Finland.'

Digitalisation in Altum Technologies

Altum Technologies has embraced the use of digital technologies in its internationalisation activities. As the marketing manager stated:

> For the business side, we use HubSpot to identify leads, deals in progress and extrapolate the future, Google analytics, and social media platforms. We use Skype for external communication, Slack for internal communication, join-me to share presentations, mobile phones, and emails.

The company routinely uses 56 technologies to support its website, including *Viewport Meta, IPhone/Mobile Compatible,* and *SSL by Default* (Crunchbase, 2022). Its website's global traffic rank is 5,148,195 among websites globally and attracts 1,912 monthly visitors from countries such as Slovenia (71 per cent site traffic), the United Arab Emirates (24 per cent site traffic), and Latvia (5 per cent) (Crunchbase, 2022). The firm has a social media team of two who create, publish, and update all the firm's social media output, one of whom is the marketing director. The social media team collaborates with the management team but retains the overarching responsibility for social media matters. The firm established a presence on Facebook, Twitter, YouTube, Instagram, and LinkedIn in 2017. According to the firm's social media strategy, it handles each social media channel differently in terms of content sharing. As reported by the marketing manager:

> … So the same thing applies with LinkedIn. Like if it's very related to the industry, something industry use, like where our firm is mentioned, then we tried to emphasise, from the professional perspective, to kind of like share the update that we are actually acting professionally as well. For example, on Instagram, we don't always put their related content. Like we don't share the same content always on all platforms. We try different approaches. And for example, Instagram it's more related to our office activities, our employee branding.

The firm has a blog, updated at least once a month. It uses LinkedIn for employee branding and networking. It uses Twitter mostly to comment on industry-related matters related to the firm's blog sites and images shared on Instagram. It also uses the YouTube channel to share videos of its operations and specific events, such as Slush 100 and the Nordic Cleantech Open Finals. According to the firm's social media strategic plan, LinkedIn is the number one priority, followed by Twitter, Instagram, Facebook, and finally, YouTube.

Drivers of social media usage

First, the decision on social media usage was based on brand awareness. As reported by marketing:

> I would say, of course, brand awareness and recognition because, nowadays, the majority of marketing activities happen online and that way it's so much easier to reach to a different audience, whether it is industry-related or event related, no matter the case. It's just so easy to reach with a keyword with hashtags and also by being present there. So that's one thing.

In the firm's early years, it had an online presence but no social media strategy per se. The situation changed after winning the Slush 100 Award in 2017, following which the firm invested resources to create a social media strategy. The marketing manager explained:

> We were, of course, present on social media before the event [Slush 100], but after that, when we received so much recognition, from media companies, from potential customers and from other stakeholders that were super interested in our solution. So, it dawned on us to maintain the image and develop reachability. And being on social media, it is one of the steps that help us be reachable.

Second, the decision on social media usage was based on a desire to network. As reported by marketing:

> We decided to use social media for connectivity and also to reach out to the audience, and a variety of segments … Most firms … especially industrial firms, no matter the industry, no matter their solution, but those that we see as a potential partner and potential customer are very much active on social media …

Table 8.2   Social media profile of Altum Technologies (as of 2022)

Firm	LinkedIn	Twitter	Instagram	Facebook	YouTube
Alpha	912 followers	219 followers 215 following 414 tweets	149 followers 262 following 137 posts	97 followers	15 subscribers 4 videos
Target	Clients, industrial experts	Clients, industrial experts, fans	Employee, clients	Clients, fans	Clients, fans
Successful entrepreneurial activities	Networking, sharing of industrial news, building brand awareness and recognition	Building brand awareness and recognition, sharing industrial news	Employee branding	Building brand awareness and recognition	Building brand awareness and recognition via videos

Social media: the next entrepreneurial opportunity recognition tool?

Since the intensification of social media usage, Altum Technologies has attracted massive attention, as reflected in the number of online followers and the success it has amassed (Table 8.2). Social media has enabled the firm to build a closer connection with potential customers, search for information on competitors, and to broaden its knowledge. As reported by the marketing manager:

> Using Twitter has extended our ability to reach companies from industries that have problems we can solve with our technology …With Twitter, it is so much easier to find our competitors with a single hashtag. So, as you are already aware, our solution is unique, so there are not yet really other providers of similar technology solutions. When I add a certain hashtag that describes our solution or the type of problem we're working with, I find many companies that are not doing the same as we do. Not providing the same offer, but at least like working in the same context. It was so much easier to reach out and just search, and it really took me less than an hour to figure that out instead of really doing a Google search, which would be completely not even close to the time efficient.

The firm's primary goal is to keep investing in social media to reach potential foreign clients and improve its brand awareness in target markets. Last year, it participated in a business and innovation development project called BID4E-project to acquire information on developing a high-level social media strategy.

Is it wise for Altum Technologies to put more resources and attention into social media? Will Altum Technologies not fall into a virtuality trap? Can Altum Technologies achieve the same success in recognising opportunities in the foreign market as B2B companies like Maersk Line?[3] With the upsurge of social media fake news where firms' competitors hire people and use non-human algorithms such as social bots and cyborgs to generate malicious content to smear the image of firms, what are the potential challenges that can hamper the survival of Altum Technologies in the foreign market? How can Altum Technologies address these challenges?

LEARNING OUTCOMES

Scholars became interested in early internationalisation (i.e., in our case, via Born Globals) in the early 1990s. The topic is now prominent in international entrepreneurship and international business research (Knight and Cavusgil, 2004; Knight and Liesch, 2016). Both the Born Global phenomenon and the adoption of digital technology have recently attracted research interest in the international entrepreneurship and international business fields (Jean et al., 2020). This has prompted scholars to call for more research on digitalisation's impact on internationalisation (Coviello et al., 2017; Katsikeas et al., 2020). By using this case study, the readers should have gained an understanding of the importance of social media in the international activities of Born Globals.

Moreover, readers should now be aware of the useful concepts related to Born Global internationalisation and social media usage during global expansion. The readers should also be aware of the contemporary challenges associated with social media usage and how Born Globals can mitigate them. Furthermore, this case study cross-fertilises perspectives from international business, international entrepreneurship, and information systems to enhance the understanding of readers on early internationalisation in the digital context, which represents a widespread, ongoing trend. Therefore, it is expected that readers should have deepened their understanding of interdisciplinary studies (Cavusgil and Knight, 2015; Etemad, 2017). Finally, the case should nurture readers' skills in resolving issues raised by business cases and improve their creative thinking, innovativeness, collaboration, and communication in teams.

SUPPLEMENTARY INFORMATION NEEDED TO ANSWER THE CASE QUESTIONS

5 powerful business opportunities on social media. Accessed 19 October 2022 at: https://www.struto.io/blog/social-media-business-opportunities.

Altum Blogs. Accessed 19 October 2022 at: https://altumtechnologies.com/company/news-and-blog/

B2B case study: Maersk gets social media right. Accessed 19 October 2022 at: https://www.business2community.com/b2b-marketing/b2b-case-study-maersk-gets-social-media-right-0442328.

BBC News: Restaurant hit by 'human meat' fake news claims. Accessed 19 October 2022 at: https://www.bbc.com/news/newsbeat-39966215.

Finland – a leading cleantech country. Accessed 19 October 2022 at: https://www.finlandcleantech.fi/.

Five from Finland: Cleantech. Accessed 19 October 2022 at: https://www.goodnewsfinland.com/feature/five-from-finland-cleantech/.

How Social media helps Maersk Line sell more stuff. Accessed 19 October 2022 at: https://thebrandgym.com/how-social-media-helps-maersk-line-sell-more-stuff/.

Kietzmann, J.H., Hermkens, K., McCarthy, I.P. and Silvestre, B.S. (2011). Social media? Get serious! Understanding the functional building blocks of social media, *Business Horizons*, 54(3), 241–51.

Maersk: the value of social media. Accessed 19 October 2022 at: https://cmr.berkeley.edu/2015/10/maersk/

McMullen, J.S., Plummer, L.A. and Acs, Z.J. (2007) What is an entrepreneurial opportunity? *Small Business Economics*, 28(4), 273–83. Available at: https://doi.org/10.1007/s11187-006-9040-z

Risk Management Magazine – fake facts: What the rise of disinformation campaigns means for businesses. Accessed 19 October 2022 at: http://www.rmmagazine.com/articles/article/2020/04/01/-Fake-Facts-What-the-Rise-of-Disinformation-Campaigns-Means-for-Businesses-

Social media business opportunities and challenges.. Accessed 19 October 2022 at: https://www
.nibusinessinfo.co.uk/content/social-media-business-opportunities-and-challengesv

Sustainability is good business. Accessed 19 October 2022 at: https://www.businessfinland.fi/en/do
-business-with-finland/invest-in-finland/business-opportunities/cleantech.

What can we learn from Maersk Line's social media presence? . Accessed 19 October 2022 at: https://
www.business2community.com/social-media-articles/can-learn-maersk-lines-social-media-presence
-0634290

Why social media will fundamentally change business. Accessed 19 October 2022 at: http://sloanreview
.mit.edu/article/why-social-media-will-fundamentally-changebusiness/

TEACHING NOTES

TARGET AUDIENCE

This case is suitable for students at universities and other higher education institutions, and a secondary audience would be researchers in the fields of international business and entrepreneurship. All will be challenged to think strategically about internationalisation at the interface of digitalisation. The case will suit both Bachelor's and Master's level students equally well. More importantly, it challenges Master's level students, including MBA candidates, to think outside the box. Thus, how to approach and conceptualise problems and solutions in innovative ways. The case has different applications in class, such as teaching knowledge/practices, particularly concerning the international business field, including subfields like international entrepreneurship and management.

SUGGESTED TEACHING STRATEGIES

It was decided that a learning café would offer the best teaching environment to study this case. The learning café environment helps improve creative thinking, innovativeness, collaboration, and team communication. The learning café process typically involves the following:

First, the instructor divides the readers into groups, ideally of at least four people, so that each can contribute. Each group should be seated around a table and be supplied with paper and post-it notes, and marker pens.

Second, the instructor spends at least five minutes setting the context, explaining learning café etiquette, and introducing the case.

Third, the instructor circulates from group to group to monitor each group's discussions on the case. The instructor engages group members by asking questions during the rounds. The group discussions will probably last for at least one hour.

Fourth, when the group discussions are complete, each group nominates presenters who inform the class how they solved the case and share solutions, insights, and observations from the case.

Finally, the instructor takes at least ten minutes to summarise the various insights and discoveries from the presentations before ending the session.

DISCUSSION QUESTIONS AND SUGGESTED ANSWERS

1. Is it wise for Altum Technologies to devote more resources and attention to social media?

Suggested Response: Yes, investing in social media will provide Altum Technologies with an opportunity to have direct engagement with stakeholders, flexibility in the coordination of international activities, and scaling. Social media can also serve as a support system for sales and marketing subsidiaries in target markets and can therefore reduce the resources required and costs in foreign marketing activities. Finally, the open-access structure of social media facilitates easy connection for the firm to other networks in the foreign market (see McFarland and Ployhart, 2015).

2. Will Altum Technologies not fall into a virtuality trap?

Suggested Response: Yes, the company could fall into the virtuality trap if it prioritises social media activities, such as online communication and networking, when searching for online opportunities, online sales channels, and online brand building at the expense of similar activities that can be organised offline (see Sinkovics et al., 2013; Yamin and Sinkovics, 2006). However, the virtuality trap can be mitigated by complementing online activities with offline activities.

3. Can Altum Technologies achieve the same success in recognising opportunities in the foreign market as B2B companies like Maersk Line?

Suggested Response: Yes, it can if the right strategies and structures are implemented. As reported by the Head of Social Media, Maersk Line: 'In our original strategy, we accounted for what we could achieve via social media, including brand awareness, insight into the market and increased employee satisfaction. But our primary goal has always been "to get closer to our customers".'

4. With the upsurge of social media fake news where existing competitors of firms hire people and non-human algorithms such as social bots and cyborgs to generate malicious content to smear the image of firms, what are the potential challenges that can hamper the survival of Altum Technologies in the foreign market?

Suggested Response: Competitors in the foreign market could use social media as a predatory tool to smear the company's image by associating it with fake news. For example, in the high-technology industry, Apple temporarily lost market share when a fake news story was posted on a blog claiming that the firm was deleting its music collections. (This is not exhaustive; readers are encouraged to list similar examples and provide other challenges.)

5. How should Altum Technologies address these challenges as they arise?

Suggested Response: The firm should be strategically flexible when affected by fake social media news. Strategic flexibility might involve addressing such issues proactively and promptly by applying a denial strategy supported by social media posts (see Gupta and Batra, 2016). (This is not exhaustive; readers are encouraged to list other related measures.)

NOTES

1. Digibarometer is a study which evaluates how well countries utilise digitalisation and how they compare to one another in that respect.
2. Slush 100 Award (Prize given to a startup for emerging as the first among 100 startups in terms of novelty of business idea in a pitching competition). Slush is a student-driven, not-for-profit movement originally founded to change attitudes toward entrepreneurship.
3. Maersk Line is a Born Global B2B company operating in the shipping industry. According to Davina Rapaport, Social Media Manager of the company, Maersk Line has a digital ecosystem which encompasses different social media channels. All the different social media channels in the ecosystem contribute to the Maersk Line's marketing mix to generate leads for new business. The company considers social media as a commercial channel not a communication channel. For example, it organises online campaigns and webinars via LinkedIn and Twitter around business issues targeted for potential customers in order to generate new business leads.

BIBLIOGRAPHY

Andersen, O. (1993) On the internationalisation process of firms: A critical analysis, *Journal of International Business Studies*, 24(2), 209–31.

Andersson, S., Evers, N. and Kuivalainen, O. (2014) International new ventures: Rapid internationalisation across different industry contexts, *European Business Review*, 26(5), 390–405.

Ardichvili, A., Cardozo, R. and Ray, S. (2003) A theory of entrepreneurial opportunity identification and development, *Journal of Business Venturing*, 18(1), 105–23.

Autio, E., Sapienza, H.J. and Almeida, J.G. (2000) Effects of age at entry, knowledge intensity, and imitability on international growth, *Academy of Management Journal*, 43(5), 909–24.

Autio, E., Mudambi, R. and Yoo, Y. (2021) Digitalisation and globalisation in a turbulent world: Centrifugal and centripetal forces, *Global Strategy Journal*, 11(1), 3–16.

Bilkey, W. and Tesar, G. (1977) The export behavior of smaller-sized Wisconsin manufacturing firms, *Journal of International Business Studies*, 8(1), 93–8.

Business Finland. (2022) Sustainability is good business. Accessed 19 October 2022 at: https://www.businessfinland.fi/en/do-business-with-finland/invest-in-finland/business-opportunities/cleantech

Calof, J.L. and Beamish, P.W. (1995) Adapting to foreign markets: Explaining internationalisation, *International Business Review*, 4(2), 115–31.

Cavusgil, S.T. (1980) On the internationalisation process of firms, *European Research*, 8, 273–81.

Cavusgil, S.T. (1994) From the Editor in Chief, *Journal of International Marketing*, 2(3), 4–6.

Cavusgil, S.T. and Knight, G. (2015) The Born Global firm: An entrepreneurial and capabilities perspective on early and rapid internationalisation, *Journal of International Business Studies*, 46(1), 3–16.

Chetty, S.K. (1999) Dimensions of internationalisation of manufacturing firms in the apparel industry, *European Journal of Marketing*, 33(1/2), 121–42.

Cleantech Finland. (2022) Finland – a leading cleantech country. Accessed 19 October 2022 at: https://www.finlandcleantech.fi/

Costa, E., Soares, A.L. and de Sousa, J.P. (2017) Institutional networks for supporting the internationalisation of SMEs: The case of industrial business association, *Journal of Business and Industrial Marketing*, 32(8), 1182–202.

Coviello, N., Kano, L. and Liesch, P.W. (2017) Adapting the Uppsala model to a modern world: Macro-context and microfoundations, *Journal of International Business Studies*, 48(9), 1151–64.

Crick, D. (2009) The internationalisation of born global and international new venture SMEs, *International Marketing Review*, 26(4/5), 453–76.

Crunchbase. (2022). Altum Technologies. Accessed 21 October 2022 at: https://www.crunchbase.com/organization/altum-technologies/technology

Cunliff, C. and Hart, D.M. (2019) The Global Energy Innovation Index: National contributions to the global clean energy innovation system. Accesssed 19 October 2022 at: https://itif.org/publications/2019/08/26/global-energy-innovation-index-national-contributions-global-clean-energy/

Etemad, H. (2017) The emergence of online global market place and the multilayered view of international entrepreneurship, *Journal of International Entrepreneurship*, 15(4), 353–65.

Fletcher, R. (2008) The internationalisation from a network perspective: A longitudinal study, *Industrial Marketing Management*, 37(8), 953–64.

Gupta, V.K. and Batra, S. (2016) Entrepreneurial orientation and firm performance in Indian SMEs: Universal and contingency perspectives, *International Small Business Journal*, 34(5), 660–82.

Gupta, V.K., Niranjan, S., Goktan, B.A. and Eriskon, J. (2015) Individual entrepreneurial orientation role in shaping reactions to new technologies, *International Entrepreneurship and Management Journal*, 12(4), 935–61.

Holm, D.B., Johanson, M. and Kao, P. (2015) From outsider to insider: Opportunity development in foreign market networks, *Journal of International Entrepreneurship*, 13(3), 337–59.

Jagongo, A. and Kinyua, C. (2013) The social media and entrepreneurship growth: A new business communication paradigm among SMEs in Nairobi, *International Journal of Humanities and Social Science*, 3(10), 213–27.

Jean, R.-J.B., Kim, D. and Cavusgil, E. (2020) Antecedents and outcomes of digital platform risk for international new ventures' internationalisation, *Journal of World Business*, 55(1), 101021.

Johanson, J. and Vahlne, J.-E. (1977) The internationalisation process of the firm – a model of knowledge development and increasing foreign market commitments, *Journal of International Business Studies*, 8(1), 23–32.

Johanson, J. and Vahlne, J.-E. (2009) The Uppsala Internationalization Process Model Revisited: From liability of foreignness to liability of outsidership, *Journal of International Business Studies*, 40(9), 1411–31.

Johanson, J. and Wiedersheim-Paul, F. (1975) The internationalisation of the firm? Four Swedish cases, *Journal of Management Studies*, 12(3), 305–23.

Johns, G. (2006) The essential impact of context on organisational behavior, *Academy of Management Review*, 31(2), 386–408.

Kaplan, A.M. and Haenlein, M. (2010) Users of the world, unite! The challenges and opportunities of social media, *Business Horizons*, 53(1), 59–68.

Katsikeas, C., Leonidou, L. and Zeriti, A. (2020) Revisiting international marketing strategy in a digital era, *International Marketing Review*, 37(3), 405–24.

Kietzmann, J.H, Hermkens, K., McCarthy, I.P. and Silvestre, B.S. (2011) Social media? Get serious! Understanding the functional building blocks of social media, *Business Horizons*, 54(3), 241–51.

Kirzner, I.M. (1973) *Competition and Entrepreneurship*, Chicago, IL: University of Chicago Press.

Knight, G.A. and Cavusgil, S.T. (1996) The born global firm: A challenge to traditional internationalisation theory, *Advances in International Marketing*, 8, 11–26.

Knight, G.A. and Cavusgil, S.T. (2004) Innovation, organisational capabilities, and the born-global firm, *Journal of International Business Studies*, 35(2), 124–41.

Knight, G.A. and Liesch, P.W. (2016) Internationalisation: From incremental to born global, *Journal of World Business*, 51(1), 93–102.

Kocak, A. and Abimbola, T. (2009) The effects of entrepreneurial marketing on Born Global performance, *International Marketing Review*, 26(4/5), 439–52.

Korhonen, H. (1999) Inward-outward internationalization of small and medium enterprises (unpublished doctoral dissertation), School of Economics Helsinki, Helsinki.

Luostarinen, R. (1979) Internationalisation of the firm (unpublished doctoral dissertation), Helsinki School of Economics, Helsinki.

Luostarinen, R. (1994) Internationalisation of Finnish firms and their response to global challenges, *WIDER Working Papers* 295309, United Nations University, World Institute for Development Economic Research (UNU-WIDER).

Madsen, T.K. and Servais, P. (1997) The internationalization of Born Globals: An evolutionary process? *International Business Review*, 6(6), 561–83.

Mainela, T., Puhakka, V. and Servais, P. (2014) The concept of international opportunity in international entrepreneurship: A review and a research agenda, *International Journal of Management Reviews*, 16(1), 105–29.

Manyika, J., Lund, S., Bughin, J., Woetzel, J., Stamenov, K. and Dhingra, D. (2016) Digital globalisation: The new era of global flows. Accessed 27 September 2022 at: https://www.mckinsey.com/~/media/mckinsey/business%20functions/mckinsey%20digital/our%20insights/digital%20globalization%20the%20new%20era%20of%20global%20flows/mgi-digital-globalization-full-report.as

McDougall, P.P. (1989) International versus domestic entrepreneurship: New venture strategic behavior and industry structure, *Journal of Business Venturing*, 4(6), 387–400.

McDougall, P.P., Shane, S. and Oviatt, B.M. (1994) Explaining the formation of International New Ventures: The limits of theories from International Business Research, *Journal of Business Venturing*, 9(6), 469–87.

McFarland, L.A. and Ployhart, R.E. (2015) Social media: A contextual framework to guide research and practice, *Journal of Applied Psychology*, 100(6), 1653–77.

McKinsey and Company. (1993) Emerging Exporters: Australia's High Value-added Manufacturing Exporters, Australian Manufacturing Council, Melbourne.

McMullen, J.S., Plummer, L.A. and Acs, Z.J. (2007) What is an entrepreneurial opportunity?, *Small Business Economics*, 28(4), 273–83.

Official Statistics Finland. (2020) Official Statistics of Finland (OSF): Finnish affiliates abroad [e-publication]. Accessed 9 September 2020 at: http://www.stat.fi/til/stu/index_en.html

O'Sullivan, J. (2020) Five from Finland: Cleantech. Accessed 20 October 2022 at: https://www.goodnewsfinland.com/feature/five-from-finland-cleantech/

Oviatt, B.M. and McDougall, P.P. (1994) Toward a theory of international new ventures, *Journal of International Business Studies*, 25(1), 45–64.

Oviatt, B. and McDougall, P. (1997) Challenges for Internationalization Process Theory: The case of International New Ventures, *MIR: Management International Review*, 37, 85–99.

Rennie, M.W. (1993) Born global, *The McKinsey Quarterly*, 4(45).

Schumpeter, J.A. (1934) *The Theory of Economic Development*, Cambridge, MA: Harvard University Press.

Shane, S. and Venkataraman, S. (2000). The promise of entrepreneurship as a field of research, *The Academy of Management Review*, 25(1), 217–26.

Short, J.C., Ketchen, D.J. Jr, Shook, CL. and Ireland, R.D. (2010) The concept of 'Opportunity' in entrepreneurship research: Past accomplishments and future challenges, *Journal of Management*, 36(1), 40–65.

Sinkovics, N., Sinkovics, R.R. and Jean, B.J. (2013) The internet as an alternative path to internationalization?, *International Marketing Review*, 30(2), 130–55.

Souza, M.P., Hoeltz, M., Benitez, L.B., Machado, Ê.L. and Schneider, C.S.R. (2019) Microalgae and clean technologies: A review, *Clean – Soil, Air, Water*, 47(11), 1–18.

Welch, L. and Luostarinen, R. (1988) Internationalization evolution of a concept, *Journal of General Management*, 14, 34–55.

Welch, L. and Luostarinen, R. (1993) Inward-outward connections in internationalisation, *Journal of International Marketing*, 1(1), 44–58.

Yamin, M. and Sinkovics, R. (2006) Online internationalisation, psychic distance reduction and the virtuality trap, *International Business Review*, 15(4), 339–60.

9
The influence of decision-making logic on the internationalisation of Born Globals: Bolt

Tairi Leis

CASE SUMMARY

Bolt is the first European mobility super-app, offering ride-hailing, shared cars and scooters, food, and grocery delivery. The company is operating in over 500 cities in more than 45 countries in Europe, Africa, Western Asia, and Latin America and in 2022 was worth €7.4 billion. This chapter presents a case study of Bolt from the perspective of the decision-making logic's influence on the internationalisation of Born Globals (BG). Behind a company's success and failure may be many different factors. Still, this case study is focused on the influence of decision-making logic used in Bolt company in the VUCA (volatility, uncertainty, complexity, ambiguity) and non-VUCA environment. The case is presented through semi-structured in-depth interviews conducted with the founders and management of the company. The chapter presents the widely used decision-making logic of effectuation and causation, outlining their main differences and suggesting scenarios for using them.

LEARNING OUTCOMES

The main learning outcomes of this case study are to:

- Understand different approaches to managerial decision-making logic.
- Discuss the causes and consequences of the decision-making logic.
- To understand how VUCA influences managerial decision-making and business performance.

THE CONTEXT

Travelling through shared rides started centuries ago with horses, carriages, and boats. Nowadays, Shared Mobility is a significant industry in which the shared rides market includes

Table 9.1   Entries into the car-sharing market in 2001–13

Year	Company and country
2001	Carpooling (Germany)
2006	BlablaCar (France)
2007	Carma (Ireland)
2009	Cabforce (Finland), MyTaxi (Germany)
2010	Wheely (Switzerland), Drive (Denmark), GetTaxi (Israel), Flinck (Germany)
2011	Cabify (Spain), Hailo (UK), Taxibeat (Greece), Buzzcar (France), CompareMyFare (UK), Blacklane (Germany), Kabbee (UK), Minicabster (UK)
2012	LeCab (France), Ants (Norway), Snapcar (France), Talixi (Germany)
2013	TripnDrive (France), Wundercar (Germany), Drive (France), Taxify (Estonia)

Source: Compiled by the author (based on public sources).

bookings from car rentals, ride-hailing & taxi, car-sharing, bike-sharing, and e-scooter sharing. Bike- and car-sharing vehicles are usually owned by sharing service providers and booked independently by customers who need to enter a contract with the sharing service provider to book vehicles via a smartphone app, the website, or by telephone, which is a huge technological advancement compared to two-way radio ordering system used before.

Many companies have developed advanced technologies to make travel safe, comfortable, and cheap. New technology involving solutions for carpooling came shortly after the millennium started. By 2014, many well-known platforms were launched, and at least 25 startups already in Europe entered the race by trying to fix transportation with new technology. Many startups across the globe were trying to help people to minimise vehicle emissions to the taxi ordering services available and were tackling the taxi-hailing space.

Bolt, formerly known as Taxify, entered the car-sharing market in 2013, among many others, although several companies were on the market earlier. Many startups across the globe have aimed to go global, but not many have succeeded in this. Bolt is an excellent example of a Born Global (BG) company, entering the international market very quickly, only half a year after the establishment of the company. The company's main rival is Uber, but the global market is shared between large companies like Lyft, Via, DiDi, Gett, Grab, Careem, Cabify, and many others. For more detailed information, see Tables 9.1 and 9.2.

BOLT

The company's background and motivation

Bolt, formerly named Taxify, was founded in Estonia by brothers Markus and Martin Villig with the help of their parents. Markus borrowed €5,000 from his parents and developed the first version of ride-hailing software. The service was launched in August 2013, and after a few months, Markus' brother Martin Villig and technical co-founder Oliver Leisalu joined the team. Together they started to build one of the fastest-growing technology businesses in European history.

Table 9.2   Industry projections 2022–26

Indicator	Amount	Year(s)
Revenue in the shared rides segment	US$379.20bn	2022
Annual growth rate revenue (CAGR)	8.06%	2022–26
Projected market volume	US$517.10bn	2026
The number of users in the shared rides segment	2,274.5m	2026
User penetration	24.5%–28.9%	2022–26
The average revenue per user (ARPU)	US$203.30	2022
Shared rides segment total revenue generated through online sales	60%	2026
Globally, most revenue will be generated in China	US$128.90bn	2022
Shared rides segment growth in the world	8.06%	2022–26
Market volume of the shared rides segment	US$517.10bn	2026

Source: Compiled by the author (based on Statista).

The motivation for international expansion was driven by the ambitions of young founders to grow and develop the company. At first, the company expanded incrementally, but as the experience base grew, it expanded radically. The local market's small size was restricting, and at first, the company expanded to nearby markets (Baltics) but quite soon also to large and attractive markets farther away. Internationalisation information was gathered from the internet and partners from their destination country. They got their first partners during the process of international expansion. Initially, they were actively searching for partners for cooperation, but later the importance of cooperation decreased.

The company used both effectual and causal logic in its decision-making. It used different logic at different points in time. As its experience grew, the company began to analyse markets before entering them. Still, it was also ready to change as the market changed, reacting quickly to great opportunities. The company's management was able to learn quickly from failures and had a strict plan for expanding internationally. In the VUCA environment (volatility, uncertainty, complexity, ambiguity), managers were flexible, adjusting earlier plans in response to changed circumstances.

Issues in different markets

The challenges of foreign market entry were mainly related to limited funding, lacking market knowledge, challenges in the regulatory environment, changes in the competitive scene, and product handicaps.

- The regulations in England were highly complex, resulting in the company failing to comply in 2017 and losing access to the market for almost two years.
- A weak understanding of the competitive market scene in Egypt resulted in the company shutting its services down just a few months after launch.
- A tough regulatory environment forced the company to shut the Netherlands operations down back in 2015.

- Fierce competition after the emergence of new players in Australia and the focus at the time on core markets in EMEA (Europe, Middle East, Africa) resulted in the eventual shutdown of the Australian market.
- Realising political risks in Russia and Belarus ultimately led to market exit in 2021 and 2022, respectively.

The most significant factors that slowed down the company's subsequent expansion were mistakes in hiring the team and the need for more resources during the beginning of the expansion phase. As a result of the self-analysis of the failures, the company's management came to the understanding that it is necessary to be able to evaluate the destination market very well; hired employees must fit the management and company culture and value propositions; it is necessary to assess the realistic amount of capital necessary to pull it off and grow the market to achieve critical mass; investigate product conformity in regards to local regulations and competition; non-working models must be changed. A business model must be abandoned or changed if it does not work well enough for a long time. Bolt learned from mistakes made, and they did exit from loss-making markets.

A short history of the firm

The firm was established in August 2013 in Estonia, and already in 2014, the company was abroad with a vision to aggregate all Tallinn and Riga taxis into one platform. Real growth started after the company raised funding up to 2 million euros in 2014. The investment came from several angel investors from the US, Asia, Estonia, and Finland. After that, the company struggled to raise money for two and a half years.

New investment was received in 2017, and the company started strategic cooperation with the world's leading ride-sharing company, Didi Chuxing, who supported the company's further growth in Africa and Europe. In 2017, the company emerged in London by acquiring a local taxi company with a licence to operate but was forced to shut down its services.

In 2018 the company got 175 million dollars in funding from a German car manufacturer Daimler, and this transaction increased the company's value to one billion dollars, catapulting Bolt to unicorn status. In the same year, in September, they launched an electric scooters rental business in Paris.

In March 2019, the company name changed from Taxify to the name Bolt because, in addition to taxi services, other modes of transportation were also offered, and the previous name remained narrow. In June 2019, the service was reopened in London with 20,000 registered drivers, and in August, it launched in Tallinn its food delivery service, Bolt Food. In September 2019, Bolt announced its 'Green Plan' strategy goals, including an initiative to reduce the transportation sector's ecological footprint by reducing emissions and adding more green ride types for passengers.

In January 2020, the European Investment Bank (EIB) made a €50 million venture debt facility available for Bolt to boost R&D and develop new products. The goal of financing, supported by the European Fund for Strategic Investments (EFSI), was to support Bolt's product development and research in areas where the use of technology can improve the safety, reliability, and sustainability of its services while maintaining the high efficiency of operations. The company raised €150 million from investors in December 2020. This included investments in services like ride-hailing and personalised mobility services like food delivery.

In March 2021, Bolt raised €20 million from IFC, a World Bank Group member, for further emerging markets push. In May 2021, Bolt launched a car-sharing service, Bolt Drive, and in August 2021, Bolt announced the raising of an investment of €600 million. The company raised funds from new investors Sequoia, Tekne, Ghisallo, and existing investors G Squared, G1 Capital, and Naya.

In January 2022, Bolt raised the €628 million investment round, led by Sequoia Capital and Fidelity Management and Research Company LLC, with participation from Whale Rock, Owl Rock (a division of Blue Owl), D1, G Squared, Tekne, Ghisallo, and others, taking the company's valuation to €7.4 billion.

Today, Bolt offers a wide range of mobility services designed to cater to different distances and needs, including ride-hailing, micro mobility rental with scooters and e-bikes, Bolt Food, delivering ready-made meals and items from restaurants and stores, Bolt Market, grocery delivery, and Bolt Drive, a short-term car rental service. Bolt has more than 3,000 employees worldwide from more than 70 different nationalities. In 2021, Bolt increased its turnover by 126 per cent to €500 million. However, the loss was €547.2 million.

In March 2019 and 2020, Bolt was ranked third in the FT 1000: Europe's Fastest Growing Companies published by the *Financial Times*.

THE PROBLEM

At the company's first stage, Bolt's founders had yet to gain experience.

> When I was 19, I was certain that I wanted to start a company … but having no experience, no funding, no connections or network, and quite limited tech skills, it wasn't the best success. (Markus Villig, 2019)

The company lacked money, and the founders started understanding the need for change.

> So, I thought, we need to change something, and we expanded to Amsterdam right away by burning 100 000 euros per month … and the business didn't work. … If we see something not working, we are not investing more, trying to figure out why it is not working and what we should do to improve. (Martin Villig, 2018)

The company quickly assessed the value proposition's importance and drew conclusions from mistakes, which helped prevent more significant losses.

> In Latvia, we invested one million dollars, and it took us about 6 months to understand that we needed to improve the service and not do more marketing. … We have seen that if the business is not growing, then something is wrong with the value propositions. It's not that you are lacking money on marketing. (Martin Villig, 2018)

> We spent the first 2–3 years making sure we got our product right. So, we would know exactly why customers want to use it and why drivers prefer us to other platforms. (Markus Villig, 2020)

From day one, the company has been very lean and cost-effective, understanding the importance of differentiation and localisation.

> Differentiation is our culture; the whole company is entrepreneurial and cost-efficient because we did not have that luxury to have money. If new employees come, they put together their own chairs, their own tables, that's how we started. We always put the drivers first, and building a sustainable company can also come with lower commissions. (Martin Villig, 2018)

> If you manage to localise, then you manage to build the best product for the customers. ... Each country is very different, and the biggest advantage is localisation. ... So, we used to be very lean, being in a high competition state, automating as much as possible. ... So, we are still able to keep up that lean operation, localise, and at the end of the day, it ends up with a better platform for drivers and riders as well. (Markus Villig, 2019)

> Our focus has always been on operating our business as cost-effectively as we can. We are the leaders of this on the world stage. ... Our business strategy is that we earn a low percentage profit on each product, but we get a large amount of it as a result. (Markus Villig, 2022)

The company started to research and analyse the market as knowledge and experience grew by learning from failures.

> There have been many failures. For example, decisions where I have been pushing to get approval to enter some specific market, and ultimately it did not work out. And looking back, I would tell you that there was not enough research at that time. ... I should have been more open-minded and taken a slower approach to take more time to research, compare, and look at more markets. Maybe I should have had more teams to help me with advice. Maybe, if we would have double decisions. (Jevgeni Beloussov, 2022)

> Later on, when we were smarter and could analyse more, we took on bigger markets and ... we analysed every market before we went ... and we looked at least ten or fifteen parameters. (Martin Villig, 2020)

The company emerged ambitiously in a developed London market without conducting in-depth research and was forced to exit.

> In England, the regulator closed us down at the beginning. That was something we could not have foreseen. The regulation was more complicated there. ... We had to make a new application and license and spend a lot of money on legal costs. It took us a year and a half, even two years, to get it straightened out so we could reopen. ... But we also experimented

in other markets, more in the early years. We used all the methods that were possible. (Martin Villig, 2020)

London overall is one of the most regulated right-heading markets in the world. And it took us more than two years to prepare to launch finally. (Markus Villig, 2020)

The company was able to draw conclusions from failures and learn from them.

I was responsible for 95% of all business then, and the main markets were profitable, so I had some voice. ... I did not need to convince them because they saw that many markets were performing well in the past and were profitable, so it was repeating the same. ... Sometimes, some of those decisions fail, and that's when we realise that we need to do better than this. ... Everything in the failure of market expansion has had some experience of understanding that I try to use and communicate to all the other teams so that they would not make the same mistakes. So, absolutely it was a learning experience, but the only question is, how much is okay to pay for mistakes? It can be fifty thousand, half a million, but sometimes it can be a 10 million loss. ... When you look at where we are now while operating in a few dozen markets, it may feel like expansion has been a walk in the park. The reality is that we made quite a lot of mistakes on the way, which sometimes even forced us to quit some of the markets while writing off multi-million € losses ... On the bright side, every mistake resulted in us reviewing our approach to market expansion and figuring out what went wrong. ... We have a solid record of re-entering the markets and operating there success-fully (Hungary, Netherlands, Finland) which proves this point. (Jevgeni Beloussov, 2022)

The decision-making process in the company evolved as the business developed in interna-tional markets.

We have been evolving our expansion framework over time based on the experience. In the beginning, it was more like that: okay, Markus, here is the research, what do you think about it? ... It would generally be a high-level presentation or Word document with the pros, cons, and budget estimates. ... These decisions were more about an agreement between 2 people, never about a discussion with a wider group of experts. ... At one point, as our functional teams grew and were able to provide better support, the market expansion greenlighting process went through big changes. ... We wanted it to be formalised to help us move fast while getting necessary expert opinions and sign-off from different teams. ... Now we have a committee reviewing a detailed report on every expansion opportunity and making a decision upon a thorough discussion. (Jevgeni Beloussov, 2022)

Management was deciding on essential issues in a very small circle due to a need for more highly qualified staff.

One of the biggest challenges has been finding the team. ... I first made mistakes in finding talents, but over time, the good thing is that you learn and understand what talent it takes to succeed. ... Back in the days when we did not have functional teams' support at the necessary level, many decisions would have to be made by myself or after consulting with Markus. ... Now, when we are a much bigger company, the cost of mistakes is much higher, and we must involve more people in the decision-making process to limit our risks. ... Also, company culture-wise, it's important to give voice to different related teams. (Jevgeni Beloussov, 2022)

The company started to make quick and bold decisions, which benefited the whole organisation.

Mindset of investors in 2015 and 2016 was difficult. They saw that Uber was raising billions, and we were some unknown guys in eastern Europe. Why should we succeed? ... For our first angels, we said we need €70,000 to expand to 5 countries. So, in the next round, we said that we need one million to expand to 10 countries. (Martin Villig, 2018)

In 2017, huge investments were received, and the company started a strategic partnership with Didi Chuxing but remained independent in its decision-making.

Didi was the third investor with whom we spoke. Two previous investors turned down. ... They did their due diligence, and with the negotiations, we grew out of the evaluation so much that we asked are you willing to improve your offer, and they said no. So, we took the next investor and the same process for another 6 months. ... And we were saying that guys, growing organically faster than with your funding, maybe you will improve your offer, and they said that they don't. And then we turned them down. And then Didi came ... and we raised 175 million dollars. (Martin Villig, 2018)

From day one, we have been very clear to our investors that we value our independence. ... It's fully up to us where we go and operate. (Markus Villig, 2019)

In 2020, with the widespread outbreak of the Covid-19 pandemic worldwide, the company ran into financial difficulties, despite previous investor involvement, and had to decide how to deal with the crisis quickly.

During this time when Covid happened, we dropped in volume by 90% in the first week. ... It was a very difficult time for us but also for many other companies. ... We started figuring out what we should do and how long it would last. So, we had a lot of management-level discussions and decisions which had to be made to cut our costs as much as we could. ... There were some hard decisions we had to make to survive. ... We realised that if the volumes are going back up eventually, we need to keep our team. It was decided to cut everyones' salaries by 20% for a few months to limit our costs. ... In the end, looking back, it was a good call as we did not have to let go of anyone during Covid times. ... Besides Covid-19, we had to face a massive shortage of cars (a result of global chip shortage), a workforce crisis (many drivers gave up on driving during Covid times), and more recently energy crisis and the war in Ukraine. ... VUCA framework wise, all this uncertainty had to be dealt with improved clarity and frequency of communication and a bigger focus on vision and quick execution. (Jevgeni Beloussov, 2022)

The company learned from previous financial difficulties and decided to keep its cash reserves in better shape for the future.

> We noticed that the need for money escalated in proportion to growth. As the company grew more than twofold in the last year, we always want an adequate cash buffer. Thereby, we can use this strategically: for example, if we want to develop a new product line or if there is a new crisis equivalent to the Covid crisis, so ultimately, our company will have certainty. … The main reason we were able to attract investors and why our value has grown is that our results are the greatest they have ever been. We are growing in every aspect of our business; we are rapidly adding new countries and cities. (Markus Villig, 2022)

Despite VUCA challenges, the company could survive and even grow because opportunities were seen and exploited, the company was very flexible, and decisions were made quickly.

> When Covid happened … it was clear that new launches and expansion should be delayed until the time is clearer and there is less ambiguity. And we started thinking … is there any random country we have just missed from our horizon? Maybe we consider doing research and launching there with minimum effort by doing it remotely 100%, with a €30,000 budget? Our normal country budget would be about a million or something. So, it sounded like a nice challenge, and we did it … and some of those markets have quickly become the top 10 markets. … We did not have a research-intensive launch. … So, it was opportunistic from our side to use this time. … We just saw that time window and realised we had to move quickly. (Jevgeni Beloussov, 2022)

> How did we do it? Well, we didn't spend time on bureaucracy. Instead, we moved fast in small teams. Teams, where everybody acts like an owner. (Aastha Yadav, 2022)

The company has five different verticals: ride-sharing, car-sharing, food delivery, grocery delivery, and scooters, and those different verticals have helped to ease the way out of crises. The company's management was able to find solutions to unexpected crises.

> When Covid happened, everyone started staying at home, ride-hailing volumes dropped a lot, and there was much less work to be done for our operations teams … so we quickly repositioned them to focus on food delivery verticals and help us launch Bolt Food. … Restaurants didn't have customers coming over, and they were willing to join any platform this time. … Sometimes, we still needed to do some sales work, but Covid made it easy. … Every challenge forces you to come up with some plan. We had to update the year's plan and budget to the new reality. … The budgeting process it's not only using the money that we take externally but also distributing money from profitable ones to those who need more investments. My job was to work with multi-million budgets and distribute the money from one group to another based on the research done. (Jevgeni Beloussov, 2022)

The company coped well in crises through flexibility and making intelligent and quick decisions.

> So, on one side, you have the market where you need to increase the prices because the energy prices are high, and, on the other hand, you understand that people don't have money, inflation is high, and this is the hard situation we are in right now. ... We have approached this in a very data-driven way where we list all the market expansions from different verticals and try to standardise the impact of the launch. ... Our data science teams always work to ensure that we have enough data to make decisions. ... At the start, it was a lot more subjective, but I learned over time and tried to make it more objective through the research to have a trustworthy solid list. ... There is always a probability of something going wrong, but if we take this measurable approach, we limit the probability of failures. But things still happen, and you never know. (Jevgeni Beloussov, 2022)

Looking back on the various failures in Bolt's history, the manager, who has been with the company for eight years, admitted:

> There were cases when we did not do enough research and then failed. There were cases where we did not hire a good enough manager or a team and then failed. There were also cases when we got value propositions wrong in the market, resulting in us failing with our pricing, quality, or availability is suboptimal. ... It's super important that you do the right research, hire a great value-breathing team and understand what makes customers like and use your service. ... Companies succeed because they have a smart enough team, are hard-working, and do not give up. (Jevgeni Beloussov, 2022)

DISCUSSION QUESTIONS

Questions for students to discuss and tasks to solve:

1. Which decision-making logic has Bolt been using in their different phases?
2. Could different decision-making logic be involved in Bolt's success and failure?
3. Which decision-making logic do you suggest for a BG to use in a VUCA and non-VUCA environment?
4. Please fill in the matrix (Table 9.3) by selecting the decision-making logic for different scenarios (success and failure episodes) using the Bolt case example.

Learning outcomes

- Review the two most used decision-making logics.
- Discuss differences between effectuation and causation.
- Describe the causes and consequences of a wrongly chosen logic.
- Identify key factors involved in the choice of decision-making logic.
- Identify key factors involved in VUCA and non-VUCA environments.

Table 9.3   Matrix for students to select the decision-making logic Bolt has used

Scenarios	Effectuation	Causation
The early stage of the company's development		
The mature stage of company's development		
Inexperienced management (learning phase of expansion)		
Experienced management with international know-how		
Emerging markets (Africa) in VUCA environment		
Developed markets (UK) in non-VUCA environment		

TEACHING NOTES

TARGET AUDIENCE

This case study should be taught in international business courses for Masters and doctoral students.

SUGGESTED TEACHING STRATEGIES

When teaching this case study, it is appropriate to divide the students into small groups and discuss the decision-making logic used by the company during the periods highlighted in the case. Role-plays are also well suited for case analysis, where, for example, 1–2 people in the group are the company's founders, one is the team leader, one is an analyst, one is an investor, etc.

SUGGESTED ANSWERS TO DISCUSSION QUESTIONS

Q1 Which decision-making logic has Bolt been using in their different phases?

Suggested answer: Bolt used effectuation in the company's development phase, and as their experience grew, there was a shift from effectuation towards causation. In the mature development phase, Bolt used more causation, and during the VUCA period, both decision-making logics were used in parallel.

Q2 Could different decision-making logic be involved in Bolt's success and failure?

Suggested answer: Yes, it could. Decision-making logic can cause success (effectuation with expansion in VUCA time to Africa) and failure (effectuation expansion to London 2017). For more information, see Table 9.4.

Q3 Which decision-making logic do you recommend for a BG to use in a VUCA environment?

Suggested answer: It depends on the market. In the VUCA environment in emerging markets, it is recommended to use effectuation, but in developed markets, both – causation and effectuation. For more information, see Table 9.4.

Q4 Which decision-making logic do you suggest for a BG to use in a non-VUCA environment?

Suggested answer: It depends on the market. In a non-VUCA environment in developed markets, it is recommended to use causation, but in emerging markets, both – causation and effectuation. For more information, see Table 9.4.

Table 9.4 Matrix for students to select the decision-making logic Bolt has used – completed

Scenarios	Effectuation	Causation
The early stage of the company's development	x	
The mature stage of company's development	x	x
Inexperienced management (learning phase of expansion)	x	
Experienced management with international knowhow	x	x
Emerging markets (Africa) in VUCA environment	x	
Developed markets (UK) in non-VUCA environment	x	

SUPPLEMENTARY INFORMATION

VUCA

VUCA stands for volatility, uncertainty, complexity, and ambiguity, encompassing many challenges that can put companies in a challenging position. The volatility challenges are unexpected and unstable situations without knowing how long the problematic period will last. Uncertainty is expressed in situations with a lack of information, though the cause and outcome of an event are known and there is a clear need for changes. Complexity arises from the many interrelated parties and variables for which some information is available or predictable, but the size or nature of that information makes it difficult to implement. In ambiguity, causal relationships are unclear because there are no previous precedents, and companies face 'unknown unknowns' and learn through experiments (Bennett and Lemoine, 2014).

Every company must deal with its VUCA environment, even if some organisations are unaware of its existence. To survive in the VUCA conditions, companies should be flexible, make necessary changes, and focus on their strengths. One of the key competencies is the ability to develop and adapt digital technologies to the organisation's needs or the ability to flexibly switch thinking between various problems (Baran and Woznyj, 2021).

Decision-making logic

The most widely used decision-making logics are causation and effectuation, which are quite opposing but are sometimes used interchangeably or even in parallel. The most cited author on that topic is Saras D. Sarasvathy, who brought next to causation also effectuation logic

Table 9.5   Comparison of effectuation and causation

Indicator	Effectuation	Causation
Resources	Outputs are chosen according to the resources available because resources drive outputs and targets by showing what is achievable.	The resources will be selected according to the pre-defined outputs. The business goals drive the resources needed to achieve specific outcomes.
Risk	A firm can risk what it is ready to lose. The company invests gradually so that risks are more hedged. The company cannot invest more than the affiliated groups are ready to risk losing.	Continuous analysis and calculation, where decisions are made based on expected returns and influenced by positive and negative sides. Investing broadly and all at once. The firm can risk what it is ready to lose.
Uncertainty	Unpredictable situations will contribute to achieving outputs, and strategies can be changed. It is impossible to project the future and make prognoses.	Unpredictable situations are more pre-planned and plan-driven. Unforeseen situations and the future are predicted by various analyses, which are used to make prognoses.
Control	The future cannot be predicted by analysis, but with new goals and opportunities, it is possible to change direction, as plans and goals are not strictly implemented.	Constant analysis and strategising, and planning for the future. The company will make plans to follow. The plans also identify the partners that are important for the company.

Source: Compiled by the author (based on Brettel et al., 2012; Chandler et al., 2011; Dew et al., 2009; Fisher, 2012; Kerr and Coviello, 2020; Prashantham et al., 2019; Sarasvathy, 2001, 2008; Sarasvathy et al., 2014; Skorupski et al., 2019).

(Sarasvathy, 2001, 2008; Schweizer et al., 2010), and whose 2001 and 2008 published articles have been widely cited (Andersson, 2011; Chandler et al., 2011; Chetty et al., 2015; Harms and Schiele, 2012). In addition, several more recent scientific works are also based on Sarasvathy's articles (Cui et al., 2019; Cussen and Cooney, 2019; Kerr and Coviello, 2020; Laskovaia et al., 2019). The main differences between effectual and causal decision-making logics are shown in comparative Table 9.5.

Sarasvathy (2001) has highlighted that companies that have been using effectuation will start using more causation as their uncertainty decreases and experience increases. Using effectuation, available resources are first reviewed, and then the choice is made (Chandler et al., 2011; Sarasvathy, 2001, 2008). Companies should start by answering the questions: (1) 'Who am I?'; (2) 'What do I know?'; 3) 'Whom do I know?' to determine what is achievable with the existing resources (Kerr and Coviello, 2020; Sarasvathy, 2001), and rely primarily on the resources and opportunities that are available (Fisher, 2012; Sarasvathy, 2001, 2008; Sarasvathy et al., 2014; Skorupski et al., 2019).

It is important to use existing resources and to find new ideas, opportunities, etc., including expanding internationally (Dew et al., 2009; Sarasvathy, 2001). However, a BG bases its decision-making on both. The skills and knowledge of the company's manager play a significant role in adapting to different environments to recognise opportunities and make decisions according to the situations. From an effectuation logic perspective, a BG finds opportunities and offers exciting solutions. Conversely, causation helps set objectives and change business strategies according to the information available (Nemkova, 2017).

Table 9.6 Recommendations on which circumstances effectuation (E) or causation (C) to use

Circumstances	E	C
Possibility to get information (Fisher, 2012; Gruber, 2007) to set objectives and change business strategies (Nemkova, 2017) and to predict the future with analysis, ensuring more control and clarity in the company (Galkina and Chetty, 2015).		x
Market is volatile (Cussen and Cooney, 2019), and the future is uncertain and unpredictable or cannot be analysed or measured (Fisher, 2012), and there is time pressure by making decisions, without a certain market to operate (Nummela et al., 2014).	x	
Uncertainty is decreasing and managerial skills are increasing (Sarasvathy, 2001) in emerging economies and in a less uncertain environment (Yu et al., 2018).		x
Skilled managers in high uncertainty, by using opportunities etc., including expanding the international market (Dew et al., 2009; Sarasvathy, 2001) in emerging economies with high uncertain environments (Yu et al., 2018).	x	
Less experienced managers in high uncertainty (Cui et al., 2019; Vissak et al., 2020); because it does not require so much planning and forecasting (Fisher, 2012).	x	
Companies with a lack of experience on the international market (Evers and O'Gorman, 2011) or at an early stage of development (Prashantham et al., 2019).	x	
Experienced and active companies in foreign markets (Matalamäki, 2017; Nummela et al., 2014).		x
Finding opportunities and coming up with exciting solutions (Nemkova, 2017) to adapt better to change in uncertainty, as goals and opportunities constantly change (Prashantham et al., 2019).	x	

Source: Compiled by the author (based on Cui et al., 2019; Cussen and Cooney, 2019; Dew et al., 2009; Evers and O'Gorman, 2011; Fisher, 2012; Galkina and Chetty, 2015; Matalamäki, 2017; Nemkova, 2017; Nummela et al., 2014; Prashantham et al., 2019; Sarasvathy, 2001; Sarasvathy et al., 2014; Vissak et al., 2020).

The decision logic to be used depends on several factors, such as the availability of information, the competence of the management, the stage of development and experience in the international market, as well as the level of maturity of the target market and the environment in which the company operates (VUCA or non-VUCA environment). Table 9.6 sets out the different circumstances and recommendations on which decision logic to adopt.

The choice of decision-making logic does not depend on the company's size but on the decision context and ability to choose between effectuation or causation (Hauser et al., 2020). Thus, companies may use the combination of two decision-making logics, and many studies have focused mainly on the positive side, and the negative side is less covered (Galkina and Lundgren-Henriksson, 2017). In case of failure, companies, based on effectuation, face it earlier and with fewer losses. Causation requires more investment; therefore, the losses are higher, and the company may not recover from failure (Fisher, 2012).

Causation or effectuation changes according to the situation and the company's environment (Gil-Barragan et al., 2020). Choosing the decision-making logic, companies should consider how much uncertainty is in the market and how many resources they have (Futterer et al., 2018). In high environmental uncertainty, causation and effectuation have a positive interaction effect on a company's performance and using decision-making logic strategically helps companies to cope with uncertainty (Yu et al., 2018). Causation firms may be unable to cope well in a crisis because of lacking flexibility or adaptability and the incapacity to make fast changes. Their longer-term plans and goals may prevent them from making important decisions in a crisis and may negatively impact the firm (Laskovaia et al., 2019).

Public sources

https://tech.eu/2014/08/26/european-transportation-startups-taxi-carsharing-ridesharing/ (accessed 24 July 2023).

https://www.statista.com/outlook/mmo/shared-mobility/shared-rides/worldwide (accessed 24 July 2023).

https://estonianworld.com/technology/estonian-taxi%c2%adbooking-app-taxify-raises-100k/ (accessed 24 July 2023).

https://www.businessinsider.com/didi-chuxing-taxify-uber-europe-africa-2017-8 (accessed 24 July 2023).

https://fortune.com/2017/09/08/london-uber-taxify-licensing-tfl-khan/ (accesed 24 July 2023).

https://www.vanguardngr.com/2018/05/taxify-closes-175m-investment-led-by-daimler-now-worth -1bn/ (accessed 24 July 2023).

https://phys.org/news/2018-06-electric-scooters-paris-europe.html (accessed 24 July 2023).

https://investinestonia.com/estonias-taxify-is-now-called-bolt/ (accessed 24 July 2023).

https://www.cnbc.com/2019/06/11/uber-european-rival-bolt-taxify-launches-in-london.html (accessed 24 July 2023).

https://www.cnbc.com/2019/08/21/uber-rival-bolt-launches-food-delivery-service-bolt-food-in-europe .html (accessed 24 July 2023).

https://the-european.eu/story-19027/bolt-launches-environmental-impact-fund-with-maiden -transaction-in-uk.html (accessed 24 July 2023).

https://ec.europa.eu/commission/presscorner/detail/en/IP_20_74 (accessed 24 July 2023).

https://investinestonia.com/estonias-unicorn-bolt-raises-e150m/ (accessed 24 July 2023).

https://www.forbes.com/sites/jonathankeane/2021/03/04/bolt-lands-20-million-from-the-world-banks -ifc-for-emerging-market-push/?sh=7f28bf721097 (accessed 24 July 2023).

https://www.eu-startups.com/2021/05/tallinn-based-bolt-launches-its-car-sharing-service-bolt-drive/

https://blog.bolt.eu/en/bolt-closes-a-600m-funding-round/ (accessed 24 July 2023).

https://www.eu-startups.com/2022/01/tallinns-bolt-jets-off-with-e628-million-to-accelerate-the -transition-from-owned-cars-to-shared-mobility/ (accessed 24 July 2023).

https://www.ft.com/content/691390ca-53d9-11ea-90ad-25e377c0ee1f (accessed 24 July 2023).

Interviews available online

The Kenyan Wallstreet, 2020. The thinking behind the investor. Interview with Markus Villig, CEO and Co-founder, Bolt. https://www.youtube.com/watch?v=NXTE00zbBD4 (accessed 24 July 2023).

Schrader, A., 2018. LIFTOFF: 5 startup stories from 'Europe's Top Founders'. Episode 5: LIFTOFF Live with Martin Villig. https://www.lift99.co/blog/liftoff-startup-stories-from-europes-top-founders (accessed 24 July 2023).

The Story of Taxify & 'Europe's Youngest Unicorn Founder', 2019. https://www.youtube.com/watch?v= bnzsJKCIHf0 (accessed 24 July 2023).

Sunny Business, 2022. Markus Villig: Bolt has become one of the largest companies in Europe. https:// www.sunnybusiness.ee/markus-villig-bolt-has-become-one-of-the-largest-companies-in-europe/ (accessed 24 July 2023).

We are Bolt, 2021. https://www.dropbox.com/sh/wnlkwd5x47rd7bf/AADkC7dSEf4d03NQ1tTybvgha/ b%20roll%20footage/Team%20clips?dl=0&preview=We_Are_Bolt_2021.mp4&subfolder_nav _tracking=1 (accessed 24 July 2023).

Personally conducted interviews

Personal interview with Jevgeni Beloussov, 11 October 2022. Length of interview: 137 minutes.
Personal interview with Martin Villig, 31 March 2020. Length of interview: 40 minutes.

Suggestions for literature that can be used for a case discussion

Bennett, N. and Lemoine, J., 2014. What VUCA really means for you. *Harvard Business Review*, 92(1/2), 1.
Sarasvathy, S.D., 2001. Causation and effectuation: Toward a theoretical shift from economic inevitability to entrepreneurial contingency. *Academy of Management Review*, 26(2), 243–63.
Sarasvathy, S.D., 2008. Entrepreneurship theory and practice. In *Effectuation: Elements of Entrepreneurial Expertise*. Edward Elgar Publishing, 58–147.

ACKNOWLEDGEMENT

This work was supported by the Estonian Research Council's grant PRG 1418.

BIBLIOGRAPHY

Andersson, S., 2011. International entrepreneurship, born globals and the theory of effectuation. *Journal of Small Business and Enterprise Developmen*, 18(3), 627–43.
Baran, B.E. and Woznyj, H.M., 2021. Managing VUCA: The human dynamics of agility. *Organisational Dynamics*, 50(2), 100787.
Bennett, N. and Lemoine, J., 2014. What VUCA really means for you. *Harvard Business Review*, 92(1/2), 1.
Brettel, M., Mauer, R., Engelen, A. and Küpper, D., 2012. Corporate effectuation: Entrepreneurial action and its impact on R&D project performance. *Journal of Business Venturing*, 27(2), 167–84.
Chandler, G.N., DeTienne, D.R., McKelvie, A. and Mumford, T.V., 2011. Causation and effectuation processes: A validation study. *Journal of Business Venturing*, 26(3), 375–90.
Chetty, S., Ojala, A. and Leppäaho, T., 2015. Effectuation and foreign market entry of entrepreneurial firms. *European Journal of Marketing*, 49(9/10), 1436–59.
Cui, L., Su, S.I.I., Feng, Y. and Hertz, S., 2019. Causal or effectual? Dynamics of decision making logics in servitization. *Industrial Marketing Management*, 82, 15–26.
Cussen, N. and Cooney, T., 2019. Exploring alternative approaches to entrepreneurial exporting: Internationalisation through an effectual lens. *Small Enterprise Research*, 26(2), 164–78.
Dew, N., Read, S., Sarasvathy, S.D. and Wiltbank, R., 2009. Effectual versus predictive logics in entrepreneurial decision-making: Differences between experts and novices. *Journal of Business Venturing*, 24(4), 287–309.
Evers, N. and O'Gorman, C., 2011. Improvised internationalisation in new ventures: The role of prior knowledge and networks. *Entrepreneurship & Regional Development*, 23(7–8), 549–74.
Fisher, G., 2012. Effectuation, causation, and bricolage: A behavioral comparison of emerging theories in entrepreneurship research. *Entrepreneurship Theory and Practice*, 36(5), 1019–51.
Futterer, F., Schmidt, J. and Heidenreich, S., 2018. Effectuation or causation as the key to corporate venture success? Investigating effects of entrepreneurial behaviors on business model innovation and venture performance. *Long Range Planning*, 51(1), 64–81.
Galkina, T. and Chetty, S., 2015. Effectuation and networking of internationalising SMEs. *Management International Review*, 55(5), 647–76.
Galkina, T. and Lundgren-Henriksson, E.L., 2017. Coopetition as an entrepreneurial process: Interplay of causation and effectuation. *Industrial Marketing Management*, 67, 158–73.

Gil-Barragan, J.M., Belso-Martínez, J.A. and Mas-Verdú, F., 2020. When do domestic networks cause accelerated internationalisation under different decision-making logic? Evidence from weak institutional environment. *European Business Review*, 32(2), 227–56.

Gruber, M., 2007. Uncovering the value of planning in new venture creation: A process and contingency perspective. *Journal of Business Venturing*, 22(6), 782–807.

Harms, R. and Schiele, H., 2012. Antecedents and consequences of effectuation and causation in the international new venture creation process. *Journal of International Entrepreneurship*, 10(2), 95–116.

Hauser, A., Eggers, F. and Güldenberg, S., 2020. Strategic decision-making in SMEs: Effectuation, causation, and the absence of strategy. *Small Business Economics*, 54(3), 775–90.

Kerr, J. and Coviello, N., 2020. Weaving network theory into effectuation: A multi-level reconceptualisation of effectual dynamics. *Journal of Business Venturing*, 35(2), 105937.

Laskovaia, A., Marino, L., Shirokova, G. and Wales, W., 2019. Expect the unexpected: Examining the shaping role of entrepreneurial orientation on causal and effectual decision-making logic during economic crisis. *Entrepreneurship & Regional Development*, 31(5–6), 456–75.

Matalamäki, M.J., 2017. Effectuation, an emerging theory of entrepreneurship – towards a mature stage of the development. *Journal of Small Business and Enterprise Development*, 24(4), 928–49.

Nemkova, E., 2017. The impact of agility on the market performance of born-global firms: An exploratory study of the 'Tech City' innovation cluster. *Journal of Business Research*, 80, 257–65.

Nummela, N., Saarenketo, S., Jokela, P. and Loane, S., 2014. Strategic decision-making of a born global: A comparative study from three small open economies. *Management International Review*, 54(4), 527–50.

Prashantham, S. and Floyd, S.W., 2019. Navigating liminality in new venture internationalisation. *Journal of Business Venturing*, 34(3), 513–27.

Prashantham, S., Kumar, K., Bhagavatula, S. and Sarasvathy, S.D., 2019. Effectuation, network-building and internationalisation speed. *International Small Business Journal*, 37(1), 3–21.

Sarasvathy, S.D., 2001. Causation and effectuation: Toward a theoretical shift from economic inevitability to entrepreneurial contingency. *Academy of management Review*, 26(2), 243–63.

Sarasvathy, S.D., 2008. Entrepreneurship theory and practice. In *Effectuation: Elements of Entrepreneurial Expertise*. Edward Elgar Publishing, 58–147.

Sarasvathy, S., Kumar, K., York, J.G. and Bhagavatula, S., 2014. An effectual approach to international entrepreneurship: Overlaps, challenges, and provocative possibilities. *Entrepreneurship Theory and Practice*, 38(1), 71–93.

Schweizer, R., Vahlne, J.E. and Johanson, J., 2010. Internationalization as an entrepreneurial process. *Journal of International Entrepreneurship*, 8(4), 343–70.

Skorupski, R., Secches Kogut, C. and de Mello, R.D.C., 2019. Do entrepreneurs from institutionally distinct countries apply different decision logic when internationalising their companies? A multiple-case analysis. *Journal of Transnational Management*, 24(2), 142–62.

Vissak, T., Francioni, B. and Freeman, S., 2020. Foreign market entries, exits and re-entries: The role of knowledge, network relationships and decision-making logic. *International Business Review*, 29(1), 101592. https://doi.org/10.1016/j.ibusrev.2019.101592.

Yu, X., Tao, Y., Tao, X., Xia, F. and Li, Y., 2018. Managing uncertainty in emerging economies: The interaction effects between causation and effectuation on firm performance. *Technological Forecasting and Social Change*, 135, 121–31.https://doi.org/10.1016/j.techfore.2017.11.017.

APPENDIX 9A

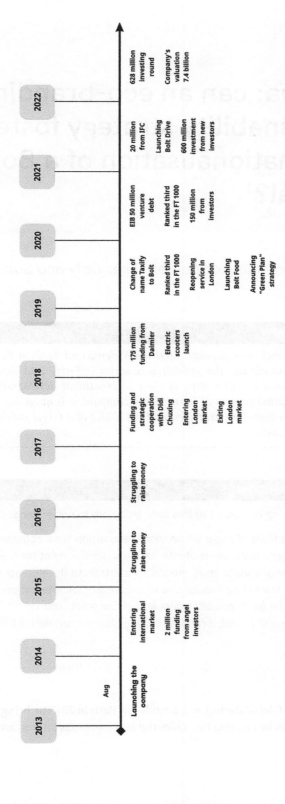

Figure 9A.1 Timeline of the company Bolt

10

Cabaïa: can an eco-branding sustainability strategy foster the internationalisation of a Born Global?[1]

Véronique Boulocher-Passet, Peter Daly and Sabine Ruaud

CASE SUMMARY

Two young French entrepreneurs, Bastien Valensi and Emilien Foiret, founded Cabaïa in 2015 to revolutionise the fashion accessories industry and internationalise quickly. The case discusses the first steps of their international development and addresses the internationalisation process of Born Global companies. It questions the role of marketing capabilities, eco-branding strategies, and the choice of a target market to succeed in rapid internationalisation.

LEARNING OUTCOMES

The main learning outcomes of this case study are to understand:

- the antecedents of rapid international expansion for a company
- the most adapted models of international development for startups
- the most appropriate entry modes for startups to develop abroad
- the use of marketing capabilities to enhance quick internationalisation
- the potential existence of targets at a global level, and
- if the choice of an eco-branding strategy is appropriate for a Born Global company.

INTRODUCTION

Cabaïa, the Born Global startup, was founded in Paris in 2015 to 'bring a dose of happiness into people's daily lives by creating fun, colourful and ingenious fashion accessories'. Committed to environmental issues and animal welfare, Cabaïa had created an eco-fashion brand for trendy, urban targets with an international lifestyle. The global fashion accessories market is expected to grow by 12.3 per cent from 2022 over the next five years (Mordor Intelligence, 2022). Cabaïa, having a strong European base, wanted to accelerate their international development to conquer the American market.

THE BIRTH OF CABAÏA

One evening in December 2015, while riding the Paris metro, Bastien Valensi (27) lost his favourite woolly cap, which his grandmother had knitted for him. What a drama! So, he set out to look for a new cap. Even as an expert in the textile industry working for a major clothing brand in Paris, he had no idea where to find a cool and original woolly cap. After days and days of looking, he was not very convinced by what he had found. No one specialised in this segment that seemed to be neglected by the fashion industry, and for which there was no major reference; the department store models were bland, soulless and of poor quality. Valensi saw only three options: (1) abandon the idea of ever finding a cool woolly cap, (2) learn how to knit, or (3) create his own brand. As he had always dreamt of setting up his own label, the penny dropped: why not create colourful, woolly caps with eccentric pompoms? And that is how Cabaïa was born! The new entrepreneur left his job at a Parisian boutique and threw himself fully into the adventure of starting his own label of woolly caps. On Microsoft Paint, he drew four cap models that reminded him of the one knitted by his granny. He added an interchange-able magnetic pompom. He only needed to find a supplier to meet quality requirements and strict environmental and social standards and integrate the magnet for the interchangeable pompom. Cabaïa's woolly cap saw the light of day.

To launch the new product, Valensi was inspired by nail bars, those little stalls in the middle of shopping aisles where you can choose nail colours from large charts. The Woolly Cap Bar was intended to be a place to choose your unique cap and pompoms. Each model had a cocktail name: Parrot, Mojito, Creamy Gin, Long Island, Manhattan, Appletini, B52, etc. and was sold in a shaker-shaped box with three interchangeable pompoms, which enabled you to change and customise your cap. The cap was more than just a piece of headgear; it was a genuine well-being accessory with a mindset. In his first 40 m2 pop-up store, Valensi sold 300 hats; three and a half months later, he sold 5,000 items.

Meanwhile, Emilien Foiret, bored in his job as a nuclear engineer, was looking for a new project. While out for a drink, he met Valensi, and the duo teamed up in 2016, intending to flood the market with Cabaïa woolly caps. Lorraine Borriello later joined the duo as their product director.

A socially and environmentally responsible brand

Valensi wanted to create a brand that respected his cheerful and honest values. He drew his inspiration from Havaianas, the Brazilian brand that transformed the flip-flop into a must-have for all the family. Hence, he created the name, Cabaïa, which conjured up a scent of summer and sun, a colourful, cheerful, festive, fun and global brand. The logo was endowed with a flagship colour, a deep blue, and depicted a beach hut, a symbol with a universal appeal internationally.

Cabaïa had five fundamental values that were inherent to their brands, namely, fun, colour, ingenuity, honesty and animal welfare:

1. *Fun* – Cabaïa believed that you did not have to take yourself too seriously to make quality products;
2. *Colour* – Cabaïa saw the world in all the colours of the rainbow;
3. *Ingenuity* – Cabaïa loved to integrate ingenious little novelties into their brand, such as interchangeable pompoms;
4. *Honesty* – Cabaïa were honest in their product, in their communication and in life;
5. *Animal welfare* – Cabaïa loved animals, and their mascot was Marty, the cat.

Cabaïa was an engaged and eco-responsible brand that wanted to contribute to the conscientious fashion brands. They espoused animal welfare and cruelty-free practices, with almost 100 per cent of Cabaïa products made without animal materials. They had even received the EVE Vegan Label.[2] Foiret explained:

> I have been a horse rider since the age of five. The animal cause was always my thing, which was why at the end of 2018, we created a partnership with the Society for the Protection of Animals (SPA) by developing limited collections, the funds of which were entirely donated to this association.

In the first two years, Cabaïa donated more than €55,000 to the SPA, making it possible to build a new refuge and carry out two surveys in order to fight against illegal breeding.

Since 2020, Cabaïa has been heavily involved in upcycling, and recycled materials (such as rubber and textile) that were GRS (Global Recycled Standard)[3] certified were used in caps. Cabaïa also had a 'no-plastic' policy, and all disposable plastic was prohibited as they used Kraft paper or starch in all their packaging. The only plastic component that remained was the small element used to attach the label, but the teams were looking for a lasting solution so that these could also be replaced. In order to reduce their carbon footprint, 90 per cent of all products were manufactured in Europe, with the remaining 10 per cent being transported by boat. Valensi explained:

> Our hats are produced in Poland, our socks in Turkey, and our bags in China, where there is a real know-how in leather goods. We tried to manufacture them closer, but the costs are not the same; a bag of the same quality would sell for more than €200 otherwise. In fact, we focus on 'made how' rather than 'made in' because we want to maintain an accessible price for our family customers. All the factories we work with are part of the Fair Wear Foundation.[4]

Cabaïa's ecological battle was not based on relocation but on sustainability. Therefore, all defective products were repaired in a factory in the Rhone-Alpes region in France and sold as second-hand items at a lower price. Unsold items were given to partner associations so that they could be distributed to those in need. Cabaïa's ecological engagement did not stop there. In 2021, they changed the status of their company with their *raison d'être* now enshrined in the company statutes: 'To create the incredible by offering ultra-colourful, ingenious accessories that are respectful of animals and the planet.' Cabaïa undertook to (1) develop even more sustainable products to achieve 80 per cent eco-responsibility by 2024; (2) continue to engage in the circular economy (repair products, sell on the second-hand market, sell prototypes, etc.); and (3) support new partnerships in order to protect biodiversity. In 2022, Cabaïa launched its first eco-responsible caps for men and women, made from recycled and ethical materials with a low environmental impact. The startup joined B Corp™ and became B certified® officially.[5]

The products

The woolly cap was a mass-market product, sold all over the world, suitable for men, women and children; it was also a niche product. The key to Cabaïa's success, the DNA if you wish, lay in its ability to disrupt, surprise and find creative ways to sell its products. Valensi explained:

> Anyone can sell woolly caps. Our added value is neither in the design nor in the quality because other brands also know how to do this. We conceptualise our ideas and dramatise our products; that is our secret.

Cabaïa's success was based on storytelling, built around the products. Cabaïa was a seller of stories, not of products. Cabaïa also developed other innovative products such as:

1. Colourful socks with wooden buttons to put together before washing them, preventing them from being mysteriously separated forever. The socks had names of couples such as Alice & Paul, Iris & Rodolphe or Maryline & John.
2. The beach towel called 'Paillote', which could be round or rectangular with a zipped pocket on the back for your phone, keys, credit cards, etc., kept in a waterproof carrying pouch.
3. The timeless and trans-generational, 100 per cent vegan, nylon backpack, Adventurer, with a 'shopping bag' opening that allows easy access, flashy colours and secure side pockets that could be attached to store small items without having to open the backpack.

In 2022, the brand had about 15 products in its catalogue. Its flagship products were the woolly cap (which accounted for 30 per cent of its turnover) and the backpack (50 per cent of turnover). It took two years to have a production rate that could meet 80 per cent of the demand for backpacks. At the end of the summer of 2021, more than 400,000 backpacks were sold. In May 2022, nearly 600,000 were sold. The Cabaïa backpack was now in second position on the French market, far behind the unbeatable Eastpak but ahead of trendy brands such as Rains or Herschel.

Since the failure of flip-flops with interchangeable straps, the production of which was stopped indefinitely due to a saturated market and lack of demand, Cabaïa implemented a new strategy based on co-creation. Hence, it developed each of its ranges in co-creation with its customers. By including them in the process, customers felt involved and talked about the brand, creating a virtuous circle. Suggestions abounded: aperitif bags, neck warmers, caps with interchangeable visors, etc. Their co-creation processes enabled Cabaïa to understand consumer expectations; however, they also had to establish the market potential for a specific product.

That is how, in November 2021, Cabaïa launched a resistant and hygienic water bottle. Valensi explained:

> Many of our customers told us that they ended up getting rid of their water bottles because they were difficult to wash, and the tea ended up tasting like coffee mixed with lemon water from the day before. Not to mention the suspicious stains that were impossible to get rid of.

Guaranteed free of bisphenol A (BPA),[6] Cabaïa's water bottle was equipped with a double insulating wall, keeping the contents hot and cold, and an ingenious specificity that allowed the bottle to be washed thoroughly and efficiently.

Distribution

After opening its first pop-up store in Velizy (Paris) in November 2016, Cabaïa continued its expansion by opening eight other pop-up stores all over France, from Paris to Bordeaux, via Toulouse, Lyon and Metz. If these spaces did not bring in much money initially, they helped the startup to generate traffic to the brand's merchant site and to impact the conversion rate. Valensi testified:

> When the site was launched, the only customers who connected to it were those who had known the brand through physical contact.

After this adaptation phase, pop-up stores were better controlled and grew exponentially; they became a real channel for growth, turnover and profitability. Cabaïa created about 20 pop-up stores a year. In addition to pop-up stores, Cabaïa had approached retail outlets such as Princess Lala. Very quickly, as of 2017, the brand was picked up by Printemps, Galeries Lafayette, BHV Marais and Bon Marché, the large Parisian department stores. As Valensi explained:

> While the channel of resellers could be perceived as "old school" because distribution was not controlled, it was very profitable, and the fixed costs were low. This meant that we could quickly earn money and reinvest it.

Cabaïa also positioned their products at airports via the services of Lagardère Travel Retail France. In the spring of 2021, to meet consumer expectations, who demanded to be able to find the brand's products in a real store, Cabaïa opened its first two permanent points of sale in Paris (30 m2 at 60, rue Vieille du Temple, in the heart of the Marais, and 50 m2 in Italie 2 Shopping Centre in the 13th district). The Cabaïa retail stores involved an immersive shopping experience that told a story and turned situational purchases into destination purchases. As of May 2022, Cabaïa had seven shops in the Paris area. The first shop to open outside Paris was in Lille in December 2021, and this store attracted a lot of Belgian customers. Valensi and Foiret aimed for 80 shops by 2025: 'The objective is to have a French network of stores. We want to satisfy our existing customers but also to capture new customers. Since opening real stores, it is roughly 50/50 between our existing customers and new ones.'

CABAÏA'S INTERNATIONAL EXPANSION

In 2019, Cabaïa launched its first international website, going beyond national and European borders. Bastien explained:

> I always wanted to create a global brand. It had always been my goal. A year after the creation of Cabaïa in 2017, we opened a pop-up store in Germany and another in Sweden. But it was much too early. What's more, we made the mistake of thinking that what worked in France would work in Germany and Sweden. We didn't take the time to test the market and anticipate customer expectations. So, we screwed up. Since 2019, we have been in a different context: we were famous enough in France to say to ourselves that we could take the next step, expanding beyond France to Eastern and Northern Europe. Then we would continue to the US. It was really exciting to start the Cabaïa story from scratch in other countries.

Internationalisation was a major challenge for Cabaïa as the investment was significant in terms of marketing, and each country had a different culture. From one culture to another across Europe, consumption patterns differed, as did the approach to a specific product. For example, ecological expectations were ten times higher in Germany than in France. Valensi added:

> We had to adapt to the habits and the customs of the different countries in which we operated. For example, our European customers were confronted with a brand and a website that they did not know. In order to establish a climate of trust and to retain this clientele, we decided to offer them the means of payment that they usually used. Also, in France, we had the culture of the carambar joke.[7] In Germany, they didn't understand these jokes at all. The jokes integrated at the bottom of emails were misunderstood. What's more, in France, language was not controlled, whereas, in Germany, they had their own style, like a Nordic or Swedish style. So, the question we had to ask was how to keep the DNA of the brand without creating a whole new brand platform to adhere to local criteria.

Cabaïa realised the limits of text when they expanded internationally. On their packaging for one of their products, their wool hats with pompoms, they had designed a tube with many expressions in French (*Tes cheveux ont fait la fête sans toi;*[8] *Foutez-moi la pêche;*[9] *Bar à bonnets;*[10] *Avant l'hiver, c'était nul et puis, on a inventé Cabaïa;*[11] *L'abus de bonnets n'est pas dangereux pour la santé;*[12] *#OKLM*[13]) and in English (*Hello; Let's go; Bad hair day; Serious is boring; Enjoy it; Smile; Happy Life; Cabaïa Spirit*), but they soon realised the limits of this when internationalising. They could not maintain the French language on the packaging in foreign markets due to the cultural specificity of the references, and translation each time would have been time-consuming and costly. Therefore, they decided to use internationally recognisable icons, images and signs rather than text on all their packaging to ease communication with their target market.

Cabaïa also realised that knowing the specificities relating to payment behaviour in a market was essential if you wanted to develop a business sustainably in a country. They developed a fundamental marketing strategy and a marketing mix, allowing them to succeed in the internationalisation of their business and consistently accelerate their export development. Cabaïa implemented a four-stage international strategy, namely:

1. A standardised customer recruitment campaign via Facebook, whereby they sent advertisements to their target (i.e., 15–35-year-old trendy, urban, city dwellers) in many European countries.
2. An analysis of the return on investment from each country, followed by the translation of their website into the languages of the chosen market.
3. A recruitment campaign of trilingual customer support staff to answer all queries in the languages of the chosen countries.
4. The setting up of pop-up stores in the chosen countries to promote their image and to recruit a network of resellers. This strategy was firmly based on a test-and-learn approach.

DEPLOYMENT STRATEGY OF CABAÏA

Driven by the success of their products, Cabaïa was profitable as of 2019. In July 2020, they raised €2.3 million, including €1 million in bank debt, from Spring Invest, a venture capital company. Cabaïa had 1,500 resellers (including 900 in France) in ten countries. The brand was present, among other countries, in leading European markets such as Germany, Belgium, Spain, Switzerland and Italy. In addition to its resellers, it also had 15 long-term pop-up stores (on average, one a year) in different shopping centres. In 2021, 80 per cent of its turnover came from France, 15 per cent from Europe and the last 5 per cent from the rest of the world. Valensi analysed the situation:

> The objective was to develop an omnichannel distribution approach, with the emphasis in 2022 on the opening of around ten permanent stores because customer acquisition costs were exploding in e-commerce.

The brand grew by targeting a trendy, urban family clientele. In 2022, its target was six billion customers, with no limit on distribution or on geographical location. And a clear ambition to next conquer the US market. Could their choice of developing an eco-branding sustainability strategy help with this ambitious objective?

DISCUSSION QUESTIONS

1. Which internal and external factors drove the startup Cabaïa to develop internationally from inception?
2. To what extent did Cabaïa follow a 'Born Global' internationalisation model?
3. Assess Cabaïa's decision to enter international markets via business partner stores.
4. Evaluate how Cabaïa's marketing capabilities enhanced their quick entry into European markets.
5. Is Cabaïa's choice to address a relatively homogeneous international target relevant to expand in the United States?
6. Is Cabaïa's eco-branding sustainability strategy an asset to further develop abroad?

TEACHING NOTES

LEARNING OUTCOMES

This case aims at exposing entrepreneurship students to the challenges faced by the international expansion of startup companies. By tracing the narrative of how an INV (International New Venture) was created and developed, students can appreciate the steps of its internationalisation. The Cabaïa case highlights critical topics related to understanding:

- the antecedents of rapid international expansion for a company
- the most adapted models of international development for startups
- the most appropriate entry modes for startups to develop abroad
- the use of marketing capabilities to enhance quick internationalisation
- the potential existence of targets at a global level, and
- if the choice of an eco-branding strategy is appropriate for a Born Global company.

CASE POSITIONING

This case can be used in undergraduate and postgraduate-level programmes. It is particularly suited for courses such as entrepreneurship, international business and management of small businesses. The case can be used to help students discuss and understand the Born Global model of internationalisation and the preferred choices of entry modes for SMEs. It can also help discuss the benefits and opportunities of addressing a global target and using an eco-branding strategy to internationalise.

ELEMENTS OF ANSWERS TO QUESTIONS

Q1 Which internal and external factors drove the startup Cabaïa to develop internationally from inception?

Globalisation is a source of opportunity for all businesses, regardless of size. The common reasons and circumstances leading to the distinctive early internationalisation of startup companies are well documented in the literature (Baronchelli and Cassia, 2014; Cavusgil and Knight, 2015; Ciravegna et al., 2018). The instructor can highlight that the reasons startups wish to internationalise will first be internal to the firm but that external and facilitating factors will play a part in this decision.

Among internal factors, students will identify Valensi's international ambition as the main reason why Cabaïa internationalised from its inception. Much is played out in the mindset that drives the entrepreneur. Valensi's personality, experience and vision for developing an international business played a key role here. The case, in developing the history of the nascent entrepreneurship, illustrates well how the aspiring entrepreneur had high levels of confidence in his abilities to start the venture and engage in subsequent activities to successfully bring it to life (Carsrud and Brännback, 2011). In the discussion, one can insist on entrepreneurship as an economic behaviour in which new venture organising activities are contingent on the characteristics of the nascent entrepreneur (Hopp and Sonderegger, 2015). Literature indicates that passion is critical and prevalent among entrepreneurs (Cardon et al., 2009; Cardon et al., 2012; Thorgren and Wincent, 2015), which is the case here. Scholars who draw from the entrepreneurship literature underline among internal factors the importance of entrepreneurs' attitudes – whether they perceive foreign markets to be risky or profitable, bringing additional market opportunities – as well as the resources a firm can deploy to go abroad in shaping decisions on when to internationalise (Ciravegna et al., 2018).

Among external factors, students can argue the case that the international as well as competitive nature of the fashion accessories industry, the required economies of scale, the small size of the domestic market and some homogeneity of the international market might have played a role in making Cabaïa rapidly wish to go global. They will agree that targeting a niche market acted as a catalyst for quick internationalisation. According to the literature, market-based antecedents of early internationalisation include the size of the domestic market, availability of opportunities in other markets, capturing a key market before competitors, preventing competitors from acquiring a dominant position in a market, receiving unsolicited orders, market knowledge, product innovation and operating in a niche market (Baronchelli and Cassia, 2014; Ciravegna et al., 2018). With this question, the instructor can lead a discussion on whether it is easier to internationalise when young and small and whether internationalisation can bring a competitive advantage. The international development question is often crucial and challenging to solve in a startup's life. However, it has become unavoidable. Nowadays, creating a startup means offering a solution to a problem that has been identified, which is often not only national. As soon as you formulate a value proposition, you must fit into the international ecosystem. Integrating an international dimension within a startup corresponds directly with the startup DNA and today's digital world. For innovative projects, it is a way to win new customers, accelerate the company's growth and position itself as a leader. Growth requires significant resources and continuous innovation of the offer to remain at the forefront of what can be achieved globally. Therefore, the number of people to whom the product or service is offered should be as large as possible to generate significant profits, making it possible to finance innovation and raise financial investments for further growth. An INV will indeed derive a competitive advantage from using specific resources and selling outputs in multiple countries (Oviatt and McDougall, 1994, 2005). It would be dangerous to wait for profitability in one country before extending into another because you would be leaving markets to other players, given that the 'first mover advantage' is crucial in several markets. Cabaïa's choice of an omnichannel strategy and developing an international website from the early beginnings of the company venture will testify that Valensi was well aware of how he needed to deploy the business internationally to reach rapid growth.

Q2 To what extent did Cabaïa follow a 'Born Global' internationalisation model?

Literature on small and medium-sized enterprises' (SMEs) internationalisation is often divided into the 'Uppsala School' and the 'Born Global School'. The Uppsala School advocates a gradual process of commitment in which experienced-based learning grows out of actions and relations developed in domestic and foreign markets. On the contrary, the key element from the Born Global School is that firms should not rest on or learn from their home market. Instead, many entrepreneurs would commit to international activities from their first years of existence, if not inception (Klyver et al., 2012). With this question, instructors can encourage students to review both theories to isolate their distinctive features, as developed by Chetty and Campbell-Hunt (2004).

In the 1990s, the seminal paper by Oviatt and McDougall (1994) identified an emerging phenomenon: 'INVs' (new ventures internationalising at or near inception). Also often named 'Born Globals' (BGs) (Rennie, 1993), these young firms experience an accelerated internationalisation process. While traditional startups used to originate as domestic firms and gradually evolved into multinational enterprises, contemporary startups increasingly began as international firms and made the world their market. The primary differentiating characteristic is the firm's age when it becomes international. Hardly created, those startups go abroad to reach larger markets. What was considered the privilege of large multinational groups had become the development model for these agile and ambitious entrepreneurs. Nowadays, companies with international status from their inception are abundant in many countries (Cavusgil and Knight, 2015). This early process of internationalisation is disruptive and calls into question the universality of the traditional Uppsala stage model (Johanson and Vahlne, 1977), which suggests companies master current business activities first, acquire certain know-how on their birth market perimeter before exporting and a good knowledge of the foreign market before deciding to engage in it. According to this model, companies would start exporting to nearby countries regarding distance, language and culture to gain experience beyond national borders gradually. The organisation would be ready to expand to more distant and complex country markets. Suppose the Uppsala internationalisation model is widely used because of its simplicity and applicability. In that case, the literature shows that company strategies (targeting, e.g., a niche market) and its resources (e.g., an excellent brand image) can reduce barriers to entry, thus facilitating faster international development.

The instructor can ask students to compare the BG model and INVs by researching the literature and initiating a class debate to differentiate them. Based on Crick (2009), BGs could be judged to have a level of commitment in the triad markets of North America, Western Europe and Southeast Asia, including Japan, within their first three years and demonstrate commitment to each market by having a turnover within three years of at least 10 per cent in each region. INVs would only need outward internationalisation within three years of business startup, representing 30 per cent of turnover to at least three overseas markets, irrespective of their geographic location. Students can list elements of Cabaïa's case study that support the BG model and those that contradict the model. The case that Cabaïa follows a BG international development model can be argued, as few early internationalising firms develop 'global' footprints; instead, they limit their export activities to a limited geography. According to Cavusgil and Knight (2015), most BG firms internationalise on a regional basis, at least in their early years. Based on the company's story, students could conclude that Cabaïa was truly 'born' with the intent to serve multiple foreign markets quickly (Coviello, 2015).

Q3 Assess Cabaïa's decision to enter international markets via business partner stores

The operational form used to enter foreign markets, called 'entry mode', represents a key issue in internationalisation. Basically, firms may choose to enter foreign markets on their own through direct exports, in partnership with other companies via contracts with distributors, or by making a direct investment in the foreign country. This complex decision is necessarily a trade-off between the resources available and the customer's support requirements. Research points to differences in entry mode strategies between large firms and SMEs. Many factors are involved in this choice. A complete review of antecedents to entry mode choice by SMEs can be found in Bruneel and De Cock (2016). Students should be encouraged to discuss which antecedents of Cabaïa can explain their choices. Being young and resource-poor, most BG firms employ exporting as their primary international entry mode (Cavusgil and Knight, 2015). Export is the least risky and cheapest way to enter an international market and often the preferred choice of entry mode for SMEs abroad. Cabaïa chose to export as its entry mode.

The benefits of direct export (via commercial partners or not) are generally:

- Access to local market experience, a form of direct contact with potential consumers which enables the acquisition of market knowledge, is an important factor for Cabaïa, as mentioned in the case of the difficulties encountered when entering Germany.
- With a shorter distribution channel and better control of the marketing mix (in comparison with indirect export via an agent), Cabaïa's marketing approach to European markets was standardised via progressive steps in distribution, leading to the recruitment of resellers.

The main limitation of this mode of entry, compared with more expensive modes such as establishing a subsidiary or a joint venture, is the lack of control over prices (customs duties).

Exporting directly through its trading partners allowed Cabaïa to overcome the constraints of limited resources that do not allow the opening of subsidiaries when expanding in a new market. Networks are influential in helping SMEs overcome these resource constraints and isolation and enabling rapid internationalisation at an early stage of a startup. New ventures that achieve instant internationalisation have tended to demonstrate higher levels of strategic pro-activeness in networking (Coviello, 2006). SMEs can counterbalance the limitations of their small size through networking (Tang, 2011).

Q4 Evaluate how Cabaïa's marketing capabilities enhanced their quick entry into European markets

In order to enjoy superior performance, a firm should first develop marketing capabilities that allow the delivery of its products/services better than competitors. Marketing capabilities include the skills and accumulated knowledge that companies use to:

- develop and launch new products (product capability)
- manage pricing tactics (pricing capability)
- provide support to distributors, and develop a close relationship with them (distribution capability)
- effectively deliver marketing messages (communication capability).

BG firms represent an optimistic, contemporary trend for international business in which any firm – of any size, the base of experience or resources – can participate actively in cross-border trade (Cavusgil and Knight, 2015). As firms increasingly internationalise and the competition in the global markets intensifies, possessing the capabilities to meet foreign customer requirements more effectively than competitors becomes more important (Tan and Sousa, 2015). Marketing capabilities are indeed likely to provide a firm with a differentiation advantage and export performance.

Students should note Cabaïa's capability to design unique, innovative products highly valued by customers (e.g., hygienic water bottles and backpacks). Cabaïa's success was also based on storytelling built around the products, which made them unique, thereby ensuring a differentiation advantage. Storytelling is often central to the legitimacy-creating efforts of new ventures (Andersen and Rask, 2014). The startup exploited image, colour and written signs as part of their semiotic resources to make meaning as they began telling their story in new markets. Using this multimodal, semiotic language strategy in the form of internationally recognisable signs, pictograms, iconography, design and visuals on packaging and labels and in their advertising was a creative way to avoid using text. Co-creating products with consumers enabled a good understanding of customer expectations. Finally, adaptation to the habits and customs of the different European countries also enabled success in their internationalisation. Innovations are often highlighted as essential to compete successfully in foreign markets (Paul et al., 2017). Students should also see that Cabaïa adopted an appropriate pricing strategy by maintaining an accessible price for families, made possible via their choice of sourcing suppliers in foreign countries. As a small company, Cabaïa offered superior value based on focused non-price differentiation rather than low cost, which is an appropriate strategy for a small company.

Distribution of Cabaïa enabled its quick internationalisation via a translated website and pop-up stores that helped recruit resellers. Securing their products positioned at airports via the services of Lagardère Travel Retail France also helped create international demand for the target market. Regarding communication, students will research Cabaïa's social media in different countries. They will be able to evaluate how Instagram, a picture-based social media, eases communication in international markets. Advances in international communication have reduced barriers to internationalisation for BGs. Social media are embedded in today's internationalisation strategies. Companies extend their reach into foreign countries by posting and tweeting. Social media networks provide founders with immediate access to a large international community of potential customers, partners, employees and competitors. They offer opportunities to create trust and reach a large audience quickly and cheaply (Leeflang et al., 2014). Instagram, in particular, has become popular for businesses as it enables them to narrate visual storytelling rather than simply present written information (Sukunesan et al., 2020). Picture-based vivid interaction with brands creates high brand engagement. Recent Millennial-focused research in the United States shows that 81 per cent of respondents agree that social media is the most effective way to reach them. Of those, 40 per cent feel Instagram is the best and most effective social media outlet to connect to brands (Richards, 2017). So, as analysed by Maltby (2012), using social media is an excellent way to accelerate the internationalisation of a startup from inception. Cabaïa understood this with their use of Facebook to broadcast their standardised customer recruitment campaign in different countries.

Q5 Is Cabaïa's choice to address a relatively homogeneous international target relevant to expand in the United States?

Homogeneity of the targets is a condition of standardisation of the international offer. If international targets are similar, for example, Cabaïa's target of trendy, urban clientele, standardisation is easier than if, as well as cultural differences, there are also differences in psychographics. What motivates the leadership of BG firms is the reach of a worldwide clientele, a transnational profile of customers around the globe, for their innovative, differentiated and unique offerings (Cavusgil and Knight, 2015).

This question is particularly interesting to discuss with students being part of the target market of Cabaïa. According to Ha (2019), with more than five billion inhabitants living in urban areas by 2030, city consumers, with their rising earning and spending power, make up most global consumption and are the driver of major consumer trends. Urban spending patterns gear towards more travel, and sophisticated urban consumers seek more varied, personalised and instantaneous experiences. They also take social and environmental issues seriously and expect businesses to be transparent and accountable for their environmental and social impact. These commonalities identified in the city consumer behaviour worldwide seem to confirm that they are a force to be reckoned with for companies. A debate can be organised with students on the homogeneity of this target. City consumers' behaviour in different regions of the world may vary. Significant differences might occur between city consumers in developed and developing countries.

Does the market show similar consumer trends among city consumers all over the globe? The discussion will then address the US market more specifically and mention the essential risk, namely, launching Cabaïa in the United States without understanding the real expectations of consumers on the market, or the power of existing local competition, at the risk of failing to succeed. Students could conclude on the relevance of addressing a specific homogeneous target internationally and recommend that Cabaïa enters other geographies like the United States by using a city-based approach to avoid getting caught up in the logistics of targeting entire countries, which leads to better work and greater relevance with the target audience. Moreover, marketers should forget about going multinational and go multi-city instead (Hayward, 2019).

Q6 Is Cabaïa's eco-branding sustainability strategy an asset to further develop abroad?

In recent years, sustainable consumerism has grown more important than ever to increasingly green-minded consumers, who at the same time, have evolved to become well informed enough to disdain 'greenwashing', or insincere brand displays of concern for the environment. Green marketing has become one of the key developments in modern business, which is more applied in developed countries than in lower and middle-income countries (Hasan et al., 2019). Eco-branding, a market instrument that mutually supports companies and consumers for recognising sustainable goals and subsidising environmental upgradation (Hayat et al., 2022), has become an interesting differentiation strategy for attaining a competitive advantage in many markets (Orsato, 2006). The main question for Cabaïa, however, is whether consumer purchase intention on green products in other parts of the world is as developed as in mainland Europe generally and if an eco-brand has the same value everywhere from a consumer perspective on the planet. Are all consumers worldwide willing to pay for the costs of ecological differentiation, and will they perceive a clear benefit to environmental investments of Cabaïa?

Cabaïa had realised with their experience in Germany that, from one culture to another, across Europe for a start, consumption patterns differed, as did the approach to a specific product. In Germany, ecological expectations were ten times higher than in France. A major study across 17 countries, The Global Sustainability Study 2021, conducted by Simon-Kucher & Partners consultancy, showed that sustainability was becoming increasingly important in consumers' purchasing decisions. It revealed generational differences in willingness to pay for sustainable products and services: higher shares of Generation Z (39 per cent) and Millennials (42 per cent) were willing to pay for sustainability, compared to Generation X (31 per cent) and Baby Boomers (26 per cent), and pay more. Attitudes towards sustainability also varied across countries – when looking at consumers who had either made significant changes to their purchasing behaviour or completely changed their way of living to be more sustainable, Austria led the way (42 per cent) among the European countries. For the United States, 22 per cent of consumers indicated major changes to their behaviour (Businesswire.com, 2021). The trends are sufficiently positive to conclude that an eco-branding sustainability strategy will help Cabaïa develop abroad.

NOTES

1. This case study was written based on one-to-one interviews with the founders of Cabaïa. The authors would like to thank Bastien Valensi and Emilien Foiret for the time they devoted to those interviews.

2. EVE Vegan Label, Source: https://www.certification-vegan.org/en/

3. Global Recycled Standard. Source: https://certifications.controlunion.com/en/certification-programs/certification-programs/grs-global-recycle-standard

4. Fair Ware Foundation. Source: https://www.fairwear.org/

5. B Corp™ is a French and international community of impact businesses, a management and impact measurement tool as well as a label that certifies companies that meet high social and environmental standards. Source: https://rainbowcollection.nl/b-corp/ consulted on 28 October 2022.

6. Bisphenol A. See: https://www.efsa.europa.eu/en/topics/topic/bisphenol

7. Carambar joke: Carambar is a French chewy caramel sweet. In 1961, the company included jokes in the sweets in the form of riddles or quick jokes. These jokes are famous for their poor quality and hence, the expression 'carambar joke' entered French culture to refer to a bad or childish joke.

8. Your hair partied without you.

9. Mix of two French expressions 'Foutez moi la paix' (leave me alone) and 'avoir la pêche' (to be in great form).

10. A cap bar/bar of caps.

11. Before winter was rubbish, then we invented Cabaïa.

12. The abuse of caps is not bad for your health, which refers to the French public health warning 'l'abus d'alcool est dangereux pour la santé' (alcohol abuse is dangerous for your health).

13. sms language [o.klm] – 'au calme' in French, 'relaxed, calm' in English, the title of a song by the French rapper Booba.

BIBLIOGRAPHY

Andersen PH and Rask M (2014) Creating legitimacy across international contexts: the role of storytelling for international new ventures. *Journal of International Entrepreneurship* 12(4): 365–88.

Baron RA (2008) The role of affect in the entrepreneurial process. *Academy of Management Review* 33(2): 328–40.

Baronchelli G and Cassia F (2014) Exploring the antecedents of born-global companies' international development. *International Entrepreneurship and Management Journal* 10(1): 67–79.

Biraglia A and Kadile V (2017) The role of entrepreneurial passion and creativity in developing entrepreneurial intentions: insights from American homebrewers. *Journal of Small Business Management* 55(1): 170–88.

Bruneel J and De Cock R (2016) Entry mode research and SMEs: a review and future research agenda. *Journal of Small Business Management* 54: 135–67.

Businesswire.com (2021) Recent study reveals more than a third of global consumers are willing to pay more for sustainability as demand grows for environmentally-friendly alternatives, https://www.businesswire.com/news/home/20211014005090/en/Recent-Study-Reveals-More-Than-a-Third-of-Global-Consumers-Are-Willing-to-Pay-More-for-Sustainability-as-Demand-Grows-for-Environmentally-Friendly-Alternatives (accessed 30 November 2022).

Cardon MS, Wincent J, Singh J, et al. (2009) The nature and experience of entrepreneurial passion. *Academy of Management Review* 34(3): 511–32.

Cardon MS, Foo MD, Shepherd D, et al. (2012) Exploring the heart: entrepreneurial emotion is a hot topic. *Entrepreneurship Theory and Practice* 36(1): 1–10.

Carsrud A and Brännback M (2011) Entrepreneurial motivations: what do we still need to know? *Journal of Small Business Management* 49(1): 9–26.

Cavusgil ST and Knight G (2015) The born global firm: an entrepreneurial and capabilities perspective on early and rapid internationalisation. *Journal of International Business Studies* 46(1): 3–16.

Chetty S and Campbell-Hunt C (2004) A strategic approach to internationalisation: a traditional versus a 'born-global' approach. *Journal of International Marketing* 12(1): 57–81.

Ciravegna L, Kuivalainen O, Kundu SK, et al. (2018) The antecedents of early internationalisation: a configurational perspective. *International Business Review* 27(6): 1200–12.

Coviello N (2006) The network dynamics of international new ventures. *Journal of International Business Studies* 37: 713–31.

Coviello N (2015) Re-thinking research on born globals. *Journal of International Business Studies* 46(1): 17–26.

Crick D (2009) The internationalisation of born global and international new venture SMEs. *International Marketing Review* 26(4/5): 453–76.

Ha L (2019) How to target evolving urban consumers. *Euromonitor International.*

Hasan MM, Nekmahmud M, Yajuan L, and Patwary MA (2019) Green business value chain: a systematic review. *Sustainable Production and Consumption* 20: 326–39.

Hayat K, Jianjun Z, and Ali S (2022) Reinforcing purchase behaviors through CSR and ethical practices. *Marketing Intelligence & Planning* 40(2): 256–72.

Hayward G (2019) Global campaigns should target cities, not countries, The Drum, https://www .thedrum.com/opinion/2019/02/25/global-campaigns-should-target-cities-not-countries (accessed 24 November 2022).

Hopp C and Sonderegger R (2015) Understanding the dynamics of nascent entrepreneurship – prestart-up experience, intentions, and entrepreneurial success. *Journal of Small Business Management* 53(4): 1076–96.

Johanson J and Vahlne JE (1977) The internationalisation process of the firm – a model of knowledge development and increasing foreign market commitment. *Journal of International Business Studies* 8(2): 23–32.

Klyver K, Hunter E and Watne T (2012) Entrepreneurial ties and innovativeness in the start-up decision. *The International Journal of Entrepreneurship and Innovation* 13(3): 153–63.

Leeflang PS, Verhoef PC, Dahlström P, et al. (2014) Challenges and solutions for marketing in a digital era. *European Management Journal* 32(1): 1–12.

Maltby T (2012) Using social media to accelerate the internationalisation of startups from inception. *Technology Innovation Management Review* 2(10): 22–6.

Mitteness C, Sudek R and Cardon MS (2012) Angel investor characteristics that determine whether perceived passion leads to higher evaluations of funding potential. *Journal of Business Venturing* 27(5): 592–606.

Moen Ø and Rialp-Criado A (2018) European SMEs and the born global concept. In *The Routledge Companion to European Business* (pp. 79–90). London: Routledge.

Mordor Intelligence (2022) Fashion accessories market – growth, trends, covid-19 impact, and forecasts (2022–2027), https://www.mordorintelligence.com/industry-reports/fashion-accessories-market (accessed 27 November 2022).

Orsato RJ (2006) Competitive environmental strategies: when does it pay to be green? *California Management Review* 48(2): 127–43.

Oviatt BM and McDougall PP (1994) Toward a theory of international new ventures. *Journal of International Business Studies* 25(1): 45–64.

Oviatt BM and McDougall PP (2005) Defining international entrepreneurship and modeling the speed of internationalisation. *Entrepreneurship Theory and Practice* 29(5): 537–54.

Paul J, Parthasarathy S, and Gupta P (2017) Exporting challenges of SMEs: a review and future research agenda. *Journal of World Business* 52(3): 327–42.

Rennie MW (1993) Born global. *McKinsey Quarterly* 4: 45–52.

Richards K (2017) 40 per cent of Millennial women say Instagram is the best way for brands to reach them, per bustle. *Adweek*, 13 December, https://www.adweek.com/brand-mar keting/40-of-m illennial-women-say-instagram-is-the-best- way-for-brands-to-reach-them-per-bustle/ (accessed 27 November 2022).

Sukunesan S, Selvarajah C, and Mellstrom Z (2020) Internationalization via Instagram: an exploratory study of small and medium enterprises. *Contemporary Management Research* 16(2): 77–121.

Tan Q and Sousa CM (2015) Leveraging marketing capabilities into competitive advantage and export performance. *International Marketing Review* 32(1): 78–102.

Tang YK (2011) The influence of networking on the internationalisation of SMEs: evidence from inter-nationalised Chinese firms. *International Small Business Journal* 29(4): 374–98.

Thorgren S and Wincent J (2015) Passion and habitual entrepreneurship. *International Small Business Journal* 33(2): 216–27.

Zhang M, Tansuhaj P, and McCullough J (2009) International entrepreneurial capability: the measurement and a comparison between born global firms and traditional exporters in China. *Journal of International Entrepreneurship* 7(4): 292–322.

11

Boris & Rufus: hotspot on screen and costs on the backyard[1]

Sílvio Luís de Vasconcellos, Clarice Zimmermann and Gérson Tontini

CASE SUMMARY

Boris & Rufus is a Brazilian animation series produced by Bell Studio in Blumenau, aimed at children aged six to ten. This teaching case addresses the company as a born-again global firm, its rapid spread across Disney channels in Latin America and digital platforms, and the dilemma of turning the characters into licensable products worldwide. Boris & Rufus aired first in 2018. In 2023, episodes are available in 80 countries and dubbed into multiple languages. However, in 2023 the licence of its products remains restricted to the Brazilian market, bringing dilemmas to keep the business sustainable in the coming years.

LEARNING OUTCOMES

The main learning outcomes of this case study are to understand Born Globals and their comparison with born-again global firms, and the transformation of online disclosure into products sold in the real world.

BELLI STUDIO

This case is not just another study applied to internationalisation or brand licensing classes. It establishes a parallel between Aline and Rubens's dilemma and their company, Belli Studio, a small Brazilian audiovisual production studio in Blumenau, a medium-sized city in southern Brazil. Its foundation occurred in 1999 when the owners decided to turn their dreams into a lifestyle. After years of working as an outsourced contractor for other audiovisual production studios, the couple and partners realised that a change in Brazilian legislation could be the opportunity to take a step forward to produce original content abroad. The internationalisation process began with a decisive event several years after the company's foundation, which international business studies call a born-again global firm. In 2018 they debuted on Disney Plus with *Boris & Rufus*, an animated children's series, and have not stopped since. As of 2023, *Boris & Rufus'* episodes are available in around 80 countries and dubbed in multiple languages.

After serving other production companies for years, the partners planned to become original content producers. Belli Studio achieved its goal by signing a contract with Disney to appear on the programming schedule with the animation *Boris & Rufus* for Latin America in 2018. Also, in 2018, the series received the Animacción Chilemonos trophy for being the most voted among children of eight to thirteen years (BRAVI, 2021). In 2019, Belli Studio launched its *Boris & Rufus* channel on Amazon Prime. Belli Studio leveraged access to technology and took advantage of institutional changes to launch *Boris & Rufus* worldwide, initially through Disney channels. In 2023, *Boris & Rufus* will be available on Disney Channel and streaming platforms such as Amazon Prime Video, Vivo Play, and Now Online TV in Latin America, North America, China, and Russia.

Producing animated television series in emerging markets is a challenge. Competitors are large producers from developed countries that traditionally produce content for TV, and competition is spreading globally. To compete, producers must seek the standards expected by distributors and simultaneously deliver something original. However, while distribution across channels and platforms is a notable achievement, it does not guarantee performance. In addition to delivering quality videos and good stories – embracing universal themes to discuss in homes worldwide – Belli Studio should translate its episodes into almost every market it enters. The narration of the original version is in Portuguese, a language spoken in less populous countries, except for Brazil. In addition, other costs, such as attracting talent to deliver new seasons quickly, are always on the table.

As highlighted, despite the relevance of being on screen in recognised international channels and platforms, this is not enough to sustain the business. Remuneration for channels and platforms pays no more than 10 per cent of production costs. The constant dilemma is how to cover the remaining 90 per cent. As a rule, this type of production is rewarded with licensing, as are *Peppa Pig* and *Lottie Dottie Chicken*. Licensing to manufacture toys, games, backpacks, and other school items is the alternative to profit from the operation. In this sense, the biggest challenge for an animated television series is distributing it and choosing licensees and distributors in all countries where they appear on the screen. The dilemma is how to move forward and explore other niches.

AUDIOVISUAL PRODUCTION: IS IT A GLOBALISED INDUSTRY?

The audiovisual industry is part of the Creative Economy and, for a long time, was considered an industry with high production costs (Doyle, 2013). With the evolution of the internet and digital media, the sector has been expanding borders, developing multi-platform channels, changing consumer behaviour, reformulating the supply chain, and transforming the media industry. At the same time that such changes facilitated the entry of new and small companies, the number of countries exporting audiovisual products also grew, more because of production costs than creativity.

Considering only the animation industry, Japan, Germany, France, England, China, Canada, the United States, and South Korea are the central producing and consuming countries (Nyko et al., 2019). In 2017, global animation consumption reached US$305.75 billion, with a projection of around US$405 billion by 2023 (Research and Markets, 2018). The growth of this industry is due to several factors, such as continuous technological advancement which provides high-quality movies and series at a low cost. In addition, the expansion of the use of 3D and 4D and the increase in internet speed allows them to be presented on different platforms and multimedia channels, with the advantage of generating revenue from product licensing and consequently generating effects in other industries (Nyko et al., 2019; Research and Markets, 2018).

One of the leading players in the audiovisual industry is the Walt Disney Company (WDC). According to Walt Disney Reports released on 8 November 2022, subscribers who select WDC channels are growing consistently. Specifically, in this teaching case, attention should be given to Disney Channel, Disney Channel International, Disney Junior, and Disney XD.

BRAZILIAN AUDIOVISUAL PRODUCTION: IS IT GOING GLOBAL?

In Brazil in 2016, only 5 per cent of all animations released in cinemas were Brazilian. There was a steep increase in 2017, due to a more favourable scenario in terms of laws and funding, in 2017, when the total was 20 per cent. Furthermore, ANCINE (Agência de Cinema) recorded an increase in subscriptions to animated series on TV of 110 per cent between 2013 and 2017 (Nyko et al., 2019). Indeed, the results have been auspicious. In 2016, the Brazilian animation *O Menino e o Mundo* was nominated for an Oscar for the best animation category (Nyko et al., 2019).

According to BNDES[2] (2016), several factors contributed to the development of this industry in Brazil. Brazilian independent production companies have turned to the TV series market, which is easier to enter because the big studios dedicate to producing feature films. In addition, Video on Demand platforms began to demand original content. There was also an increase in subscription channels, including those exclusively for children. In addition, in 2011, Law 12485/11, 2011 established the minimum quota of Brazilian content in the programming schedule of pay-TV channels, providing visibility to national content and great acceptance by children in Brazil (Nyko et al., 2019).

ALINE AND RUBENS TALK ABOUT THE CASE

One of the barriers to producing original content is that channels and platforms seek to hire studios that operate in large centres, believing they are the best. However, small studios like Belli Studio are outsourced suppliers for these production companies in cities like São Paulo and Rio de Janeiro. When the legislation changed, it was possible to access banks' credit lines and have official agencies' support to promote audiovisual production, such as ANCINE. Thus, Belli Studio could offer its original content directly to channels and platforms, strengthening its brand and obtaining greater financial returns.

Law 12,485/2011 was a milestone for opening up the animation market in the country. In order to gain scale, it attracted large distributors to Brazil who began to idealise viable products in other markets. If there were not a law that forced the insertion of national content in international channels, these channels would not run the risk of accepting new projects. They would stick to content made available and tested in other markets that yield a lot in licensing with effects throughout the production chain of marketable products for people who consume video production as consumer products.

With the quotas, national producers became attractive to large international groups interested in exploring the national market, taking audiovisual production from different parts of the world. In addition, the law has changed the audiovisual market. It brought learning about what Brazilians like to watch. The companies that own the content distribution channels and platforms were able to verify that Brazilians like Brazilian productions, which meant that other national productions could develop and expand. More recently, they perceived that the production of emerging countries has an international appeal that transcends the production made in a few countries for decades.

'We looked for characters that could be of interest to channels and platforms', said Aline. Belli Studio learned about the *Boris & Rufus* project through pitching in 2015 at a local event where new professionals could share their creations. Elisa Baasch (illustrator) and Felipe Cargnin (screenwriter), who studied together, were starting in the profession. The inspiration for the original idea came from videos of cats that are successful on the internet. Did they wonder what it would be like if the dogs got jealous of this situation and started competing with the cats for 'likes'? Also, Boris and Rufus were animals that used technology to communicate. In summary, *Boris & Rufus* is an animated series about the adventures of Boris, a grumpy dog, and Rufus, a ferret who believes he is a dog. The two live in the backyard of Enzo, a teenager who is in love with his neighbour, Jennifer, who owns a famous internet cat, Leopoldo.

When Aline and Rubens realised they had an excellent opportunity to produce original content, they promoted Belli Studio, then proposed that the authors keep a percentage without Belli Studio having to buy the work. The authors could develop the production together with the production company. 'In January 2016, I went to Argentina, the headquarters of Disney Latin America, and presented the project. Disney approved it and announced that they would make the contract available in two weeks', said Rubens.

When he returned to Brazil and received the contract, they asked themselves how they would close the budget. They realised that Disney would pay 10 per cent of the budget to be the first showcase, with delivery in two languages, neutral Spanish and Portuguese, for distribution in Latin America, with the right to three years of exclusivity for the Latin American cable channel. However, they would have to raise funds to deliver within the agreed time frame.

The first season would consist of 26 11-minute episodes and a 22-minute Christmas Special, with an estimated budget of around $650,000. Aline and Rubens still did not know how to raise the remaining 90 per cent. They were in a gridlock; if they signed with Disney, Aline and

Rubens would have to meet deadlines, as Belli Studio already had a fixed delivery date, or they would try to take the budget amount and start producing first, then close a deal with Disney, taking the risk to miss the long-awaited chance.

After overcoming the difficulties and with a series of loans assumed, they were aired on Disney XD, making the *Boris & Rufus* brand known. In addition, several awards that Belli Studio competed for and won were helping to lend credibility to the series. These events created more possibilities for licensing the brand and distributing the series on other channels. Brand licensing transforms series into products such as T-shirts, notebooks, and other products and is an essential source of income for the audiovisual industry. Licensing and distributing the series on other channels returns in features and promotion. Thus, the more channels the series aired, the more brand licensing it yields, with possibilities of reaching markets that the company could try to evaluate.

In 2019, the first season premiered on streaming platforms such as Looke, Now Online, and Vivo Play (Siqueira, 2019). Thus, the series was also distributed by Amazon Prime in Latin America. Launching the series on streaming channels was crucial for making it more accessible to the public. According to the Center for Studies on the Development of the Information Society (Cetic, 2023), in 2012, 49 per cent of people had the habit of watching videos online; in 2017, it grew to 71 per cent. In 2020, Amazon Prime Video in Brazil increased the number of views by 800 per cent compared to the previous semester (Lopes, 2020).

After developing the English dub, the series began airing on streaming channels in several English-speaking countries, further expanding airtime through Amazon Prime. Depending on the negotiation, the company that licenses the series pays for dubbing into other languages. Usually, the channel itself pays for the dubbing. Even if the licensor pays, the production company receives the dubbing done when the licence ends. Since 2020, *Boris & Rufus* has been available in Russia, with dubbing paid by the licensor.

INTERNATIONALISATION BETWEEN ONLINE AND THE REAL WORLD

The first step of internationalisation was not a plan. Belli Studio only intended to broadcast its original content on TV and internet platforms. Located in an emerging market like Brazil, it means being known as a content producer that can deliver a season even if distributors only pay 10 per cent of the costs, given the Brazilian market is enormous with a considerable population between six and ten years old. Furthermore, this is not the first time Brazilian animation has become internationally known. Using platforms and pay-tv, *The Fishnaut* became a worldwide sensation in 2004, and *Lottie Dottie Chicken* has been a hit since 2006 (Pinho & Pinho, 2019), following pioneer *Monica & Friends*, who have experimented with international markets since the early 1970s. After a long history in cartoons around the world, they started offering online content in 2014 (de Aguillar Pinho et al., 2017). In common, they all raised funds from the BNDES.

The challenge of licensing internationally

As in the chicken and egg dilemma, the brand must be known to license a product. To be known, the characters must appear on TV and the internet. In short, to make money, you need money. After using up its resources and taking out loans to pay for the production, Belli Studio realised that licensing its products alone could not sustain a second season while paying off loans and subcontractors. As its main characters, *Boris & Rufus*, started to become better known in the Brazilian market and their business relationships are in Brazil, it can be said that *Boris & Rufus* are in high demand on international screens but costly in the backyard. The next challenge is to spread the licences around the world. How could Aline and Rubens do this?

DISCUSSION QUESTIONS

1. As a born-again global firm, what should Belli Studio do to start growing internationally?
2. What peculiarities do global born-again firms from emerging markets have that differ from competitors in developed markets?
3. Are there specificities of global born-again firms inserted in the Creative Economy compared to companies in traditional sectors?
4. Is the flattening of technological gaps between countries still problematic in audiovisual production? Why?
5. How can internationalisation through licensing in foreign countries take advantage of the experience in the countries of origin?

TEACHING NOTES

LEARNING OUTCOMES

This teaching case can help discuss Born Globals, their comparison with born-again global firms, and the transformation of online disclosure into products sold in the real world. The teacher can access further literature on the topics below:

- Born-again global firms are related to time-threshold for a firm to become 'born-again' when they spread their operations fast after a long period without operations abroad (Sheppard, 2012), mainly when a critical event provides small firms with additional resources to face opportunities (Bell et al., 2003). Born-again global firms began to internationalise slowly and incrementally, consistent with the traditional pattern of traditional firms. However, these firms develop a proactive internationalisation pattern at a certain overturning point, more in line with the Born Global pattern (Baum et al., 2015).
- Born-again global firms from Emerging Markets took advantage of changes in the institutional context or an internal change that offers conditions to integrate global value chains led by giants in motion production. For example, when a traditional firm hires someone with international connections, this hiring can deflagrate a born-again

process that accelerates a firm's internationalisation process (Semensato et al., 2022). Specifically, in this teaching case, a change in the Brazilian regulation of film diffusion on TV occurred. It helped produce a significant opportunity for audiovisual producers to engage in international markets and with other Brazilian producers (Pinho & Pinho, 2019).

- Born-again global firms can relate to technology access or changes in the Creative Economy that internationally connects firms from this segment (de Vasconcellos et al., 2017). In parallel, the Creativity Economy has received additional attention from governments that face this sector's conditions to engage creative firms in the international digital ecosystem. For example, the Brazilian content of *Lottie Dottie Chicken* was the first entertainment and media brand to create one hundred per cent within the new media digital environment (Pinho & Pinho, 2019).

- Internationalisation by licensing in foreign countries is a phenomenon that accelerated because the digital economy enables technologies across frontiers (Gambardella & McGahan, 2010; Teece, 2018). Internationalisation by licensing results from disseminating a brand in another country that opens opportunities to license correlated products (de Aguillar Pinho et al., 2017), sometimes deriving from relational-based technological alliances (van Kranenburg et al., 2014).

- Technological gaps among countries have not only been flattening distances (Gomes et al., 2018) but also inviting international business scholars to rethink if we should discuss international business separately from a global business perspective (Meyer, 2013). Although technologically flattening distance drove the internationalisation of multinationals at the end of the last century (Gassmann & Zedtwitz, 1999), this effect is not restricted only to such organisations anymore (Warner & Wäger, 2019). Especially in the digital economy, there is a connection to the Creative Economy that enables new technologies and licensing models. Then, this interconnection enables firms geographically far apart to profit together (Teece, 2018).

POSITION IN THE COURSE

This case is suitable for MBA and undergraduate courses related to Business Administration, especially when the focus is on the internationalisation of startups, Born Globals, and small and medium-sized enterprises (SMEs). The case provokes comparisons of forces that dominate digital platforms. It also covers adapting to multiple cultural scenarios, highlighting the creativity and flexibility these companies require to obtain gains. Finally, the case may inspire students to reflect on how the free audiovisual products available on the internet cover their costs and make a profit.

TEACHING PLAN

Teachers can conduct the case keeping in mind the strategy and innovation business model perspectives. The authors elaborated on the case to frame the strategic analysis and propose alternatives to keep the business online and profitable. Students should apply some models to evaluate strategic alternatives: strengths, weaknesses, opportunities, and threats (SWOT analysis); and the organisation's value, rarity, inimitability, and readiness analysis (VRIO).

To evaluate the business model, the authors suggest the CANVAS analysis. Teachers can use cartoon examples like *Peppa Pig* or *Lottie Dottie Chicken* to discuss their business models as benchmarks. The class can list which products are derived from these designs they know. Students should suggest derivative business models that make a profit and reinforce the values that *Boris & Rufus* disseminate.

CONDUCTING A SWOT ANALYSIS OF THE BUSINESS MODEL ADOPTED BY BELLI STUDIO TO MAINTAIN THE SUSTAINABILITY OF *BORIS & RUFUS*

STRENGTHS

- Episodes have a universal context. Thus, the products can be licensed and produced on a large scale anywhere globally.
- The first season was a success, and Belli Studio is spreading the cartoon to various channels and platforms worldwide quickly, making the characters more and more internationally known.
- Belli Studio has solid licensing contracts in Brazil, a country with a large population between six and ten years old. So, scalability does not seem to be an issue.

WEAKNESSES

- Belli Studio has only 10 per cent of its costs covered by its contract with Disney. As a result, it often needs to outsource production and fails to retain talent in an industry where this is essential.
- Since the company is in a medium-sized city, there is no workforce available to hire when it needs it.
- Brazilian licensees are focused on the domestic market and cannot export on a large scale.

OPPORTUNITIES

- Other Brazilian cartoons obtained licences abroad and have already followed this path. Thus, Belli Studio could follow their trajectories and mimic their steps to disseminate production abroad.
- Brazilian law is still protecting and leveraging audiovisual production. Thus, they can create other stories and characters to build on their learning.
- As Belli Studio fulfils its contracts regularly, it can strengthen its commercial ties with major distributors.

THREATS

- Countries like South Korea, Argentina, Spain, France, Mexico, and China have laws to encourage production and protect the audiovisual industry similar to Brazilian law. Their governments created rules for the dissemination and production of native content. Thus, competition is more aggressive than in the last decade.

- Companies in emerging markets that rely on financing have higher costs than those in advanced economies.
- When a small company deals with large companies, the relationship is not symmetrical, which means that the forces are unequal and it is tricky to keep the business stable.

EVALUATE BELLI STUDIO'S FEATURES AND CAPABILITIES USING A VRIO ANALYSIS FRAMEWORK (BARNEY, 1995; ROCKWELL, 2019)

Table 11.1 explains how to interpret the VRIO framework suggested.
List resources and capabilities.

- Some examples of resources are active contracts, a network in the Brazilian Creative Economy, the capability of developing universal scope stories, and lean staff.

Evaluate how valuable resources and capabilities are.

- If the firm retains the resource, can it increase revenues or decrease costs from a long-time perspective?

Evaluate how rare they are.

- How rare is the resource or capability? Is it expandable to deal in other markets if necessary?

Evaluate how difficult to imitate they are.

- Considering the resources or capability are valuable and rare, how difficult is it for a competitor to imitate? Are there competitors in conditions to imitate this resource or capability?

Analyse if the organisation supports them.

- Is Belli Studio efficient in keeping its critical resources and capabilities available to the entire organisation? Is Belli Studio taking advantage of detaining its set of resources and capabilities?

Production of animated videos for TV or platforms is not fully sustainable because distributors do not cover all costs. This condition means that the production of audiovisual products cannot be anchored as a business model isolated from others. In this case, considering the licensed products, it is necessary to verify the nine stages of the business model proposed by Osterwalder and Pigneur (2010). Some questions can help students discuss alternatives.

CLIENT SEGMENT

- Who will benefit from the deal? Take into account the target audience of licensed products.

Table 11.1   Example of interpreting the VRIO framework

Resources or capabilities	Valuable?	Rare?	Inimitable?	Organisation?
Resource or capability 1				
Resource or capability 2				
Resource or capability 3				
Resource or capability 4				
Resource or capability 5				

VALUE PROPOSITION

- What is valuable to the consumer segment? Consider why the segment is interested in buying and benefiting from the licensed product.

DISTRIBUTION CHANNELS

- How can Belli Studio distribute the product to add value to the customer segment? Analyse how the licensee can deliver the products properly and how Belli Studio can contribute.

CLIENT RELATIONSHIPS

- How should the relationship between customers and suppliers be? Will it be a relationship of community, loyalty, or occasional sales?
- What is the best relationship to be developed between Studio Belli and the licensees in the long term, considering that Belli Studio is a leader in its value chain?

REVENUE FLOWS

- What kind of revenue can Belli Studio achieve? Some possibilities are on the table to discuss, considering licensing, franchising, and commissions. An alternative is evaluating how competitors deal because they have built their business model.

KEY RESOURCES

- Which know-how does Belli Studio need?
- What sales and contracting skills do they need?
- What knowledge must Belli Studio have before dealing with foreign licensees?

KEY ACTIVITIES

- How will Belli Studio coordinate licensees?
- Which technical specificities will licensees have to accomplish before contracting?
- How to avoid piracy?
- How can data monitoring from video access help organise production and reach suppliers?

PARTNER NETWORK

- Who will be the legal consultant in each country where production will take place?
- How can products developed by licensees be emulated around the world?

NOTES

1. This research was supported by the National Research Council (CNPq) grant number 07982/2018-3.
2. BNDES is the official Brazilian bank for social and economic development. It is the acronym from its original Portuguese name, *Banco Nacional de Desenvolvimento Econômico e Social.*

SUPPLEMENTARY INFORMATION FOR THE CASE DISCUSSION

BNDES. (2016). *No Title.* Brazilian Development Bank. https://www.bndes.gov.br/SiteBNDES/bndes/bndes_en/Institucional/Press/Noticias/2010/20100623_porte_empresa.html

BRAVI. (2021). *BRAVI - Brasil Audiovisual Independente.* Produced by Belli Studio, Boris and Rufus Cartoon Conquers the Asian Market. https://bravi.tv/produzido-pela-belli-studio-desenho-boris-e-rufus-conquista-o-mercado-asiatico/

Cetic. (2023). *Center of Studies for the Information Society Development.* Data Portal. https://data.cetic.br

de Aguillar Pinho, M. L. C., da Rocha, A. M. C., de Aguillar Pinho, C. R., & Giovannini, C. J. (2017). "Monica and Friends": the challenge to internationalize. *Emerald Emerging Markets Case Studies, 7*(2), 1–26. https://doi.org/10.1108/EEMCS-06-2016-0139

Law 12485/11. (2011). *Lei 12485/11* (pp. 1–20). https://www.planalto.gov.br/ccivil_03/_ato2011-2014/2011/lei/l12485.htm

Lopes, M. M. (2020). Animação "Boris e Rufus", produzida em Blumenau, chega à América do Norte pela Amazon Prime Video. In *NSC Total.* https://www.nsctotal.com.br/noticias/animacao-boris-e-rufus-produzida-em-blumenau-chega-a-america-do-norte-pela-amazon-prime

Nyko, D., Zendron, P., Nyko, D., & Zendron, P. (2019). *O Mercado Consumidor De Animação No Brasil.*

Pinho, M. L. C. de A., & Pinho, C. R. de A. (2019). Lottie dottie chicken goes international: How the Brazilian creative industry expands internationally via licensing. *Rutgers Business Review, 4*(1), 10–30.

Research and Markets. (2018). Global Animation Market - Forecasts from 2018 to 2023. In *Knowledge Sourcing Intelligence LLP.*

Siqueira, G. (2019). *Animação nacional Boris e Rufus disponível em streaming.* 100 Fronteiras. https://100fronteiras.com/brasil/noticia/animacao-nacional-boris-e-rufus-disponivel-em-streaming/

REFERENCES

Barney, J.B. (1995). Looking inside for competitive advantage. *Academy of Management Perspectives, 9*(4), 49–61.

Baum, M., Schwens, C., & Kabst, R. (2015). A latent class analysis of small firms' internationalisation patterns. *Journal of World Business, 50*(4), 754–68. https://doi.org/10.1016/j.jwb.2015.03.001

Bell, J., McNaughton, R., Young, S., & Crick, D. (2003). Towards an integrative model of small firm internationalisation. *Journal of International Entrepreneurship, 1*(4), 339–62.

de Aguillar Pinho, M.L.C., da Rocha, A.M.C., de Aguillar Pinho, C.R., & Giovannini, C.J. (2017). 'Monica and Friends': The challenge to internationalise. *Emerald Emerging Markets Case Studies, 7*(2), 1–26. https://doi.org/10.1108/EEMCS-06-2016-0139

de Vasconcellos, S.L., Marlon, J., Monticelli, V., Calixto, C., & Garrido, I.L. (2017). Prospecting theoretical approaches to understand internationalisation of creative economy firms. *Internext: Revista Eletrônica de Negócios Internacionais Da ESPM, 12*(3), 77–92. http://ezproxybib.pucp.edu.pe:2048/login?url=http://search.ebscohost.com/login.aspx?direct=true&db=a9h&AN=127091419&lang=es&site=eds-live&scope=site%0A10.18568/1980-4865.12377-92

Doyle, G. (2013). *Understanding Media Economics.* Sage.

Gambardella, A., & McGahan, A.M. (2010). Business-model innovation: General purpose technologies and their implications for industry structure. *Long Range Planning*, 43(2–3), 262–71. https://doi.org/10.1016/j.lrp.2009.07.009

Gassmann, O., & Zedtwitz, M. Von. (1999). New concepts and trends in international R&D organisation. *Research Policy*, 28, 231–50.

Gomes, L.A. de V., Facin, A.L.F., Salerno, M.S., & Ikenami, R.K. (2018). Unpacking the innovation ecosystem construct: Evolution, gaps and trends. *Technological Forecasting and Social Change*, 136, 30–48. https://doi.org/10.1016/j.techfore.2016.11.009

Meyer, K.E. (2013). What is, and to what purpose do we study, international business? *AIB Insights*, 13(1), 10–13.

Osterwalder, A., & Pigneur, Y. (2010). *Business Model Generation: A Handbook for Visionaires, Game Changers and Challengers*. Hoboken, NJ: John Wiley & Sons.

Pinho, M.L.C. de A., & Pinho, C.R. de A. (2019). Lottie dottie chicken goes international: How the Brazilian creative industry expands internationally via licensing. *Rutgers Business Review*, 4(1), 10–30.

Rockwell, S. (2019). A resource-based framework for strategically managing identity. *Journal of Organizational Change Management*, 32(1), 80–102. https://doi.org/10.1108/JOCM-01-2018-0012

Semensato, B.I., Oliva, F.L., & Roehrich, G. (2022). Innovation as an internationalisation determinant of Brazilian technology-based SMEs. *Journal of International Entrepreneurship*, 20(3), 404–32. https://doi.org/10.1007/s10843-022-00317-y

Sheppard, M. (2012). Born Global and born-again global firms: A comparison of internationalization patterns. In *Handbook of Research on Born Globals* (pp. 46–56). Cheltenham, UK and Northampton, MA, USA: Edward Elgar Publishing. https://doi.org/10.4337/9780857938046.00013

Teece, D.J. (2018). Profiting from innovation in the digital Economy: Enabling technologies, standards, and licensing models in the wireless world. *Research Policy*, 47(8), 1367–87. https://doi.org/10.1016/j.respol.2017.01.015

van Kranenburg, H., Hagedoorn, J., & Lorenz-Orlean, S. (2014). Distance Costs and the degree of inter-partner involvement in international relational-based technology alliances. *Global Strategy Journal*, 4(4), 280–91. https://doi.org/10.1002/gsj.1085

Warner, K.S.R., & Wäger, M. (2019). Building dynamic capabilities for digital transformation: An ongoing process of strategic renewal. *Long Range Planning*, 52(3), 326–49. https://doi.org/10.1016/j.lrp.2018.12.001

Printed and bound by CPI Group (UK) Ltd, Croydon, CR0 4YY

12/12/2024

14611567-0001